The Territory of Japan

Kentaro Serita

The Territory of Japan

Its History and Legal Basis

Second Edition

 Springer

Kentaro Serita
Kobe University
Kobe, Japan

ISBN 978-981-99-3012-8   ISBN 978-981-99-3013-5   (eBook)
https://doi.org/10.1007/978-981-99-3013-5

Preface to the English Edition

Japan first became widely known among Europeans through *The Travels of Marco Polo*, in which thirteenth century Venetian merchant Marco Polo referred to Japan as "Zipangu, the Land of Gold." Though Polo himself never travelled to Japan, he is thought to have been expressing the views held by the residents of southern China, after he had spent time in Hangzhou, which at the time was a trade hub between Japan and China.

Meanwhile, modern Japan makes an appearance in American author Herman Melville's *Moby-Dick*, as a country closed to the outside world and a refueling station for the American whaling crew that ventures out into the North Pacific, as far as the Ogasawara (Bonin) Islands. This depiction demonstrates how, as the newly modernized Japan was being pressed by the nations of Western Europe to open its doors to trade, many wanted the attribution of the islands around Japan to be clarified—not only China, but also Russia to Japan's north, various countries that had been looking East since the Age of Sail, and America to the east. Thus, efforts were made to define Japan's territories from the end of the Edo period through to the Meiji period, resulting in their present definition. This work describes the changes and current state of Japan's territories while also touching upon developments in the international community relating to maritime resources from the latter half of the twentieth century onwards.

It is well known how Japan emerged as a modern nation and vied alongside other countries to expand its territory at a time when the world was ruled by the law of survival of the fittest, before finally signing the San Francisco Peace Treaty in 1952. Consequently, a series of unresolved territorial issues continue to burden Japan. In this work, I attempted to examine the claims of the relevant countries with an open mind and strived to lay the foundation for calmly addressing the issues involved, so as to find a peaceful solution.

As was mentioned in the Epilogue of the original Japanese edition, this text was primarily an analysis of the situation up to 2002. Therefore, I would like to write a summary of the facts regarding the situation since that time as they relate to Russia, China, and the Republic of Korea (ROK).

The Northern Territories: Kunashiri Island, Etorofu Island, the Habomai Islands, and Shikotan Island

As touched on in Chapter 1, the entry into force of the Soviet-Japanese Joint Declaration put an end to the state of war with the former Soviet Union, which had not signed the Peace Treaty with Japan after World War II. However, Russia (the successor State to the former Soviet Union) continues to occupy the Northern Territories even now, as the two parties have not reached an agreement on the peace treaty negotiations referred to in the said Declaration.

In November 2010, then-Russian President Dmitry Medvedev set foot on Kunashiri Island despite protests from the Japanese government, the first time for a sitting Russian or Soviet leader to visit one of the four islands of the Northern Territories. He paid another visit again as prime minister in July 2012.

After Russia launched its "special military operation" against Ukraine on February 24, 2022, the United Nations General Assembly held an emergency special session and adopted a Resolution declaring Russia's action an "Aggression against Ukraine." Japan joined with other Western countries to impose sanctions on Russia. On September 5, 2022, with still no end in sight to the war in Ukraine, Russia announced the suspension of force of the visa-free travel agreement for former residents of the disputed islands, "as a response to the illegal sanction pressure exerted by the Japanese government and its joining the West's Russophobic policy."[1] Peace treaty negotiations remain suspended.

The Senkaku Islands

In April 2012, the then-governor of Tokyo announced his idea for the Tokyo Metropolitan Government to purchase three privately owned Senkaku Islands (Uotsuri Island, Kitakojima Island, and Minamikojima Island). Instead, the central government acquired ownership of the islands in question on September 11 of that year for more than 2 billion yen ($26 million) and ownership was transferred from the private citizens to the government. Since the acquisition of the islands, there have been incidents in China where anti-Japanese demonstrations turned violent, and the buildings of Japanese companies were set on fire.

Prior to this development, China sent two government vessels into Japanese territorial waters for the first time on December 8, 2008. (This intrusion did not result from an arbitrary decision made by the ships, according to an article in which the person in charge of the government vessels at the time was interviewed; it was planned from 2006 for the purpose of undermining Japan's valid control over the

---

[1] According to Leonid Slutsky, chairman of the international committee of the Russian State Duma. "Russia's withdrawal from agreement on Kurils seen as response to sanctions—lawmaker," September 5, 16:24 https://tass.com/politics/1503027. Accessed December 11, 2022.

islands and was carried out with the consent of the authorities.) Then, a Chinese fishing boat operating in Japanese territorial waters caused a collision on September 7, 2010 when it crashed into Japan Coast Guard patrol vessels that had called for it to leave the territorial waters. As soon as the captain of the fishing vessel was arrested for obstructing the execution of official duties, China immediately demanded an apology and compensation from Japan. Since the 2012 transfer of ownership to the Japanese government, China has reportedly sent government vessels into Japan's contiguous zone, except in rough weather, to this day.

September 11, 2022 marked 10 years since the transfer of ownership over the Senkaku Islands. During this time, it has become normal for China Coast Guard ships to stalk Japanese fishing vessels operating in Japan's territorial waters. Also, there have been 332 cases of intrusion into territorial waters over this decade, according to the Japan Coast Guard. Under these circumstances, the Japan Coast Guard remains on high alert, continuing to deploy a succession of new patrol vessels. With the confrontation between the USA and China over Taiwan intensifying, it appears that tensions in the East China Sea will be further prolonged.

Takeshima

In August 2012, ROK President Lee Myung-bak set foot on Takeshima for the first time as an incumbent president. The Japanese side protested, but ROK government officials and parliamentarians have been landing on Takeshima ever since then. ROK security personnel have been permanently stationed on the island since 1954, and the country continues its illegal occupation.

Over the years, Japan has patrolled the island (Japan Maritime Safety Agency[2] vessels on patrol were fired upon several times), sent official protests, and presently announces Japan's response in its *Diplomatic Bluebook*. Japan may be required to take additional measures to support its territorial claim, however, so that its opposition will not be deemed a "paper protest" (as one judge found France's to be in the Minquiers and Ecrehos case, contested between the United Kingdom and France at the International Court of Justice; see Chapter 4).

Moreover, Japan has proposed three times[3] since 1954 to refer the matter to the International Court of Justice for a peaceful settlement, but there has been no movement in the situation.

Yokohama, Japan   Kentaro Serita
September 2022

---

[2]The English name for Japan's Coast Guard until it was changed in 2000.

[3]September 1954, March 1962, and August 2012.

Preface

Earth, the Water Planet, is home to over six billion people. It also hosts animals, plants, and a variety of resources such as minerals. Human beings, land dwellers, are split up among around 200 countries. There they live their lives, using Earth's resources to do so. Although there are around 200 countries now, 50 years ago there were only around 100. Given that territory forms the foundation of the political entity that is a State, the past 50 years have seen significant territorial changes. Setting aside the breakup of the Union of Soviet Socialist Republics, the twentieth century has been characterized by the independence of former colonies and loss of colonial territory for the former colonizers. Starting in the sixteenth century, for 500 years the countries of Europe had sought to expand their homeland, doing so by seizing colonies. During the last 100 of those 500 years, the recently modernized Japan also took part in the scramble to seize colonies. While the colonizers lost these lands, the former colonies gained their independence, and almost all human beings came to have their own homeland.

Each country is structured in its own way. The countries that had colonies, including the United Kingdom, France, Germany, Italy, Spain, Portugal, the Netherlands, Belgium, and Japan, all vary, both in when they had colonies and when they lost them. Even among those countries that have flourished since ancient times, those that were colonized, such as India, Indonesia, or Mexico, and those that were not, such as China, Turkey, or Thailand, are all different.

But what does "homeland" even mean?

The United Nations (UN) advanced the emancipation of non-self-governing territories, i.e., colonies. During that process, Spain and Portugal argued that they had overseas provinces, not colonies, which could not be separated from the Spanish or Portuguese mainland. The UN responded in 1960 by adopting the standard whereby a non-self-governing territory is "a territory which is geographically separate and is distinct ethnically and/or culturally from the country administering it."

Since ancient times, many countries have gradually expanded their spheres of influence, eventually clashing with other powers, resulting in war. When one power comes into contact with a rival power, its expansion ceases. This process was repeated for a period of time, eventually forming proto-countries. Today that is thought to be what is meant by "homeland," and it is said to be ethnically and/or culturally unified.

In Japan's case, the feudal lords of the Sengoku ("Warring States") period established small States across the Japanese archipelago. Each had its own laws and administration. They often clashed with one another. Starting in the middle of the sixteenth century, there was a notable emergence of forces seeking to unify the Japanese archipelago. As is commonly known, Oda Nobunaga took a large step toward that goal. In order to unify the country, Japan broke off trade relations with the outside world until the sixteenth century. Toyotomi Hideyoshi turned his attention to the Asian mainland and sent troops to the Korean Peninsula, whereas Tokugawa Ieyasu sought to restore friendly diplomatic relations with the Joseon. Friendly diplomatic relations were restored in 1607 for the first time since the Muromachi period. Envoys travelled between Japan and the Joseon, and although there were ups and downs, friendly relations were maintained until the Meiji Restoration (1868). Relations with Europe, meanwhile, were limited to Dejima in Nagasaki, but despite this, Japan flourished culturally and economically in the Edo period. The beginnings of a modern market-based economy also emerged.

Examining territorial changes reveals the nature of countries. One cannot speak of a country's territory without taking into account its relations with its neighbors. This work examines the path Japan has taken as a modern State from the Meiji period onward. I intend to squarely examine the nature of Japan and thereby understand its standing in East Asia and the world.

Kobe, Japan   Kentaro Serita
May 2002

Introduction

A nation's existence is founded on a fixed area. This space is its territory. There is no nation that has no territory. The only place in which a nation can exclusively exercise its authority is within its own territory. Territory consists of territorial land, which is the land portion; territorial sea in the case of nations that face the sea, whereby a nation's sovereignty extends to a belt of sea of a fixed distance adjacent to its coast; and territorial air space, which is the air space above a nation's territorial land and sea. A nation's territory is the spatial scope within which its legal order applies. That scope is determined by international law. Depending on the nation, stipulations regarding its territory may be included in its constitution. The Constitution of Japan does not include such stipulations. Japan's domestic laws only include a law on its territorial sea. In principle, Japan's current territory is stipulated by the Potsdam Declaration of July 1945 and the Treaty of Peace with Japan of September 1951.

In addition to territorial land, sea, and air space, this work also touches upon exclusive economic zones (EEZs), continental shelves, and air defense identification zones (ADIZs), given that they are also often discussed in the context of territory. Therefore, in addition to the Treaty of Peace with Japan, this work also refers to international treaties, such as the United Nations Convention on the Law of the Sea (UNCLOS), and related domestic laws, as necessary.

Furthermore, as a result of Japan's surrender in 1945 and in accordance with the Cairo Declaration and the Potsdam Declaration, Japan's current territory was limited to Honshū, Hokkaidō, Kyūshū, Shikoku, and various small islands that were decided by the Allied powers. In other words, Japan was giving up the territory that it had added over the previous approximately 50 years through the exercise of military power, similar to Europe and the USA. Japan's quest for expansion sometimes extended to warfare, such as the First Sino-Japanese War, the Russo-Japanese War, and World War I, and was in principle reverting to the state of possessing only the territory that was firmly established at the end of the Edo period (1603–1867) and the beginning of the Meiji period (1868–1912), when Japan first embarked on becoming a modern nation; in other words Japan's inherent territory.

Though the current state of Japan's territory has already been established for approximately 60 years, it reminds one of the end of the Edo period, when Japan completed its unification and enjoyed peace; it even makes one feel that it is possible to live without digging in one's heels and to feel at ease with oneself.

The stipulations of Article 2 and 3 of Chapter II, titled "Territory," of the Treaty of Peace with Japan are as follows. (Incidentally, the significance of Article 3 has been lost following the conclusion of the Amami Reversion Treaty of 1953, the Ogasawara Reversion Treaty of 1968, and the Okinawa Reversion Treaty of 1972.)

Article 2

(a) *Japan, recognizing the independence of Korea, renounces all right, title,[4] and claim to Korea, including the islands of Quelpart, Port Hamilton and Dagelet.*

(b) *Japan renounces all right, title and claim to Formosa and the Pescadores.*

(c) *Japan renounces all right, title and claim to the Kurile Islands, and to that portion of Sakhalin and the islands adjacent to it over which Japan acquired sovereignty as a consequence of the Treaty of Portsmouth of September 5, 1905.*

(d) *Japan renounces all right, title and claim in connection with the League of Nations Mandate System, and accepts the action of the United Nations Security Council of April 2, 1947, extending the trusteeship system to the Pacific Islands formerly under mandate to Japan.*

(e) *Japan renounces all claim to any right or title to or interest in connection with any part of the Antarctic area, whether deriving from the activities of Japanese nationals or otherwise.*

(f) *Japan renounces all right, title and claim to the Spratly Islands and to the Paracel Islands.*

Article 3

Japan will concur in any proposal of the United States to the United Nations to place under its trusteeship system, with the United States as the sole administering authority, Nansei Shoto south of 29° north latitude (including the Ryukyu Islands and the Daito Islands), Nanpo Shoto south of Sofu Gan (including the Bonin Islands, Rosario Island and the Volcano Islands) and Parece Vela and Marcus Island. Pending the making of such a proposal and affirmative action thereon, the United States will have the right to exercise all and any powers of administration, legislation and jurisdiction over the territory and inhabitants of these islands, including their territorial waters.

The Treaty of Peace with Japan, though initially intended to be a peace treaty between all the Allied powers and Japan, was eventually concluded only between the nations of the free world from among the Allied powers and Japan, in light of the dramatic change in the international setting arising from the formation of the Government of the People's Republic of China (PRC) in 1949 and the outbreak of the Korean War in 1950. Unlike the peace treaties concluded in 1947 with Italy, Bulgaria, Finland, Hungary, and Romania, which involved all the Allied powers and as such established overall peace, the Treaty of Peace with Japan merely achieved plural (i.e., fragmented) peace. Japan therefore concluded subsequent bilateral peace

---

[4]"Title" refers to facts that are recognized as generating rights under law. The title to territory includes appendages, such as protrusions from the sea floor within territorial seas, accumulation of sediment, and reclaimed coastlines, as well as occupation of *terra nullius*, and cessions, and annexations.

treaties or treaties to reestablish diplomatic relations with those countries that did not participate in the Treaty of Peace with Japan,[5] which was signed in San Francisco (thus also known as the San Francisco Peace Treaty).

Although China managed to survive the war against Japan through a united national front, following the conclusion of World War II, the Government of the PRC controlled mainland China, while the Government of the Republic of China (ROC) was based in Taiwan and some other areas. Neither party was invited to participate in the San Francisco Peace Conference. Japan concluded the Treaty of Peace between Japan and the Republic of China (Japan-ROC Peace Treaty) with the ROC government in Taiwan in April 1952. Article 2 of the treaty referred to the Treaty of Peace with Japan, stating, "It is recognized that under Article 2 of the Treaty of Peace with Japan signed at the city of San Francisco in the United States of America on September 8, 1951 . . ., Japan has renounced all right, title and claim to Taiwan (Formosa) and Penghu (the Pescadores) as well as the Spratly Islands and the Paracel Islands." The Government of Japan recognized the PRC government in September 1972 and, upon issuing the Joint Communique of the Government of Japan and the Government of the PRC (Japan-China Joint Communique), declared the Japan-ROC Peace Treaty null and void. Paragraph 3 of the Japan-China Joint Communique states, "The Government of the People's Republic of China reiterates that Taiwan is an inalienable part of the territory of the People's Republic of China. The Government of Japan fully understands and respects this stand of the Government of the People's Republic of China, and it firmly maintains its stand under Article 8 of the Potsdam Proclamation."

In October 1956, Japan and the Soviet Union, which did not sign the Treaty of Peace with Japan, signed the Joint Declaration by the Union of Soviet Socialist Republics and Japan, which restored normal diplomatic relations between the two sides. Article 9 of the declaration stipulates:

> *The Union of Soviet Socialist Republics and Japan agree to continue, after the restoration of normal diplomatic relations between the Union of Soviet Socialist Republics and Japan, negotiations for the conclusion of a Peace Treaty.*
>
> *In this connexion, the Union of Soviet Socialist Republics, desiring to meet the wishes of Japan and taking into consideration the interests of the Japanese State, agrees to transfer to Japan the Habomai Islands and the island of Shikotan, the actual transfer of these islands to Japan to take place after the conclusion of a Peace Treaty between the Union of Soviet Socialist Republics and Japan.*

In general, the transfer of wartime territories is ultimately decided by a peace treaty. However, according to Article 8 of the Potsdam Declaration, which was accepted by Japan and which concluded the war, Japan was also limited by the terms of the Cairo Declaration of November 1943.[6] The Cairo Declaration made no mention of the Kurile Islands; their transfer to the Soviet Union was merely a

---

[5] Kokusaihō Jirei Kenkyūkai. 1988. *Kokkō saikai, seifu shōnin* (Restoration of Diplomatic Relations and Recognition of Governments). Tokyo: Keio University Press.

[6] See the section on the Cairo Declaration in Chapter 1.

promise shared among the leaders of the USA, Great Britain, and the Soviet Union under the secret agreements of the Yalta Conference of February 1945, of which Japan was not aware. Therefore, Japan and Russia, the successor of the Soviet Union, have yet to conclude a peace treaty, which would ultimately resolve the territorial issue between the two sides.

Thus, upon analyzing the Treaty of Peace with Japan, the current status of Japan's territories is clear. Chapter 1 of this book traces the development of Japan's territory from the past to the present, centered on the Treaty of Peace with Japan and with a focus on the international context. The chapter will clarify the process leading from the firm establishment of Japan's territories at the end of the Edo period and during the Meiji period, to their subsequent expansion and then their reduction following the end of the war, as well as the key issues. In addition, Chapter 1 in particular will discuss Antarctica, regarding which Japan has never asserted any territorial claims, taking into account the stipulations of the Treaty of Peace with Japan, and the fact that Japan is one of the parties to the Antarctic Treaty. Chapters 2, 3, and 4 examine the specific territorial topics, looking in some detail at the diplomatic challenges related to Japan's territory, namely the Northern Territories, the Senkaku Islands, and Takeshima, while also clarifying the arguments. Chapter 5 takes a comprehensive look at the issue of Japan's sovereignty and national jurisdiction in relation to the seas. Chapter 6 addresses the diplomatic factors to consider pertaining to the seas that lie between Japan and China, and between Japan and the Republic of Korea (ROK), namely the current situation in which the delimitation of EEZs between Japan and China, and Japan and the ROK is extremely difficult, as well as the points of contention and points of agreement for reaching a temporary solution. Finally, based on the points covered in the preceding chapters, Chapter 7 gives thought to what is best for future generations in terms of stability and coexistence in East Asia. It proposes designating the Senkaku Islands and Takeshima, over which the assertion of sovereignty by the relevant countries is deadlocked, as nature preserves in line with the model in Antarctica, which is only open for natural or scientific studies. Furthermore, Chapter 7 treats the difficulty of delimiting EEZs as a golden opportunity, in a sense, and proposes establishing a cooperative international structure in the area stretching from the Sea of Japan to the East China Sea and the Yellow Sea.

Chapter 8 examines territorial air space, providing an overview of the current situation and discussing ADIZs, too, given that they also pertain to territorial matters.

Translation Note

Japanese terms, including the names of persons and places, are in principle romanized according to the Hepburn system, with a macron (a bar over the letters) to indicate long vowels. An exception is made for commonly known place names, such as Tokyo, Kyoto, etc. Chinese words are romanized using the Pinyin system; exceptions include familiar historical personages, such as Chiang Kai-shek (Jiang Jieshi in Pinyin). Japanese names are written in the traditional word order, placing the family name first, e.g., Hashimoto Ryūtarō. This custom has been followed for the names of persons from other Asian countries, too. Any direct citation from a source document in English, however, retains the original wording.

Contents

About the Author

Kentaro Serita was born in 1941 in the former Manchuria. He graduated from the Faculty of Law at Kyoto University. He has served as Professor of International Law in the Faculty of Law at Kobe University from 1981; Dean of the Graduate School of International Cooperation Studies at Kobe University from 1994; and Professor Emeritus at Kobe University from 2004. He was also formerly the Dean of the Law School at Aichi Gakuin University and President of Kyoto Notre Dame University.

An expert in international law and international human rights law, he has authored many works, including *Kenpō to kokusai kankyō* (Japan's Constitution in the International Environment (revised edition)); *Kokusai jinken jōyaku shiryōshū* (The International Bill of Human Rights (document collection)); *Eijūsha no kenri* (The Rights of Permanent Residents); *Fuhenteki kokusai shakai no seiritsu to kokusaihō* (Building on the Global Community and International Law); *Shima no ryōyū to keizai suiiki no kyōkai kakutei* (Sovereignty over Islands and the Delimitation of Economic Zones); and various international treaties. In 2017, he received the Order of the Sacred Treasure, Gold Rays with Neck Ribbon for his academic achievements.

Chapter 1
Development of Japan's Territory

Delimitation and Expansion of Peripheral Territories

Delimitation of Peripheral Territories in the Late Edo and Meiji Periods

It is well known that Japan, as an independent country, has been in contact with China and the Korean Peninsula since ancient times, and it has deepened exchanges with these neighbors. However, when Western nations pressed Japan to open its doors to trade as a modern State, there was a need to clarify the sovereignty over the surrounding islands. Thus began the process of defining Japan's peripheral territory, which spanned from the late-Edo to the Meiji periods. Japan had to delineate the territories between itself and Russia, which was expanding southward from Siberia; the United States and the United Kingdom, which were approaching across the Pacific from the east and west; and also nearby China and the Korean Peninsula.

The Northern Territories, the Kurile Islands, and Sakhalin

Looking first to the north, Russia occupied the Kamchatka Peninsula at the close of the seventeenth century, then began expanding southward toward the Kurile Islands. When the Russians had come to the Northern Territories by the mid-eighteenth century, the influence of Japan's Matsumae Domain had only extended to Kunashiri Island. However, Russia's administration did not reach Etorofu Island; although it had established a colony on Uruppu Island, Russia abandoned it and withdrew in 1805. Meanwhile, the Japanese shogunate conducted a survey of Sakhalin, Kunashiri Island, Etorofu Island and Uruppu Island beginning in 1785; hardened defenses in eastern Ezo to bring the area, including the Northern Territories, under its direct control in 1799; and established a settlement on Etorofu Island the following

© Kreab K.K. 2023

K. Serita, *The Territory of Japan*, https://doi.org/10.1007/978-981-99-3013-5_1

year. Japan thus had established its sovereignty over the Northern Territories by the beginning of the nineteenth century. The 1811 Golovnin Incident further demonstrated that Japanese rule had been cemented there.[1]

The Matsumae Domain had also conducted surveys of Sakhalin in the seventeenth century. At the beginning of that century, the Qing dynasty initiated its administration of Sakhalin, already known in China in the earlier Tang and Yuan dynasties. Qing influence brushed up against Russia's in the Heilongjiang (Amur) River area. The Treaty of Nerchinsk of 1689 established the relationship between the Qing dynasty and Russia in this area, and the latter withdrew. The desolate land of Sakhalin was not of particular interest to the Qing, however, and neither Japan nor Russia was able to determine much about the region despite sending survey expeditions during this time.

As Russia sought to expand into the northern Pacific in search of trade, Adam Laxman and Nikolai Rezanov made voyages to Nemuro in 1792 and to Nagasaki in 1804. After the shogunate refused to trade with Russia, Rezanov burned down a guard station and committed other acts of violence on his return journey toward Sakhalin. In May 1805, Mamiya Rinzō, whom the shogunate had ordered to conduct a survey of Sakhalin, discovered what came to be known as the Mamiya Strait between Russia and Sakhalin, thus proving that the latter is an island. Mamiya's findings appeared in a book of maps, *Kita Ezo Zusetsu*, and this evidence was presented in Europe in a book by Philipp Franz von Siebold entitled *Nippon* (1832). However, the ownership of Sakhalin was not determined until the late Edo period. In 1727, Russia signed the Treaty of Kyakhta with the Qing dynasty. This document delimited the border between Siberia and Outer Mongolia and, together with the Treaty of Nerchinsk, kept Russia's southern expansion in check until the mid-nineteenth century.

Following the First Opium War of 1840, the Qing dynasty signed the Treaty of Nanjing in 1842. The Qing was forced to cede Hong Kong to the UK and to open the ports of Shanghai and Canton (Guangzhou). As a result, Russia's overland trade through the town of Kyakhta was suddenly threatened and Russia was forced to reconsider a policy of expanding into Qing lands. In 1843, a naval expedition under the command of Yevfimy Putyatin was planned to survey the Sea of Okhotsk and the mouth of the Amur River, ensure access to Chinese seaports, and visit Japan. The expedition was postponed due to various circumstances, but a survey of the Amur's mouth was conducted. The port of Nikolayevsk-on-Amur was built at the river's mouth in 1850, thus sparking a border dispute with the Qing about sovereignty over the Amur coastline. According to the record of a British ambassador to Russia, Russia surveyed Sakhalin (Karafuto) for coal in 1852. When word reached Russia

---

[1] Russians had conducted raids in southern Sakhalin, on Etorofu Island, and elsewhere during 1806–07. The shogunate hardened its defenses against the violence, and when Russian naval captain Vasily Golovnin sailed to Kunashiri Island under orders from the Russian Navy to survey the area, he and his subordinates were captured on Kunashiri Island by Matsumae magistrate officials and transported to Hakodate. This incident was peacefully resolved 2 years later thanks to mediation by Takadaya Kahei.

the following year of a mission to Japan undertaken by Commodore Matthew C. Perry of the US Navy, there was concern that the US would seize Sakhalin. Russia then issued a decree to occupy the island.

It was under these circumstances that Putyatin, Russia's plenipotentiary, came to Nagasaki in July 1853, where he commenced negotiations with the shogunate on delineating national borders and opening Japanese ports for trade. This mission resulted in the signing of the Treaty of Commerce, Navigation and Delimitation between Japan and Russia on February 7, 1855. This treaty, which was based upon the Japan-US Treaty of Peace and Amity, dealt with national borders in Article 2. It defined the border as lying between Etorofu Island and Uruppu Island, and it stated that Etorofu Island in its entirety belongs to Japan, that all of Uruppu Island and the "Kurile" Islands to its north belong to Russia, and with regard to Sakhalin that "the division of the land shall be performed at a later date."

In May 1858, as the Qing dynasty was in the midst of the Taiping Rebellion and fighting the Second Opium War against the British and French armies in a conflict that was sparked by the October 1856 Arrow Incident, Russia, pressing south from Siberia, signed the Treaty of Aigun with the Qing, by which Russia gained all land north of the Heilongjiang (Amur) River. Furthermore, under the Convention of Peking (Beijing) agreed between Russia and the Qing in November 1860, the Qing ceded to Russia the Primorsky Krai area east of the Ussuri River as compensation for mediating a peace with the UK and France. Due to the Qing signing the Convention of Tianjin with Russia, the US, the UK, and France in June 1858, as well as the Convention of Peking in October 1860, external powers began stationing ministers resident in Beijing, and in January 1861 the Qing established the Zongli Yamen, an institution to handle diplomatic affairs in the manner of Western States.

In the meantime, Russia was gradually pushing farther into Sakhalin and antagonizing Japan by asserting control over the entire island. After the Meiji Restoration of 1868 overthrew the Japanese shogunate, Harry Parkes, envoy extraordinary and minister plenipotentiary of the UK, displayed an interest in Russian activity in this region and advised Japan to abandon Sakhalin.

Sakhalin was shared by Japan and Russia, but there were clashes between the two countries' officials and negotiations had come to a standstill. Japanese Foreign Minister Soejima Taneomi suggested purchasing Sakhalin from Russia, participated in the *Seikanron* debate over whether to immediately send a punitive expedition to Korea, and also suggested ceding Sakhalin to Russia providing that Russia agreed to a Japanese conquest of Korea. However, Japanese figures such as Kuroda Kiyotaka, then vice director-general of the Hokkaidō Development Commission, argued in favor of abandoning Sakhalin to instead focus on administering Hokkaidō and strengthening defenses against the Russians out of concern for Japan's foreign relations and national strength at the time.

Eventually, Soejima met with the Qing dynasty in March 1873 to negotiate issues concerning the Ryūkyū Islands. He resigned that October due to the political upheaval that had resulted from the *Seikanron* debate. After the pro-invasion faction stepped down from their posts, those in favor of focusing on domestic affairs gained control of the Japanese government. The policies supported by figures like Kuroda gained widespread support. Vice Admiral Enomoto Takeaki became Minister to Russia in 1874, where he commenced negotiations that resulted in the conclusion of the Treaty for the Exchange of Sakhalin for the Kurile Islands on May 7, 1875. Under the terms of the treaty, Japan recognized that the entirety of Sakhalin was Russian territory, while Russia ceded to Japan the Kurile Islands, thus giving Japan dominion over the 18 islands stretching from Shumshu Island to Uruppu Island. Thus, in a peaceful manner, the Kurile Islands became Japanese territory and a border between Japan and Russia was finally delimited.[2]

The Ogasawara (Bonin) Islands and Okinawa

Next as we look to the south, no discussion of the Pacific Ocean during the nineteenth century can omit the role of the Chinese market. The US, the first country to pry open Japan's doors to the outside world, had conducted its trade with the Far East primarily along a route running from the Atlantic Ocean around the Cape of Good Hope and onward to the Indian Ocean. After the Mexican-American War and the signing of the Treaty of Guadalupe Hidalgo on March 10, 1848, the US received land concessions that include present-day California and Texas. It enacted a plan to open sea routes accessing the Pacific Ocean when gold was discovered in California. Like many European countries, America's capitalist mindset was one reason for seeking to open Japan's markets. Furthermore, from the 1840s to the 1850s, whaling was a thriving industry and there was a concentration of whales in the North Pacific. Some whaling vessels ended up shipwrecked on the Japanese coast, thus providing further impetus to open up Japan.

It was in this setting that Commodore Perry, in command of the East India Squadron, turned his eyes on his first voyage toward the Port of Naha as well as Port Lloyd (Port of Futami) on Chichijima Island, the chief port of the Ogasawara (Bonin) Islands. Perry had been raised in Rhode Island, the heart of the American whaling industry, and he came from a military family, with both a father and elder brother who had served in the Navy. On May 26, 1853, he arrived in Naha from Shanghai, and after paying a visit to Ryūkyū King Shō Tai at Shuri Castle he entered the Port of Futami on June 14. British and Russian warships had also visited the Ogasawara (Bonin) Islands prior to Perry's arrival, and already there were foreigners living there as immigrants. The shogunate had dispatched magistrates of foreign affairs to the islands in 1861, but the door to immigrants was mostly closed until the Meiji Restoration.

Even after the beginning of the Meiji period, the Japanese government was unable to work out a clear position on immigration, the *Seikanron* debate being a contributing factor. However, it did spell out a development and settlement policy in 1874,

---

[2]Taijudō, Kanae. 1998. *Kaikokki no ryōdo kōshō: Ryōdo kizoku no kokusaihō* (Territorial Negotiations upon the Opening of Japan: International Law on Territory). Tokyo: Tōshindō.

and in 1876 the government placed the Ogasawara Islands under the control of the Home Ministry and sent notifications to ministers resident of other nations. No other country lodged an objection to this incorporation.

Perry had also eyed the Ryūkyū Kingdom, but it had long-standing ties with the Qing dynasty and the archipelago was in a special position in the nineteenth century. That is to say, Shimazu Iehisa, the lord of the Satsuma Domain (also known then as the Kagoshima Domain), had received permission from Shogun Tokugawa Ieyasu, who had unified Japan under one ruler, to send troops to the main island of Okinawa in 1609 to apprehend King Shō Nei of the Ryūkyū Kingdom and subject his land to Japanese rule. However, Shō Nei's clan continued to maintain control over the Ryūkyū Kingdom as its kings. Their reign was regulated by the Fifteen Laws stipulated by the Shimazu clan, and for over 200 years the Satsuma Domain collected tax from the Ryūkyū Kingdom and enforced the laws of the domain. The Ryūkyū Kingdom had maintained ties with the Qing, sending tribute and engaging in a tributary relationship. However, there was no objection from the Qing over the Shimazu clan's rule, and Qing law was not enforced on the Ryūkyū Islands. In other words, the Qing dynasty did not have material control over Ryūkyū, and the islands were in practical terms a vassal State of the Satsuma Domain. However, the Satsuma Domain did permit the Ryūkyū Kingdom considerable political and religious freedom, and the kingdom maintained contact with the Qing as well as Western powers in the late Edo period.

It was in this situation that in 1854 the Ryūkyū Kingdom signed the Ryūkyū-US Treaty of Amity with Commodore Perry, along with largely similar treaties with France in 1855 and the Netherlands in 1859. Thus, despite being within the shogunate's system of domains, the Ryūkyū Kingdom was granted a degree of autonomy. After the Meiji Restoration, however, this was a source of controversy concerning the Ryūkyū Disposition.[3] In any case, Japanese control over the Ryūkyū Islands caused no problems for Japan's relations with the Qing dynasty or any other powers from 1880 onward.[4]

---

[3] A Meiji government plan to integrate the Ryūkyū Kingdom into the Empire of Japan. It comprised a series of policies implemented from the islands' incorporation under the jurisdiction of Kagoshima Prefecture in 1871 until the establishment of Okinawa Prefecture in 1879.

[4] Japan had been embroiled in a dispute with the Qing dynasty over control of the Ryūkyū Kingdom. During negotiations, Japan submitted a proposal to China it termed *Buntō Kaiyaku*. "Buntō," literally "island separation," meant conceding to China islands near Taiwan: Miyako Island and the Yaeyama Islands (also known as the Sakishima Islands). "Kaiyaku," meaning "revised terms," would redefine the relationship between Japan and the Qing dynasty by permitting the Japanese to conduct trade in China just as Western nations were allowed to. The negotiations reached a compromise that fulfilled Japanese wishes on October 21, 1880, but met with objections from Li Hongzhang, an influential Chinese politician and diplomat, and the Qing dynasty postponed signing an agreement. Thereafter, the Japanese did not respond to calls for renewed talks, and the issue faded away after the First Sino-Japanese War.

The Senkaku Islands and Takeshima

The existence of the Senkaku Islands was known since ancient times to the people of the Ryūkyū and the Chinese, as they lay along a trade route between those two kingdoms. After the Meiji Restoration, the Japanese government, while giving consideration to the overall relationship with the Qing dynasty, from 1885 on conducted thorough surveys of the Senkaku Islands through the authorities of Okinawa Prefecture and by way of other methods. It was carefully confirmed through these surveys that the Senkaku Islands had been uninhabited and showed no trace of having been under Qing control. Based on this confirmation, the Japanese government took the step of formally incorporating the Senkaku Islands into the territory of Japan in January 1895. The Treaty of Shimonoseki, the peace treaty that ended the First Sino-Japanese War, was concluded in April of that year, by which Taiwan was ceded to Japan. However, the Senkaku Islands were not among the islands ceded to Japan as a part of the territory of Taiwan.[5]

Takeshima, the uninhabited islands that lie along the line running from the Oki Islands of Shimane Prefecture to Ulleungdo of Korea, are historically associated with the Japanese economic activities on Ulleungdo. The Kingdom of Joseon in Korea adopted an "empty-island" policy with Ulleungdo from the fifteenth century to the end of the nineteenth century. During this time, Japanese people did administer Ulleungdo for around 80 years from the beginning of the seventeenth century after receiving a license from the shogunate. Disagreements arose with the Joseon, however, and in 1696 the shogunate forbade Japanese from traveling to the island. After the shogunate renounced Ulleungdo (called Takeshima at the time), it no longer prohibited travel to present-day Takeshima (called Matsushima at the time), regardless of a policy of national seclusion that had been adopted by then. After the Meiji Restoration, the Japanese government decided to place Takeshima under the jurisdiction of Shimane Prefecture in 1905, and it gave public notice thereof. Even so, no protests were lodged.[6]

Territorial Expansion During the First Sino-Japanese War, the Russo-Japanese War, and World War I

The Cession of Taiwan and the Liaodong Peninsula

Japan and the Qing dynasty settled the matter of Taiwan in October 1874: at the end of that year Japan withdrew its troops from the so-called Taiwan Expedition. The Treaty for the Exchange of Sakhalin for the Kurile Islands was signed in May of the

---

[5] See Chapter 3.
[6] See Chapter 4.

following year. These events marked the clear delimitation of Japan's peripheral territory and the beginning of Japanese expansion into the continent. Japan, seeking to open up the Korean Peninsula, dispatched a warship in September 1875 to support its negotiations with the Joseon. This sparked the Ganghwa Island Incident,[7] which was followed by the February 1876 signing of the Japan-Korea Treaty of Amity. Japan thus won the race with the Western powers to open up the Korean Peninsula. It was through this treaty that Japanese political and economic influence rapidly penetrated into the area.

However, the Joseon Kingdom was a tributary of the Qing dynasty and also part of its market, so the Korean Peninsula became a flashpoint for conflict and disputes between Japan and the Qing. The Japanese and Qing militaries became involved in the political struggle within the Joseon Kingdom between the pro-Japanese Independence Party and the pro-Qing Conservative Party. This eventually resulted in the signing of the Convention of Tianjin between Japan and the Qing in April 1885, which stipulated that both sides remove their troops from the area. Yet in 1894, the internal political turmoil within the Joseon Kingdom led to the Donghak Rebellion that spread throughout the Korean Peninsula.[8] The Joseon government requested the dispatch of Qing troops. Japan also sent in forces, and the confrontation between the two finally resulted in exchanges of fire between their armies in July. Then, on August 1, Japan declared war on the Qing.

Japan's victory that resulted in the 1895 peace treaty to end the First Sino-Japanese War not only turned the Korean Peninsula into a neutral zone, but also forced the Qing dynasty to pay a huge sum in reparations and cede Taiwan, the Pescadores Islands, and the Liaodong Peninsula to Japan. The cession of the Liaodong Peninsula, however, was not overlooked by Russia, which adopted an increasingly aggressive stance in administering the Far East after deciding to construct the Trans-Siberian Railroad in 1891. Hence, Russia, Germany, and France intervened to have Japan sign a treaty in November 1895 to return the Liaodong Peninsula.

The great powers demanded numerous concessions from the Qing once the dynasty's weakness was exposed. On the pretense of the Qing bestowing gratitude for the tripartite intervention, Russia and the Qing concluded the Sino-Russian Secret Treaty in May 1896, the treaty concerning the construction and management of the Chinese Eastern Railway in August, the so-called Cassini Treaty in

---

[7] In September 1875, the Japanese government dispatched a warship on "a cruise for the purpose of studying sea routes to the Kingdom of Joseon." As surveys of the Tsushima Strait were largely complete at this time, the gunboat *Un'yō*, on patrol along the western coast of Korea, approached Ganghwa Island, where it was met with Korean cannon fire. The *Un'yō* then responded with a disproportionate retaliatory assault.

[8] Donghak was an anti-Christian, anti-Confucian peasant religion that arose in the mid-nineteenth century. It advocated establishing Eastern (Korean) Learning (as opposed to Western Learning) and promoted the establishment of worldly benefit and an equal society. It spread widely among farmers in southern Korea, which led to a peasant rebellion involving Donghak followers and ordinary farmers.

September, as well as a treaty for the lease of Lüshun (Port Arthur) and Dalian Bay signed in March 1898, which yielded great benefits from Manchuria to Guandong (Kwantung). They also established so-called railway-affiliated land where Russia had police authority as well as the right to station troops. After the Russo-Japanese War, Japan acquired the "railway-affiliated land" along the South Manchuria Railway and the Anfeng Railway connecting Andong with Fengtian (Mukden) (present day Dandong to Shenyang). Germany used the killing of missionaries in Shandong as an excuse to occupy Jiaozhou Bay in 1897, then concluded a treaty in March the next year to lease the area. In June 1897, France obtained rights to the Yunnan extension of the Annan Railway as well as mining rights in Yunnan, Guangxi, and Guangdong. France then signed a treaty with the Qing the following November to lease Guangzhou Bay. Matching France's accomplishments, the UK signed an agreement to lease the Kowloon Peninsula in June 1898, and then, in rivalry with Russia, concluded another lease agreement for the town of Weihai in July.[9] The great powers also forced the Qing to make "non-concession declarations" so that they could monopolize the interests and lands they had acquired.

With the exchange of notes in April 1898, Japan forced the Qing dynasty to permit non-concession in Fujian, while the UK received non-concessions on the coast at the mouth of the Yangtze River and other locations, and France received them on Hainan Island and in Guangdong, Guangxi, and Yunnan. Taking advantage of this momentum, foreign powers gradually expanded and added to the number of settlements they administered, such as the Shanghai International Settlement. Japan established its first exclusive settlement in the Hangzhou concession in September 1896. Its largest was the Tianjin concession, established via a memorandum between Japan and the Qing in August 1898. Other Japanese settlements were in Suzhou, Hankou, Shashi, Fuzhou, Xiamen, and Chongqing.

The Cession of Sakhalin and the Annexation of the Korean Peninsula

Japan's victory in the First Sino-Japanese War, and its incursions into the Korean Peninsula and Manchuria, posed a threat to Russian plans for expanding into its Far East. The hostility between Japan and Russia intensified on the Korean Peninsula where the Qing dynasty had withdrawn. In March 1898, Nishi Tokujirō, foreign minister in the third Itō Hirobumi Cabinet, notified Russian Foreign Minister Baron Roman Romanovich Rosen that if Russia would leave Korea to Japan, then Japan would consider Manchuria outside the scope of its interests. Rosen's reply was that Russia would not accept the complete exclusion of its influence from Korea. The dispute ended in April with the conclusion of the Nishi-Rosen Agreement, which

---

[9]Department of Transportation, Ministry of Railways of Japan. *Shina tetsudō kankei jōyaku isan* (Collection of Treaties related to Chinese Railways). September 1926.

stipulated that Russia would allow Japanese dominance in terms of the size of commerce and industry, and the number of settlements, while Japan would give tacit approval to Russian occupation of Lüshun and Dalian.

In March 1899, however, the anti-foreigner Boxers (a faction of the ancient White Lotus religion) staged a rebellion in Shandong, China in response to Germany's leasing of Jiaozhou Bay and their movement spread across northern China. In May 1900, the legations of 11 powers in Beijing demanded that the Qing dynasty immediately quell the Boxers' revolt. Instead, in June the Qing emperor joined sides with the Boxers who had surrounded the national legations in Beijing. He then declared war on all foreign powers that had troops in Beijing. With the support of the UK and the US, Japan dispatched a large force that was joined in an alliance with other nations' troops, and this army marched into Beijing in August. The Boxer Rebellion (also known as the Boxer Uprising or the Yihequan Movement) came to an end in September 1901 with the signing of the Boxer Protocol. This document forced the complete surrender of the Qing and granted the foreign powers the right to station police and military forces in the Legation Quarter. The majority of troops supplied in the joint deployment were from the Japanese and Russian armies. Russian forces were diverted to strengthen their grip on Manchuria. Russia's indifference to objections from Japan, the UK, and the US led to greater hostility between Japan and Russia.

In January 1901, Russia proposed turning Korea into a neutral zone, to which Japan demanded that Russia first withdraw its troops from Manchuria. After concluding the Anglo-Japanese Alliance Treaty in 1902, Japan called for the recognition of the independence of the Qing dynasty and Korea and underscored the importance of preserving their territorial integrity. Japan further demanded that it be given dominant status in all areas, including politics, the economy, and military matters and be allowed to possess a foothold for entry into Manchuria. Russia only gave support to respecting the independence and territorial integrity of Korea and pushed for turning lands north of the 39th parallel into neutral territory and for Japan's full exclusion from Manchuria. At the end of 1903, Japan formulated a policy towards the Qing dynasty and Korea to be taken if negotiations were to break down. Japan made its final proposal to Russia in January the following year. An Imperial Conference was convened on February 4, which concluded that "if we waste this opportunity, we fear that we, the Empire of Japan, will fall into a disadvantageous situation both diplomatically and militarily, from which we shall not recover." The Japanese government decided to break off the talks with Russia and on February 10 issued a declaration of war against Russia. The Russians signed an agreement to surrender Lüshun to Japan on January 2, 1905. Japan emerged victorious in the Battle of Mukden on March 10, and on May 27 Japan secured a complete naval victory in the Sea of Japan. After the Battle of Mukden, however, Japan's war-fighting capabilities had reached their limit. On June 1, Japan requested that US President Theodore Roosevelt amicably mediate a Russo-Japanese peace. With Roosevelt's good offices, a conference was convened in Portsmouth, New Hampshire.

The Portsmouth Peace Treaty, signed on September 5, 1905, forced Russia to recognize Japan's special rights in Korea, stipulated that both countries would withdraw their forces from Manchuria, and guaranteed that Russia would respect Manchurian sovereignty. Furthermore, the lease on the Port of Lüshun and Dalian, as well as the railway running between Changchun and the Port of Lüshun along with its affiliated land, would be ceded to Japan. In addition, Russian territory on Sakhalin south of the 50th parallel was ceded to Japan. However, by taking over control of special interests in Manchuria from Russia, Japan continued its expansion into the Asian mainland while sowing discord over the issues of maintaining territorial integrity, the Open Door Policy, and equal opportunity as advocated by the US.

After the Russo-Japanese War, in October 1905, Japan finalized a policy of turning Korea into a protectorate. The Japan-Korea Treaty of 1905 (Japan–Korea Protectorate Treaty) was signed in November, thus establishing the Office of the Resident-General and making Korea a protectorate of Japan. Japan later annexed Korea on August 22, 1910, through the conclusion of the Japan-Korea Annexation Treaty.

Leases, Settlements, and Special Interests in China, Acquisition of the South Pacific Mandate, and the Creation of Manchukuo

The Xinhai Revolution began on October 10, 1911, in Wuchang, China. The following January, Sun Yat-sen became provisional president and established the Provisional Government of the Republic of China (ROC) in Nanjing. Qing dynasty Emperor Puyi abdicated in February and Yuan Shikai was appointed provisional president in Beijing the next month, thus marking the end of Qing rule. The US recognized the ROC in May 1913, followed by 13 other powers including Japan, the UK, Russia, Germany, and France that October. On October 10, Yuan was officially inaugurated as president of China.

On August 1, 1914, just after the outbreak of World War I, Germany declared war on Russia. The UK wished for Japan to join the fight against the German-armed merchant fleet; Japan declared war on Germany on August 23. Japan occupied German-controlled territory in Jiaozhou Bay and on South Pacific islands. Since the great powers were too distracted to pay any attention to East Asia, Japan took advantage by issuing the Twenty-One Demands to the Yuan Shikai administration in January 1915, followed by an ultimatum. China was forced to accept the demands on May 9. Japan had insisted on special interests in Shandong Province as well as various interests in Manchuria and Mongolia. Also among the demands were that the Chinese government should engage Japanese as political, financial, and military advisers. Thus, on May 25, the two sides concluded a Sino-Japanese treaty and exchanged notes concerning Shandong Province, notes concerning Fujian Province, and notes concerning leased land in Jiaozhou Bay; they also signed a Sino-Japanese treaty concerning South Manchuria and Eastern Inner Mongolia and exchanged notes on the Han-Ye-Ping Company (a company formed to manage Hanyang's iron manufacturing, Daye's gold mining and Pingxiang's coal mining). In addition to sparking anti-Japanese demonstrations in China, these moves to expand Japan's influence there met with strong opposition from the US. The signing of the Lansing-Ishii Agreement in November 1917 was an American attempt to prevent the expansion of Japan's special interests. That same month, the Soviet government was established in Russia following the October Revolution.

World War I came to an end when the Allied Powers signed an armistice with Germany on November 11, 1918. A peace conference was held in Paris in January 1919. At a meeting of five powers on January 27, Japanese plenipotentiary Makino Nobuaki demanded the unconditional cession of Jiaozhou Bay and all German territory on Pacific islands north of the equator. On May 4 in Paris he proclaimed that Shandong would be retroceded to Japan; the peace conference participants decided on May 7 to make Pacific islands north of the equator a Japanese mandate. The Treaty of Peace between the Allied and Associated Powers and Germany (Treaty of Versailles) was signed on June 28. China did not sign the treaty in light of the dissatisfaction over the treatment of Shandong as well as the rise of the May Fourth Movement back home, which called for China's refusal to sign the peace treaty (as it did not nullify the Twenty-One Demands), the nullification of said demands, and a boycott of Japanese goods.

In July 1921, the US unofficially proposed holding a conference in Washington, DC to Japan, the UK, France, and Italy to discuss arms limitations and issues concerning the Far East. This American initiative resulted in the convening of the Washington Naval Conference that November. In December Japan, the US, the UK, and France signed a document entitled the "Four-Power Treaty on Insular Possessions and Dominions in the Pacific." The signatories pledged to respect rights pertaining to these islands and to cooperate in order to resolve any disputes among them. It was also stipulated that with the entry into force of the treaty, the third Anglo-Japanese Alliance, which was signed on July 13, 1911, would be terminated. In February 1922, these four countries at the Washington Naval Conference were joined by Belgium, China, Italy, the Netherlands, and Portugal in signing the Nine-Power Treaty concerning China, which stipulated respect for China's sovereignty, maintaining its territorial integrity, support for the Open Door Policy, and equal opportunity. This treaty essentially limited the scope of the Twenty-One Demands. The return of the lease on Jiaozhou Bay was also promised at this conference. This Washington system was assembled through Japan's cooperative diplomacy with the US. Under this regime, however, conflicts over Japan's special status in East Asia with the UK and the US (the latter in particular) gradually rose to the surface. Disagreement over the issue of Manchuria became especially heated.

On the night of September 18, 1931, the Japanese army staged a bombing on the South Manchuria Railway at Liutiaohu. This led to the commencement of military operations in an event that came to be known as the Mukden Incident. It also destroyed the framework of cooperation with the US under the Washington system. On September 19, the Japanese government received reports about clashes between

Japanese and Chinese forces and decided to prevent the situation from escalating as it did not have a clear understanding of what had really happened. However, the staff of the Kwangtung Army, the Japanese force stationed in the area and led by officers that included Lieutenant Colonel Ishiwara Kanji and Colonel Itagaki Seishirō, decided to resolve the Manchuria-Inner Mongolian question on their own. US Secretary of State Henry Stimson, citing the Kellogg-Briand Pact on the renunciation of war and the Nine-Power Treaty, issued a warning to Japan on September 22 that it should take responsibility for the events in Manchuria. The Japanese Cabinet of the time was being led by Foreign Minister Shidehara Kijūrō. The Japanese government released its first announcement concerning the Mukden Incident on September 24. The Council of the League of Nations passed a resolution on October 24 calling for the withdrawal of Japanese troops from Manchuria. In response, the Japanese government issued a second announcement on the matter on October 26, citing the preconditions for the return of Japanese troops to within the South Manchuria Railway zone, or in other words the withdrawal of Japanese troops. Nevertheless, the Kwangtung Army continued to carry out military operations for up to 5 months, occupying major cities in the three provinces of Fengtian (Liaoning), Jilin, and Heilongjiang. On March 1, 1932, the Kwangtung Army declared that it was creating the State of Manchukuo. Eventually, the Japanese Ministry of War and the Army General Staff Office granted approval of the Kwangtung Army's actions. After the May 15 Incident, the Japanese government recognized the State of Manchukuo, which its military had created, on September 15 and signed the Japan-Manchukuo Protocol. In the meantime, the US Secretary of State had announced the Stimson Doctrine, a policy that withheld recognition of the new situation in Manchuria, on January 7, 1932. The League of Nations formed the Lytton Commission, a group with British, American, French, German, and Italian members who conducted an on-the-ground investigation in Japan, China, and Manchuria in February. The resulting Lytton Report was communicated to Japan, China, and other League member States on October 1, after Japan had accorded recognition to the State of Manchukuo. Based on this report, the League of Nations deliberated on a draft recommendation, and on February 24 of the following year the Assembly voted 42 to 1 in favor of approving the document. Japan announced its withdrawal from the League of Nations on March 27, and, isolated, pursued its rule over Manchuria and expansion into the Asian mainland.[10]

The Second Sino-Japanese War began on July 7, 1937, when Japanese and Chinese forces clashed on the Marco Polo Bridge outside of Beijing. The Japanese army occupied the capital of Nanjing on December 13. The Chinese government that had formed the First United Front between the Kuomintang and the Communist Party relocated to Chongqing in November and called on US, British, and Soviet support in an all-out war of resistance. The front extended all across China. Japan

---

[10]For more on Japan's recognition of Manchukuo and the US refusal to recognize the State, see Serita, Kentarō. 1996. *Fuhenteki kokusai shakai no seiritsu to kokusaihō* (Building on the Global Community and International Law). Tokyo: Yūhikaku.

occupied the island of Hainan in February 1939. Then, in July 1940, it adopted a policy of southward expansion, which would include the use of force, in order to acquire strategic resources for conducting war. Japan's reach consequently extended to the Dutch East Indies and French Indochina. Japan signed the Japanese-Soviet Neutrality Pact in Moscow on April 13, 1941. Having reduced the risk of a two-front conflict, Japan started the Pacific War by declaring hostilities against the Chongqing government's supporters, the US and the UK on December 8 (December 7 in the US).

It is useful at this juncture, before we review Japan's territory prior to the outbreak of World War II, to refer to the Four-Power Treaty on Insular Possessions and Dominions in the Pacific concluded among Japan, the US, France, and Italy, as the central part of the Washington System, which accounted for 10 years of peace between World War I and World War II. A Protocol was added to the treaty in February 1922, the year after it was signed. It states: "The term 'insular possessions and insular dominions' used in the aforesaid Treaty shall, in its application to Japan, include only Karafuto (or the Southern portion of the island of Sakhalin), Formosa and the Pescadores, and the islands under the mandate of Japan."

Other than the territories prescribed by the Four-Power Treaty, Japan also held the Korean Peninsula, and its colonial interests in China included leased land and settlements, and the Beijing Legation Quarter, as well as railway-affiliated land. In fact, Japan signed a pact on January 9, 1943, with the Chinese government in Japanese-occupied Nanjing led by Wang Jingwei concerning the retrocession of settlements and the abolition of extraterritoriality. All settlements and the Legation Quarter had reverted to China by August 1. However, the government in Chongqing led by Chiang Kai-shek refused to recognize the treaty and considered it inherently null and void. Meanwhile, the Spratly Islands, where mining operations were underway to retrieve phosphoric ore that the Japanese had discovered in 1915, were incorporated into the jurisdiction of the Taiwanese city of Kaohsiung in 1939. Although the Japanese had been mining phosphoric ore in the Paracels since 1920, Japan had never asserted its sovereignty over the islands before World War II.

The End of World War II and Territorial Issues

Territories won and lost through war are finally decided by a peace treaty. As had been the case with the Treaty of Shimonoseki, the Portsmouth Peace Treaty, and the Treaty of Versailles, the Treaty of Peace with Japan, which was signed in San Francisco in September 1951, determined the extent of Japan's territory after World War II. In the case of World War II, however, the armistice and surrender documents prior to the official peace contained clauses concerning territory and broadly outlined the political conditions for peace and reparation principles. Furthermore, the occupation of Japan lasted a lengthy period of 6 years from the end of war to the official peace. Of course, there are many instances in history when a preliminary peace was arranged, during which conditions for the official peace to come were worked out, but the timeframes ranged from a few months to at most a year, and thus 6 years was unusually long. Therefore, there is value in conducting a detailed analysis of the peace that was arranged after World War II.

Three important documents touched on the matter of Japan's territory prior to the end of the war: the Cairo Declaration of November 27, 1943, the secret Yalta Agreement of February 11, 1945, and the Potsdam Declaration of July 26, 1945. The Cairo Declaration was incorporated into the Potsdam Declaration, and the surrender document Japan signed on September 2, 1945, contained a pledge to carry out the provisions of the Potsdam Declaration in good faith. In contrast, the Yalta Agreement remained only as an agreement of the leaders of the US, the UK, and the Soviet Union, which was made public on February 11, 1946, after Japan's surrender. The Cairo Declaration and the Potsdam Declaration are decisively different in legal nature from the Yalta Agreement in terms of whether or not Japan accepted them prior to the peace treaty.

There are two other documents that stated the general goals of the Allies in the war. These were the Atlantic Charter of August 14, 1941, and the Declaration by United Nations of January 1, 1942. In both documents, the Allies advocated the principles of no territorial aggrandizement and the self-determination of peoples. This is what most definitively distinguishes World War II from the imperialistic wars fought previously.

The Allies involved used these declarations and agreements to unilaterally incorporate Japanese territory as their own and to take other measures prior to the conclusion of a peace treaty. Not only are these measures of questionable legitimacy in terms of the end to territorial aggrandizement and the self-determination the Allies had themselves advocated, but they also created a problem concerning the peace treaty's final legal validity. The following is an examination of these actions taken by the Allies, the relationship between those actions and principles, and the problems they created.

Acceptance of the Potsdam Declaration

The US, China, and the UK issued the Potsdam Declaration on July 26, 1945. The Declaration begins with the following statement: "We—the President of the United States, the President of the National Government of the Republic of China, and the Prime Minister of Great Britain, representing the hundreds of millions of our countrymen, have conferred and agree that Japan shall be given an opportunity to end this war." On July 28, however, then Prime Minister of Japan Suzuki Kantarō ignored the Potsdam Declaration and announced that the war would go on. The first atomic bomb was dropped on Hiroshima on August 6. The Soviet Union joined the war on August 9: the Red Army commenced an invasion of Manchuria, northern Korea, and Sakhalin. That same day, the second atomic bomb fell on Nagasaki. Japan finally accepted the terms of the Potsdam Declaration on August 14. On August 16, Emperor Hirohito ordered all Japanese forces to cease fighting immediately. Thereafter, the Soviet Union began landing forces on Shumshu Island on August 18; they had completed their occupation of Shikotan Island, Kunashiri Island, and the Habomai Islands by September 3. In Manchuria, Soviet forces took Fengtian, Changchun, Harbin, and Jilin on August 20, and Lüshun and Dalian on August 22. In Korea they seized Pyongyang on August 24. On September 2, Foreign Minister Shigemitsu Mamoru and Chief of the Imperial Japanese Army General Staff Umezu Yoshijirō signed the surrender documents aboard the *USS Missouri* in Tokyo Bay. Also that day, the Supreme Commander for the Allied Powers (SCAP), General Douglas MacArthur, issued his first general order to the Imperial Japanese Army and Navy.

The Potsdam Declaration was written by the US, the UK, and China, then later agreed to by the Soviet Union. It contains 13 paragraphs. Number 8, which concerns territory, reads as follows: "The terms of the Cairo Declaration shall be carried out and Japanese sovereignty shall be limited to the islands of Honshu, Hokkaido, Kyushu, Shikoku and such minor islands as we determine."

To briefly sum up how World War II started, a great war was declared in Europe on September 3, 1939. The next day, the Japanese government declared that it would not be involved in the hostilities in Europe and that it would move forward in settling the Second Sino-Japanese War. Japan, Germany, and Italy signed the Tripartite Pact in September 1940. In a speech on December 29, US President Franklin Delano Roosevelt, elected to an unprecedented third term in office in November, denounced the Tripartite Pact and declared that the US would supply arms to democratic nations. The US enacted the Lend-Lease Act in March 1941 to support the countries fighting against Germany. The Japanese-Soviet Neutrality Pact was signed on April 22. Hostilities broke out between Germany and the Soviet Union on June 22 when German forces launched an invasion of the USSR. It was at this juncture that Roosevelt and British Prime Minister Winston Churchill met in Newfoundland, where they announced the Atlantic Charter, a document that advocated the building of a new world to ensure the freedom, equality, and peace of people. The Atlantic Charter confirmed eight points of common national policy principles, which begin as follows: "First, their countries seek no aggrandizement, territorial or other; Second, they desire to see no territorial changes that do not accord with the freely expressed wishes of the peoples concerned..."

Meanwhile, Japan declared war on the US and the UK on December 8, 1941. On January 1, 1942, the US, the UK, the Soviet Union, China, and others declared the formation of an alliance whose goals would be those espoused in the Atlantic Charter. Each of the Allies vowed that they would not independently seek a ceasefire or peace settlement with the Axis powers. As they fought the war, the main Allies, including the US, the UK, China, and the Soviet Union, met to discuss the conditions for peace with Japan. Deliberations with the Soviet Union had a particular focus on the conditions under which it would join the fight against Japan, but these discussions did not go into considerable detail until 1943. The British foreign minister met with President Roosevelt in Washington, D.C. in March of that year. Roosevelt then met with Churchill in Quebec in August. In October, the foreign ministers of the US, the UK, and the Soviet Union held a meeting in Moscow. It was here that Soviet leader Joseph Stalin and the Soviet foreign minister informed US Secretary of State Cordell Hull that the USSR would go to war against Japan. Roosevelt, Churchill, and Generalissimo Chiang Kai-shek, accompanied by their military and diplomatic advisors, met in Cairo from November 22 to 25 to discuss the war against Japan. The results of their deliberations were announced on the final day of this conference. They are presented in the Cairo Declaration. It reads as follows:

> *The Three Great Allies are fighting this war to restrain and punish the aggression of Japan. They covet no gain for themselves and have no thought of territorial expansion. It is their purpose that Japan shall be stripped of all the islands in the Pacific which she has seized or occupied since the beginning of the first World War in 1914, and that all the territories Japan has stolen from the Chinese, such as Manchuria, Formosa, and The Pescadores, shall be restored to the Republic of China. Japan will also be expelled from all other territories which she has taken by violence and greed. The aforesaid three great powers, mindful of the enslavement of the people of Korea, are determined that in due course Korea shall become free and independent.*
>
> *With these objects in view the three Allies, in harmony with those of the United Nations at war with Japan, will continue to persevere in the serious and prolonged operations necessary to procure the unconditional surrender of Japan.*

The Cairo Declaration laid down two principles concerning issues related to Japan's territory. The first is opposition to territorial aggrandizement, a principle also shared with the Atlantic Charter and the Declaration by United Nations. The second principle established is that those territories of Japan that were "seized," "stolen," and "taken" (terms that are not necessarily accurate from a legal perspective) shall be stripped from Japan. These territories were those which were absorbed in Japan's expansion in the First Sino-Japanese War, the Russo-Japanese War, and in World War I.

The day after the Cairo Conference concluded, Roosevelt and Churchill held meetings with the Soviet leader in Tehran until December 1. Stalin again stated that the USSR would go to war against Japan, and he made the return of territories and special rights taken by Japan in the Russo-Japanese War an issue. However, the Soviet Union's reward for fighting Japan was not definitively finalized until the Yalta Conference in February 1945. A pact concerning Japan was made in secret at these Yalta meetings. Fearful that details of the agreement may leak out, the US, UK, and USSR did not invite Chinese officials to these deliberations, even though the topic at hand concerned their country. China was not promptly informed of the pact. The Yalta Agreement on Soviet involvement in the war against Japan states the following:

> *The leaders of the three Great Powers—the Soviet Union, the United States of America and Great Britain—have agreed that in two or three months after Germany has surrendered and the war in Europe has terminated the Soviet Union shall enter into the war against Japan on the side of the Allies on condition that:*
>
> 1. *The* status quo *in Outer-Mongolia (The Mongolian People's Republic) shall be preserved;*
> 2. *The former rights of Russia violated by the treacherous attack of Japan in 1904 shall be restored, viz:*

(a) *the southern part of Sakhalin as well as all islands adjacent to it shall be returned to the Soviet Union,*

(b) *the commercial port of Dalian shall be internationalized, the preeminent interests of the Soviet Union in this port being safeguarded and the lease of Port Arthur [Lüshun] as a naval base of the USSR restored,*

(c) *the Chinese-Eastern Railroad and the South-Manchurian Railroad which provides an outlet to Dalian shall be jointly operated by the establishment of a joint Soviet-Chinese Company it being understood that the preeminent interests of the Soviet Union shall be safeguarded and that China shall retain full sovereignty in Manchuria;*

3. *The Kuril islands shall be handed over to the Soviet Union.*

It is understood, that the agreement concerning Outer-Mongolia and the ports and railroads referred to above will require concurrence of Generalissimo Chiang Kai-Shek. The President will take measures in order to obtain this concurrence on advice from Marshal Stalin.

The Heads of the three Great Powers have agreed that these claims of the Soviet Union shall be unquestionably fulfilled after Japan has been defeated.

For its part the Soviet Union expresses its readiness to conclude with the National Government of China a pact of friendship and alliance between the USSR and China in order to render assistance to China with its armed forces for the purpose of liberating China from the Japanese yoke.

This secret pact contained rewards inserted by Roosevelt and demanded by Stalin in exchange for joining the fight against Japan. The USSR was promised to receive (1) the Japanese territories of southern Sakhalin and the Kurile Islands, and (2) Japan's interests in Manchuria.

President Harry S. Truman, who assumed office following the sudden death of Roosevelt, abided by the Yalta Agreement. As Japan's interests in Manchuria were a matter involving China, Truman informed then Minister of Foreign Affairs Soong Tzu-wen of the ROC of the agreement in Washington, D.C. on June 14, 1945, and Soong commenced negotiations with Stalin and Soviet Foreign Minister Vyacheslav Molotov in Moscow on June 30. During this time Stalin temporarily halted the negotiations to attend the conference in Potsdam on July 14. The Potsdam Declaration was issued on July 26 and negotiations between China and the Soviet Union resumed on August 5. On August 8, the USSR declared war on Japan. The Soviets invaded Manchuria on the following day and commenced military operations inside Chinese territory.

The negotiations finally wrapped up on August 14. The two sides signed the Sino-Soviet Treaty of Friendship and Alliance (the instrument of ratification was not exchanged until later in Chongqing, on December 3). This was also the date on which Japan accepted the terms of the Potsdam Declaration. Under the terms of the Japan-Soviet Treaty, the Soviet Union gained the advantageous position and interests in the Three Northeastern Provinces—roughly equivalent to Manchuria—that Russia had enjoyed during its Imperial era. This unfair treaty for China was the price for Soviet aid in the fight against Japan. When the People's Republic of China (PRC) was founded in 1949, it formed a new agreement, the Sino-Soviet Treaty of Friendship, Alliance and Mutual Assistance, which was concluded on February 14, 1950, to replace the treaties and agreements of the Republican era. Nevertheless,

Japan's leases and its interests in Manchuria were recognized by international treaties such as the Portsmouth Peace Treaty in 1905, the treaties between Japan and the Qing dynasty, and the January 20, 1925, treaty on basic rules governing relations between Japan and the Soviet Union that reaffirmed the continuing complete validity of the Portsmouth Peace Treaty that Japan had signed with Russia. Thus, the parties involved were required to take legal steps to make any changes to these treaties (hence the signing of the Treaty of Peace with Japan and the Sino-Japanese Peace Treaty).

Japan was completely unaware of the secret Yalta Agreement on southern Sakhalin and the Kurile Islands. Thus, Japan was not bound by the agreement itself. With regard to southern Sakhalin, the Cairo Declaration, which is incorporated into the Potsdam Declaration, stated that "Japan will also be expelled from all other territories which she has taken by violence and greed." Southern Sakhalin became Japanese territory in the peace treaty that ended the Russo-Japanese War. Therefore, this sentence from the Cairo Declaration can be interpreted as also referring to southern Sakhalin. However, since the Kurile Islands changed hands peacefully, this sentence from the Cairo Declaration does not apply. Instead, the islands' transfer to the Soviet Union is only in agreement with the clause in the Yalta Agreement which states: "The Heads of the three Great Powers have agreed that these claims of the Soviet Union shall be unquestionably fulfilled after Japan has been defeated." Even so, the transfer of this territory should have been postponed until a peace treaty had been signed. In any case, Japan was kept uninformed of the Yalta Agreement when it agreed to the terms of the Potsdam Declaration.

Drafting the Treaty of Peace with Japan

At the February 1947 Paris Peace Conference, the Allies signed peace treaties with Italy and other Axis States Hungary, Romania, and Bulgaria, as well as with Finland. The peace with Japan and Germany was finally put on the agenda. On March 17, SCAP Douglas MacArthur put forth a proposal in Tokyo for a prompt peace with Japan that would mark a shift from implementing a harsh peace to a magnanimous peace.

Earlier, on March 12, Truman had declared to the world the start of the "Cold War" between the US and the Soviet Union. On June 5, the US worked out the final details of the Marshall Plan, a massive aid program for Europe. In the meantime, China's civil war had intensified.

Even with these fast-paced developments occurring, the US government suggested on July 11 to national representatives on the Far Eastern Commission (FEC) in Washington, DC that preliminary meetings on the peace with Japan be held in August. However, the proposal to hold a meeting of the 11 FEC member States was at odds with the proposal for a four-way meeting of the foreign ministers of the US, the UK, the Soviet Union, and China, where the Soviets would hold veto power. Furthermore, although members of the British Commonwealth agreed on swiftly implementing a peace with Japan, the timing conflicted with the British Commonwealth Conference in Canberra in August, so the FEC meeting was, in fact, postponed. During this year and the next, the debate over peace with Japan grew international in scope as the focus turned toward the American proposal. However, the global situation was rapidly changing, as the Cold War became ever more serious. The Berlin Blockade was launched in September 1948. In August, the Republic of Korea (ROK) was founded south of the 38th parallel on the Korean Peninsula and recognized by the US; in September, the Democratic People's Republic of Korea (DPRK) was established north of the line and recognized by the Soviet Union. The US then signed an aid agreement with the ROK in December. The North Atlantic Treaty forming NATO was signed in April 1949. The Federal Republic of Germany (West Germany) was created as a provisional government in May. The PRC was founded in Beijing on October 1 and the German Democratic Republic (East Germany) was established on October 7. Then, the ROC relocated its capital to Taipei, Taiwan in December. In 1950, Mao Zedong and Stalin met in February in Moscow, where they signed the Sino-Soviet Treaty of Friendship, Alliance, and Mutual Assistance. The structural framework of opposing sides known as the Cold War eventually led to actual fighting when North Korean troops crossed the 38th parallel and pushed southward on June 25.

Little progress was made on settling the peace with Japan, but John Foster Dulles, who had been assigned as a consultant to the US State Department in April, was charged with working on the peace agreement in May. He then began exploring a multilateral (separate) peace agreement. The Americans prepared for the negotiations by drafting seven principles that outlined their thinking. These principles were based on a vast trove of past documents and draft treaties the State Department had collected over the years. The FEC member States commenced their negotiations in September.

Details of the American memorandum on the Seven Principles for Peace with Japan came out in bits and pieces in the press in October. The State Department released the document on November 24, with seven principles covering: Parties, United Nations, Territory, Security, Political and Commercial Arrangements, Claims, and Disputes. The document clearly sets forth a basic path toward a magnanimous peace that would generally rule out claims for reparations, place no limits on Japan's militarization or on industrial productive capacity, and would not consider establishing administrative organs in Japan following the peace. It states the following regarding territory[11]:

Japan would
(a) *recognize the independence of Korea;*
(b) *agree to U.N. trusteeship, with the U.S. as administering authority, of the Ryukyu and Bonin Islands and*

---

[11] *Foreign Relations of the United States, 1950*, Volume VI, East Asia and the Pacific, eds. Neal H. Petersen, et al. (Washington: Government Printing Office, 1976), Document 757. https://history.state.gov/historicaldocuments/frus1950v06/d757. Accessed on December 13, 2022.

(c) *accept the future decision of the U.K., U.S.S.R., China and U.S. with reference to the status of Formosa, Pescadores, South Sakhalin and the Kuriles. In the event of no decision within a year after the Treaty came into effect, the U.N. General Assembly would decide. Special rights and interests in China would be renounced.*

Preliminary negotiations between FEC members and the US on the seven principles wound down in late October. The Soviet Union was against the proposal for a peace based on the seven principles. It particularly voiced objections over the clause on territory. The Soviets argued that the ownership of Taiwan and the Kurile Islands had already been agreed between the Allies during the war, and they were also opposed to a trusteeship arrangement for the Ryūkyū Islands. Such a position had been anticipated, and the US expected the negotiations to proceed to another round. However, when the UN Forces seemed to be approaching the Chinese border on the Korean Peninsula in late November, Chinese volunteer troops crossed into Korea and by early 1951 had pushed the UN Forces back to a position south of the 38th parallel. This change in the military situation and escalating clashes between US and Chinese forces led to the reemergence of the view that a peace treaty was premature and the idea of allowing Chinese representatives from both Beijing and Taiwan to attend the talks was written off. Nevertheless, the US began to push even harder for a quick peace settlement with Japan.

In March 1951, after discussions with other interested parties, American officials delivered an American proposal for the Treaty of Peace with Japan to the FEC member States. The Japanese government received the same document on March 27. The 22-article draft's Preamble and Chapter III, which dealt with territory, were written as follows:

3. *Japan renounces all rights, titles and claims to Korea, Formosa and the Pescadores; and also all rights, titles and claims in connection with the mandate system or deriving from the activities of Japanese nationals in the Antarctic area. Japan accepts the action of the United Nations Security Council of April 2, 1947, in relation to extending the trusteeship system to Pacific Islands formerly under mandate to Japan.*

4. *The United States may propose to the United Nations to place under its trusteeship system, with the United States as the administering authority, the Ryukyu Islands south of 29° north latitude, the Bonin Islands, including Rosario Island, the Volcano Islands, Parece Vela and Marcus Island. Japan will concur in any such proposal. Pending the making of such a proposal and affirmative action thereon, the United States will have the right to exercise all and any powers of administration, legislation, and jurisdiction over the territory and inhabitants of these islands, including their territorial waters.*

5. *Japan will return to the Union of Soviet Socialist Republics the southern part of Sakhalin as well as all the islands adjacent to it and will hand over to the Soviet Union the Kurile Islands.*

Furthermore, Article 11 of this document stipulates that "Japan renounces all special rights and interests in China," while Article 19, the final article of Chapter VIII, states that "Except for the provisions of Article 11, the present Treaty shall not confer any rights, title or benefits to or upon any State unless and until it signs and ratifies, or adheres to, this Treaty; nor, with that exception, shall any right, title and interest of Japan be deemed to be diminished or prejudiced by any provision hereof in favor of a State which does not sign and ratify, or adhere to, this Treaty." Through these provisions, the US was clearly showing that although southern Sakhalin and the Kurile Islands had been promised to the Soviet Union in Yalta and that they had come under Soviet occupation, the confirmation of Soviet title under a peace treaty would hinge upon whether the Soviet Union participated in said peace treaty.

The British government then completed a draft treaty in April. With this document, it made clear that it recognized the PRC as the government of China. Assuming this government would be the signatory to the treaty, the document went beyond having Japan renounce sovereignty over Taiwan and the Pescadores Islands by also clearly stipulating that China was the owner of these territories. The British draft was stricter than the American one regarding territorial issues, as it stipulated that Japan's residual sovereignty of the Ryūkyū Islands and the Ogasawara (Bonin) Islands shall not be recognized, that Japan shall renounce sovereignty over them, and that Japan shall also renounce all future claims to the Antarctic region. In order to move the peace negotiations forward, the Americans and British devoted their combined energies to writing a joint US-UK draft that would meet each other halfway. From late April to early May, working level meetings were held in Washington, D.C., where a provisional joint draft was written. That draft was the basis for negotiations in London in June, where the two sides largely reached a consensus. Thereafter, this draft was shown to the Japanese. After they had met to clear up issues, the final joint US-UK draft was released on July 12. Japan had received the US-UK draft treaty on July 7. On July 20, this joint draft was officially sent along with an invitation to peace talks.

When the two sides were negotiating the provisions on territory in London, the British compromised because the US flatly denied it had any intention of exerting sovereignty over the Ryūkyū Islands. With regard to Taiwan, the UK had recognized the PRC as the government of China and argued for returning the island to China, but the US disagreed because it had recognized the ROC and wanted only for Japan to renounce sovereignty over Taiwan. As for the Kurile Islands and southern Sakhalin, the provisional draft written in May stated that these islands would be transferred to the Soviet Union as desired by the UK (although the British understanding was that the Habomai Islands and Shikotan Island were not a part of the Kurile Islands). However, the US did not want to provide any direct benefits to the Soviet Union and was concerned about becoming involved in disputes between Japan and the Soviets, who were in de facto control, over the method of transfer, should the Soviets not join the Treaty. Therefore, the US proposed that Korea, Taiwan, southern Sakhalin, the Kurile Islands and other territories be grouped together under one article only stipulating that Japan renounce sovereignty over them. This proposal was eventually adopted in the final treaty. Thus, Article 2 of the US-UK draft for the Treaty of Peace with Japan was completed and the draft was released on July 12.

Until the Treaty of Peace with Japan went into effect on April 28, 1952, Japan was under Allied occupation, during which it was under indirect rule.

However, SCAP, in a January 1946 memorandum entitled "Governmental and Administrative Separation of Certain Outlying Areas from Japan," defined Japan as follows:

3. *For the purpose of this directive, Japan is defined to include the four main islands of Japan (Hokkaido, Honshu, Shikoku and Kyushu) and the approximately 1000 smaller adjacent islands, including the Tsushima Islands and the Ryukyu (Nansei) Islands north of 30° North Latitude (excluding Kuchinoshima Island); and excluding (a) Utsuryo (Ullung) Island, Liancourt Rocks (Take Island) and Quelpart (Saishu or Cheju) Island, (b) the Ryukyu (Nansei) Islands south of 30° North Latitude (including Kuchinoshima Island), the Izu, Nanpo, Bonin (Ogasawara) and Volcano (Kazan or Iwo) Island Groups, and all the other outlying Pacific Islands [including the Daito (Ohigashi or Oagari) Island Group, and Parece Vela (Okino-tori), Marcus (Minami-tori) and Ganges (Nakano-tori) Islands], and (c) the Kurile (Chishima) Islands, the Habomai (Hapomaze) Island Group (including Suisho, Yuri, Akiyuri, Shibotsu and Taraku Islands) and Shikotan Island.*
4. *Further areas specifically excluded from the governmental and administrative jurisdiction of the Imperial Japanese Government are the following: (a) all Pacific Islands seized or occupied under mandate or otherwise by Japan since the beginning of the World War in 1914, (b) Manchuria, Formosa and the Pescadores, (c) Korea, and (d) Karafuto.*

Unless explicitly stated otherwise, all memorandums and orders issued by General Headquarters thereafter were considered to apply to the above definition of Japan. However, the sixth item of the memorandum stated, "Nothing in this directive shall be construed as an indication of Allied policy relating to the ultimate determination of the minor islands referred to in Article 8 of the Potsdam Declaration."[12]

The Current State of Japan's Territory

Renunciation of Japan's Expanded Territory: Korea, Taiwan, the Kurile Islands, Sakhalin, and the South Pacific Mandate

In accordance with Article 2 of the Treaty of Peace with Japan, Japan renounced Korea, Taiwan, the Kurile Islands, Sakhalin, and the South Pacific Mandate. Apart from the Kurile Islands, these were all territories that Japan added during the Sino-Japanese War, the Russo-Japanese War, and World War I.

Korea was placed under military administration, with the area to the south of the 38th parallel occupied by the US military and the area to the north occupied by the Soviet military. Ultimately, in 1948, the Government of the ROK was established in the south and the Government of the DPRK in the north. In accordance with the Treaty of Peace with Japan, Japan "recogniz[ed] the independence of Korea" and on the day of entry into force of the Treaty, Japan accorded implied recognition to the ROK.[13] Following lengthy negotiations between Japan and the ROK, the two sides

---

[12] For more details on these international documents, see Serita, Kentarō (ed). 2010. *Konpakuto gakushū jōyakushū* (Basic Documents in International Law). Tokyo: Shinzansha.

[13] Kokusaihō Jirei Kenkyūkai. 1983. *Kokka shōnin* (Recognition of States). Tokyo: Japan Institute of International Affairs.

concluded the Treaty on Basic Relations between Japan and the Republic of Korea in June 1965. Japan is still engaged in negotiations with the DPRK, but no diplomatic relations exist between the two sides as of now.

As for Taiwan, authority over the country was given to Chiang Kai-shek during the reallocation of Japan's occupied territories that was stipulated in SCAP General Order No. 1 of September 2, perhaps in part because the US, which had seized control of the Philippines in February 1945 towards the end of World War II, passed through Taiwan and landed in Okinawa in April of the same year. On October 25 a retrocession ceremony was held and China accepted the "surrender of the Imperial Japanese Army and Navy and supporting forces in Taiwan and Penghu," "took administrative control over the territory and people of Taiwan and Penghu, and seized the military and other assets of Taiwan and Penghu," and proclaimed that from that day "Taiwan and Penghu were again incorporated formally into the territory of the ROC and that the territory, people and administration were placed under the sovereignty of the Nationalist Government of the ROC." The ROC thus completed the reintegration of Taiwan under its own control through measures under its domestic law, thereby making Taiwan a province of the ROC. Taiwan, which was known under Japanese rule as a *shū* (Japanese for state or province), was now known as a *xian* (Chinese for county), and the Spratly Islands, which were part of Taiwan, were made part of Guangdong Province. Under the Treaty of Peace with Japan, Japan simply "renounce[d] all right, title and claim to Formosa and the Pescadores" and "to the Spratly Islands," without specifying to whom it was doing so. Subsequently, this renunciation was "recognized" in the Japan-ROC Peace Treaty of 1952. Japanese court precedent interpreted this to mean that Taiwan was transferred to the Republic of China.[14] However, in the 1972 Japan-China Joint Communique with the Government of the PRC, which considered Taiwan to be an inalienable part of its own territory, Japan merely stated that "the Government of Japan fully understands and respects this stand of the Government of the People's Republic of China, and it firmly maintains its stand under Article 8 of the Potsdam Proclamation."

The Soviet Union, which entered the war against Japan on August 9, 1945, launched an attack on South Sakhalin on August 11, and controlled all of Sakhalin by August 25. Meanwhile, Japan accepted the Potsdam Declaration on August 14 and the Emperor of Japan ordered the immediate ceasefire of all troops. However, fighting was initiated by the Soviet landing on August 16 on Shumshu Island, the island closest to the Kamchatka Peninsula, and all Japanese forces on the island surrendered on August 23. Though the Soviet literature on the matter contains different interpretations and there is no unified view, it is believed that the Soviet forces then headed south as far as Uruppu Island, which was formerly a territory of Russia and which had been transferred to Japan under the Treaty for the Exchange of Sakhalin for the Kurile Islands, occupying all 18 islands by August 28. It is said that

---

[14] See the Supreme Court Ruling on December 5, 1962, in Supreme Court of Japan, *Saikōsai keiji hanrei shū* (Collection of Supreme Court Rulings) 16, 1661.

the Soviets initially believed that Etorofu Island and other islands to the south of it were under US control and the troops that were advancing southward retreated. However, learning that US forces were not occupying the islands, the Soviet forces occupied Etorofu Island, Kunashiri Island, Shikotan Island, and the Habomai Islands by September 3, using a detached force (Fig. 1.1).

According to the 1907 Hague Convention Respecting the Laws and Customs of War on Land, under a military occupation the occupant bears a number of obligations, including respecting the laws in force in the occupied territory, respecting private rights, and protecting the property of the hostile State. However, on February 2, 1946, the Soviet Union nationalized the land and banks on South Sakhalin and the "Kurile Islands," and subsequently, on February 3, it took measures to incorporate the occupied areas as part of the territory of the Russian Soviet Federative Socialist Republic, one of its member States. The Council of People's Commissars affirmed the measures and ordered that the effects thereof be applied retroactively from September 20, 1945. In February 1947, the Soviet Constitution was revised to include provisions stipulating this change in territory, and in March of the following year, the Russian Constitution was also similarly revised. According to the 1951 Treaty of Peace with Japan, "Japan renounce[d] all right, title and claim to the Kurile Islands, and to that portion of Sakhalin and the islands adjacent to it over which Japan acquired sovereignty as a consequence of the Portsmouth Peace Treaty of September 5, 1905." However, as the Soviet Union was not a party to the treaty, no rights, titles, or benefits were conferred to it, in accordance with Article 25 of said treaty (special provisions under Article 21 apply to China and Korea, which, like Russia, were not parties to the treaty).

Meanwhile, the Pacific Islands that were formerly under mandate to Japan came under the occupation of the US and on April 2, 1947, they became a UN trust territory. The end of the Japanese mandate was not necessarily legally defined, but in any case, Japan "accept[ed] the action of the United Nations Security Council," in accordance with the Treaty of Peace with Japan.

Renunciation of the Kurile Islands and the Issue of the Northern Territories

Citing the agreements of the Yalta Conference, the Soviet Union occupied the Kurile Islands, as described above. At the same time, however, following various developments, Japan eventually accepted its renunciation of Sakhalin and the Kurile Islands under the Treaty of Peace with Japan. At the San Francisco Peace Conference, the Soviet Union had opposed the joint proposal by the UK and the US that only a renunciation be stipulated in the treaty, and had proposed a revision, which was not accepted, whereby Japan would recognize the complete sovereignty of the Soviet Union over these territories and renounce all right, title, and claim to them. As such, the question of to whom Japan would renounce these territories was not decided.

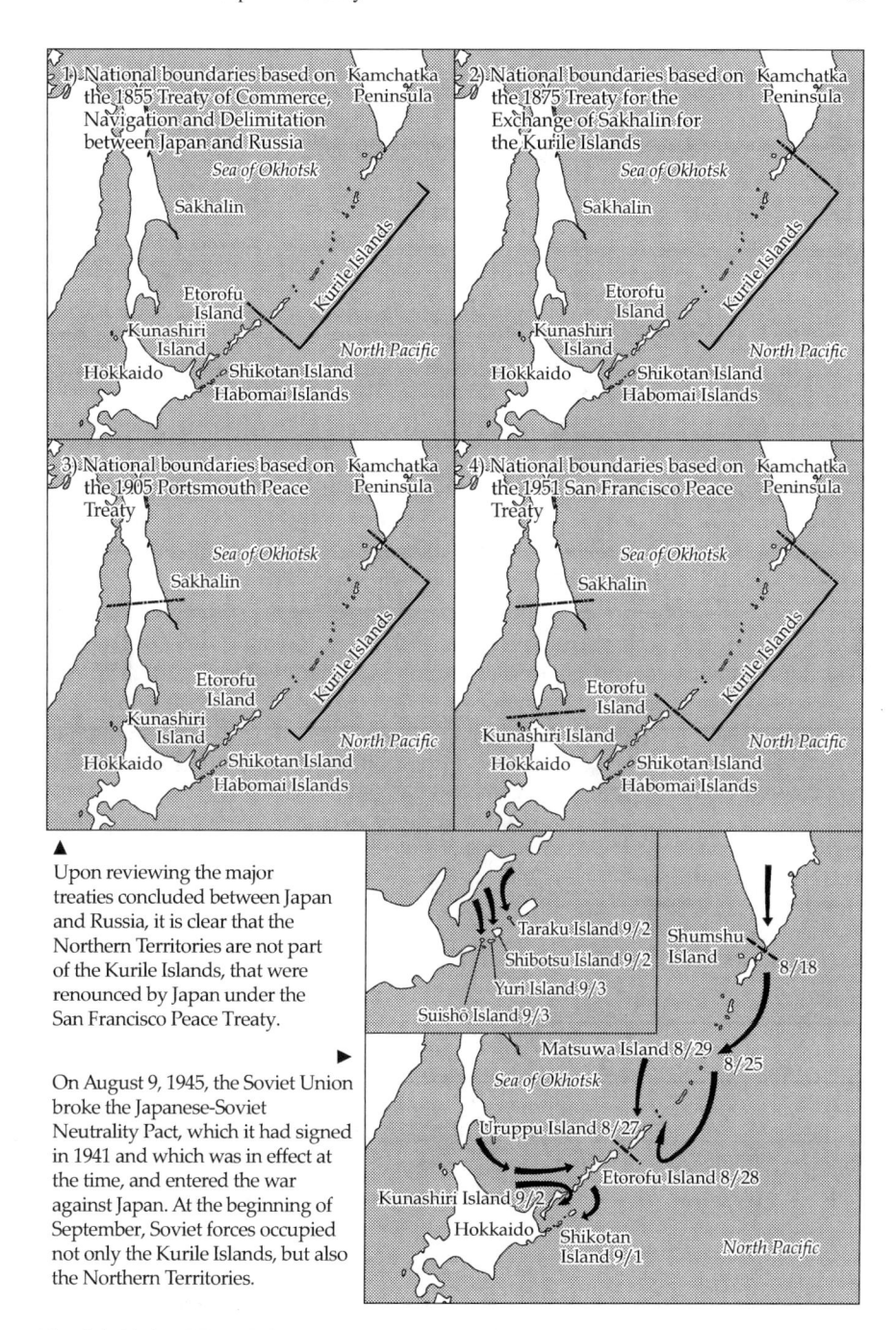

Upon reviewing the major treaties concluded between Japan and Russia, it is clear that the Northern Territories are not part of the Kurile Islands, that were renounced by Japan under the San Francisco Peace Treaty.

On August 9, 1945, the Soviet Union broke the Japanese-Soviet Neutrality Pact, which it had signed in 1941 and which was in effect at the time, and entered the war against Japan. At the beginning of September, Soviet forces occupied not only the Kurile Islands, but also the Northern Territories.

Fig. 1.1 National Boundaries with Russia

However, it is well known that the Soviet Union has in fact controlled these territories until the present day.

In light of the fact that the Soviet Union did not ratify the Treaty of Peace with Japan, in accordance with its Article 20 Japan and the Soviet Union needed to conclude a bilateral peace treaty. So, in June 1955, for the first time, the two countries commenced negotiations to conclude a peace treaty. However, it seemed unlikely that they would be able to come to an agreement on matters other than the Habomai Islands and Shikotan Island in these talks. Therefore, on September 29 of the following year, as stated in the Matsumoto-Gromyko letters, Japan and the Soviet Union agreed to resume negotiations on the conclusion of a bilateral peace treaty that included the territorial issues following the resumption of normalized diplomatic relations, and in accordance with the 1956 Japan-Soviet Joint Declaration, the state of war between the two sides was brought to an end and diplomatic relations were resumed.

The disagreement between Japan and the Soviet Union centered on the geographical scope of "the Kurile Islands" that Japan had renounced. At the San Francisco Peace Conference, the Japanese plenipotentiary Yoshida Shigeru had already stated that, "At the time of the opening of Japan, her ownership of two islands of [Etorofu] and Kunashiri of the South Kuriles was not questioned at all by the Czarist government. But the North Kuriles north of [Uruppu] and the southern half of Sakhalin were areas open to both Japanese and Russian settlers."[15] Furthermore, Yoshida drew the attention of the countries in attendance in referring to "the islands of Habomai and Shikotan, constituting part of Hokkaido, one of Japan's four main islands." Although the Treaty of Peace with Japan itself did not define the geographical scope of the Kurile Islands, Japan's interpretation was that "the Kurile Islands" referenced in the treaty did not include the Habomai Islands and Shikotan Island, nor did it include Etorofu Island and Kunashiri Island. However, it can be pointed out that a certain degree of uncertainty was evident during the interpellation sessions of the Diet around the time of the entry into force of the Treaty of Peace with Japan. In October 1951, Nishimura Kumao, director-general of the Treaties Bureau of the Ministry of Foreign Affairs, in reference to the difference between the South and North Kuriles, stated that, "I consider the North Kuriles and the two islands of the South Kuriles to be part of the scope of the Kurile Islands as stated in the treaty."[16] In May of the following year, Minister for Foreign Affairs Okazaki Katsuo stated in response to a question that, "According to the peace treaty, Japan has renounced the Kurile Islands and Sakhalin. It follows therefore, that since Japan has renounced them, we should not think about trying to recover them. That being said, the ideal outcome would be for the Allied countries to reconsider and revise the treaty.

---

[15] English from "The Delegate of Japan-Shigeru Yoshida (Prime Minister and Minister of Foreign Affairs)" September 7, 1951, Annex 33, pp. 313–314. https://www.mofa.go.jp/mofaj/annai/honsho/shiryo/archives/pdfs/heiwajouyaku4_07.pdf. Accessed on December 13, 2022.

[16] House of Representatives Special Committee on the Peace Treaty and the Japan-US Security Treaty.

Furthermore, the islands to the south of the Kuriles, such as Habomai and Shikotan, are obviously not part of the Kuriles. Therefore, regardless of Japan's renunciation of rights in Article 2 of the treaty, we of course intend to maintain to the very end the assertion that these are Japan's territories... I believe there are differing views on the definition of the Kuriles. We intend to clearly resolve these points as soon as possible in the future."[17] Subsequently, in December 1955, Nakagawa Tōru, director-general of the Treaties Bureau of the Ministry of Foreign Affairs, stated in response to a question that, "We consider the South Kuriles to not be part of the Kurile Islands. As you are aware, we are continuing to engage in the negotiations with the Soviet Union based on this stance."[18] On February 11 of the following year, at the House of Representatives Committee on Foreign Affairs, Parliamentary Vice-Minister for Foreign Affairs Morishita Kunio proclaimed the unified view of the government that the four Northern Islands of Japan's Northern Territories were not part of the Kurile Islands that Japan had renounced.

With regard to the negotiations between Japan and the Soviet Union, under the 1956 Japan-Soviet Joint Declaration, the two sides agreed to resume negotiations to conclude a bilateral peace treaty following the resumption of normalized diplomatic relations and to transfer the Habomai Islands and Shikotan Island to Japan, in line with the wishes of Japan and out of consideration for its national interests. The negotiations lost momentum, however, partly owing to Soviet opposition to the subsequent conclusion of the Japan-US Security Treaty in 1960. In October 1973, Tanaka Kakuei, the serving Japanese prime minister, visited the Soviet Union, the first such visit since Prime Minister Ichiro Hatoyama's in 1956. As a result of the summit meeting between Tanaka and General Secretary Leonid Brezhnev, the Soviet Union softened its previous stance that "the territorial question has been settled by virtue of various international agreements" and the Japanese side announced the two sides had affirmed that the issue of the four Northern Islands remained unresolved. Thereafter, however, time passed without significant developments. More recently, working groups on the peace treaty were established at the 8th Japan-Soviet Foreign Ministers meeting held in December 1988, in order to promote greater progress on peace treaty negotiations between the two foreign ministers. Although the Soviet Union's stance remained firm, the two sides were nonetheless able to hold substantive discussions on the territorial issues. Following the end of the Cold War and the collapse of the Soviet Union, Russia emerged as the successor of the former Soviet Union, and negotiations between Japan and Russia have continued until the present day.[19]

---

[17] House of Representatives Committee on Foreign Affairs.

[18] Ibid.

[19] See Chapter 2.

Reversion of the Administrative Rights from the US: Amami, Ogasawara (Bonin), and Okinawa

While the dates on which these islands came under US military occupation differ, the date on which the US military landed on the main island of Okinawa was April 1945. The major US policy of establishing military bases in Japan, in order to administrate the Ryūkyū Islands under the UN Trusteeship system and under US military occupation, was first officially announced by US Secretary of State Henry Stimson in January 1950. In September of the same year, the secretaries of state and defense addressed a joint memorandum to the president, recommending the start of preliminary negotiations for the Peace Treaty with Japan and stating the need to secure exclusive and strategic US control of the Ryūkyū Islands south of 29 degrees north latitude. The Seven Principles of Peace with Japan issued in October stated that, "Japan would ... agree to U.N. trusteeship, with the U.S. as administering authority, of the Ryukyu and Bonin Islands" and negotiations with the Allied powers were subsequently begun.

In an *aide-mémoire* dated November 20, 1950, the Soviet Union pointed out that neither in the Cairo Declaration nor the Potsdam Declaration was there any mention of removing Japan's sovereignty over the Ryūkyū and Ogasawara (Bonin) Islands, as well as the fact that the governments issuing the Cairo and Potsdam Declarations had stated the policy of not expanding territories, and therefore sought an explanation from the US regarding its rationale for placing these islands under UN trusteeship with the US as the administering authority. In response, the US issued a reply on December 28, citing Article 77 of the UN Charter and the Potsdam Declaration, explaining that trusteeship did not amount to territorial expansion, and that, in strict adherence to the Potsdam Declaration, it would determine in the peace treaty the future status of the "minor islands" referred to in the declaration. This contention between the US and the Soviet Union remained until the San Francisco Peace Conference, at which point the US plenipotentiary, John Foster Dulles, and the British plenipotentiary, Kenneth Younger, clarified that sovereignty over the Amami Islands and the Ryūkyū Islands would remain with Japan (i.e., residual sovereignty), while the Soviet plenipotentiary, Andrei Gromyko, proposed the recognition of Japan's complete sovereignty. In any case, the administrative rights over the Amami Islands, the Ogasawara (Bonin) Islands, and the Okinawa Islands, which were transferred to the US under the Treaty of Peace with Japan, were returned to Japan through the respective reversion agreements concluded in 1953, 1968, and 1972, without it ever being proposed that they be placed under UN trusteeship. Japan currently has complete sovereignty over these islands.

Nevertheless, it was not entirely inconceivable that the conclusion of an agreement only between Japan and the US regarding the reversion of the administrative rights over these islands, which can be considered as changing the provisions of the Treaty of Peace with Japan, would give rise to legal issues in relations with other parties to the treaty. However, Article 3 of the treaty states that "Japan will concur in any proposal of the United States to the United Nations to place [the islands] under

Fig. 1.2 The Ogasawara (Bonin) Islands and Okinawa

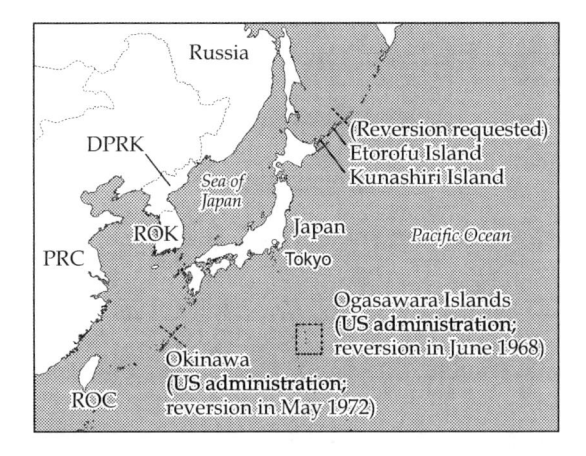

its trusteeship system, with the United States as the sole administering authority." As such, Japan must concur with any such "proposal," but if no such proposal is made, then Japan will not be made to bear any obligations. Furthermore, the US would not be obligated to make such a proposal, nor would there be any issue with the US making a direct reversion to Japan, the original sovereignty holder. Moreover, as evidenced in the interpellation sessions of the Japanese Diet, from the very beginning, the possibility was discussed of the reversion of the islands to Japan, if and when their strategic necessity was lost (Fig. 1.2).

Treaties Bureau Director-General Nishimura Kumao stated that "The United States has expressed, as its rationale for placing the Nansei Shotō Islands under the trusteeship system, the need for the United States to administrate the islands for the present time for the sake of maintaining peace and security, and has never once expressed the need to improve the political, economic, and cultural standards of our brethren living on these islands, and make them autonomous or independent."[20] In addition, 2 days after, in response to a question, Nishimura stated that, "As the U.S. Government has officially explained, the purpose of Article 3 is not permanent, and is solely intended for the maintenance of peace and security in the Far East. Therefore... we believe it is necessary to make continual efforts to ensure the stability of the Far East as soon as possible, to bring about the day where measures such as those of Article 3 are no longer necessary, and to enable the region to revert to its original state."[21]

It can therefore be said that the legal status of the Nansei Shotō Islands and the Nanpō Shotō Islands, as defined in Article 3 of the Treaty of Peace with Japan, is unique, in terms of the question of its consistency with the basic purpose of the UN trusteeship system, and the fact that it was the result of the political situation in the Far East.

---

[20] House of Councillors Special Committee on the Peace Treaty and the Japan-US Security Treaty, November 5, 1951.

[21] Ibid., November 7, 1951.

Clashes with Other Countries' Sovereignty: Takeshima and the Senkaku Islands

For the sake of the administration of the occupation of Japan by the Allied powers, Takeshima was included among the regions separated from Japan politically and in terms of administration where the exercise of the rights of the Japanese government was suspended, in accordance with an instruction note issued by SCAP on January 29, 1946.

Once the Treaty of Peace with Japan was signed on September 8, 1951, and the restoration of Japanese sovereignty became certain, the ROK took steps to strengthen its regulations of activities by foreign fishing vessels, and on January 18, 1952, ROK President Syngman Rhee issued the Proclamation of Sovereignty over Adjacent Seas (also known as the proclamation of the Syngman Rhee Line), a unilateral declaration of sovereignty over waters that included Takeshima. Japan immediately lodged a protest with the ROK side on January 28, stating that, while the ROK declaration appeared to assume territorial rights over Takeshima, "the Japanese government does not recognize any such assumption or claim by the ROK concerning these islets which are without question Japanese territory." In response to Japan's protest, the ROK stated by the *note verbale* on February 12 that the ROK "merely wished to remind the Japanese Government that SCAP, by SCAPIN No. 677 dated January 29, 1946, explicitly excluded the islets from the territorial possessions of Japan and that again the same islets have been left on the Korean side of the MacArthur Line, facts that endorse and confirm the Korean claim to them, which is beyond any dispute." On April 25 of the same year, the Japanese government refuted the ROK response, stating that the SCAP instruction note was irrelevant to the sovereignty of Takeshima.[22]

Thereafter, from 1954 onwards, ROK authorities have been stationed on Takeshima, and armed incidents have even occurred. As the ROK's "illegal occupation" of Takeshima continues, the Japanese government has taken a variety of measures to date, including lodging protests each year.[23]

The Senkaku Islands, meanwhile, did not appear to have any particular natural resources, nor were subject to much interest by the world. However, in the autumn of 1968, the United Nations Economic Commission for Asia and the Far East (now the United Nations Economic and Social Commission for Asia and the Pacific) conducted a geophysical survey led primarily by Japanese, ROK, and Taiwanese scientists. The survey indicated the possibility of the existence of abundant petroleum resources in an area approximately 200,000 km^2 in size, mostly due northeast from Taiwan, attracting much attention from other countries. Precisely at this time, the negotiations between Japan and the US for the reversion of Okinawa were

---

[22] See the section on the SCAP instruction note in Chapter 1.

[23] See Chapter 4.

ongoing, and in June 1971 an agreement was reached on the Okinawa Reversion Treaty, and administrative control of Okinawa reverted to Japan in 1972.

Following the conclusion of the Okinawa Reversion Treaty in June 1971, on December 30 of the same year the Chinese Ministry of Foreign Affairs issued a statement asserting that, "Not long ago, the U.S. Congress and the Japanese Diet one after the other approved the agreement on the 'reversion' of Okinawa. In this agreement, the Governments of the United States and Japan flagrantly included the Diaoyu and other islands in the 'area of reversion.' This is a gross encroachment upon China's territorial integrity and sovereignty. The Chinese people absolutely will not tolerate this!" and furthermore, that, "After World War II, the Japanese Government illicitly handed over to the United States the Diaoyu and other islands appertaining to Taiwan, and the United States Government unilaterally declared that it enjoyed the so-called 'administrative rights' over these islands. This in itself was illegal."[24]

In response, the Japanese Ministry of Foreign Affairs in March 1972 issued a statement entitled "Basic View on the Sovereignty over the Senkaku Islands," in which it stated that, since their incorporation into Japan's territory in 1895, "Historically, the Senkaku Islands have continuously been an integral part of the Nansei Shotō Islands, which are the territory of Japan. These islands were neither part of Taiwan nor part of the Pescadores Islands, which were ceded to Japan from the Qing dynasty in accordance with Article 2 of the Treaty of Shimonoseki, which came into effect in May of 1895;" that, "Accordingly, the Senkaku Islands are not included in the territory which Japan renounced under Article II of the San Francisco Peace Treaty. They were placed under the administration of the United States of America as part of the Nansei Shotō Islands, in accordance with Article III of the said treaty" and that, "The fact that China expressed no objection to the status of the Islands being under the administration of the United States under Article III of the San Francisco Peace Treaty clearly indicates that China did not consider the Senkaku Islands as part of Taiwan."

While Japan has continued to control the Senkaku Islands, Japan and China did hold various exchanges on the matter around the time of the conclusion of the Treaty of Peace and Friendship between Japan and the People's Republic of China. On October 25, 1978, then Vice Premier Deng Xiaoping, who was visiting Japan for the exchange of the instruments of ratification for the treaty, stated that "Even if... the issue is temporarily shelved, I don't think I mind." In the first place, the idea that during the negotiations on the Treaty of Peace and Friendship between Japan and China, Japan arrived at the tacit understanding that the issue of the Senkaku Islands would not be mentioned in the treaty and would instead be shelved, is, as Minister of Foreign Affairs Miyazawa Kiichi stated in 1975, in response to a question on the matter, "a mistaken recognition, and it is not in fact the case that the negotiations on

---

[24]"Statement of the Ministry of Foreign Affairs of the People's Republic of China," December 30, 1971. English translation in *Peking Review*, January 7, 1972, p. 12. http://www.massline.org/PekingReview/PR1972/PR1972-01.pdf. Accessed on November 30, 2022.

the treaty were held amid the issue being shelved."[25] In addition, more recently, Treaties Bureau Director-General Saitō Kunihiko stated, in response to a question on the matter, that, "Since the Senkaku Islands are under the valid control of Japan and a part of Japan's territory, the idea of shelving the issue is completely unthinkable. Thus, there was absolutely no agreement between Japan and China to shelve the issue."[26]

The Antarctic and Japan

Since the beginning of the twentieth century, all continents on Earth, apart from the Arctic and the Antarctic, have been divided up by different countries. Since 1908, the UK and six other countries have set up sectors in parts of the Antarctic, over which they have asserted their sovereignty, citing discoveries of coastlines or past expeditions as evidence. Sectors are fan-shaped areas determined by two lines drawn poleward from both extremes of the coastline or other geographic features on which the country in question bases its claim and a latitudinal line. "Sectorism" asserts that the laws of occupation,[27] which were established as a means by which human beings could acquire land for regular living, are inapplicable or inappropriate for the polar regions (Fig. 1.3).

However, the effectiveness of sectorism has not yet been commonly recognized and jurisdiction over the polar regions remains uncertain. Thus, in order to avoid clashes over sovereignty among the countries concerned and to prevent territorial disputes, in the spirit of international cooperation realized by the International Geophysical Year, the Antarctic Treaty was signed in 1959 and entered into force in 1961. Under the treaty, all countries' claims to territorial rights or territories south of 60 degrees south latitude were frozen and the whole region was opened up for peaceful use, resulting in the establishment of a completely unprecedented international regime. As for the Arctic, Canada and the Soviet Union established sectors therein, and have at present established their territorial rights over the land areas inside these sectors.

Japan, meanwhile, had at one point asserted its territorial rights over the Antarctic prior to World War II based on the exploration led by Lieutenant Shirase Nobu but had not taken measures to incorporate the area into its territory. However, in accordance with Article 2, paragraph (e) of the Treaty of Peace with Japan, Japan

---

[25] House of Representatives Committee on Budget, October 22, 1975.

[26] House of Representatives Committee on Foreign Affairs, November 8, 1985.

[27] Occupation: A mode of title to the acquisition of land, alongside, for example, cession or annexation. Occupation is the exercise of authority over and acquisition of a land with no sovereign title by a country. In order to ensure that the occupation is effective, the country must effectively control the *terra nullius* with the intention of making it part of its sovereign territory, but it need not necessarily notify other countries thereof.

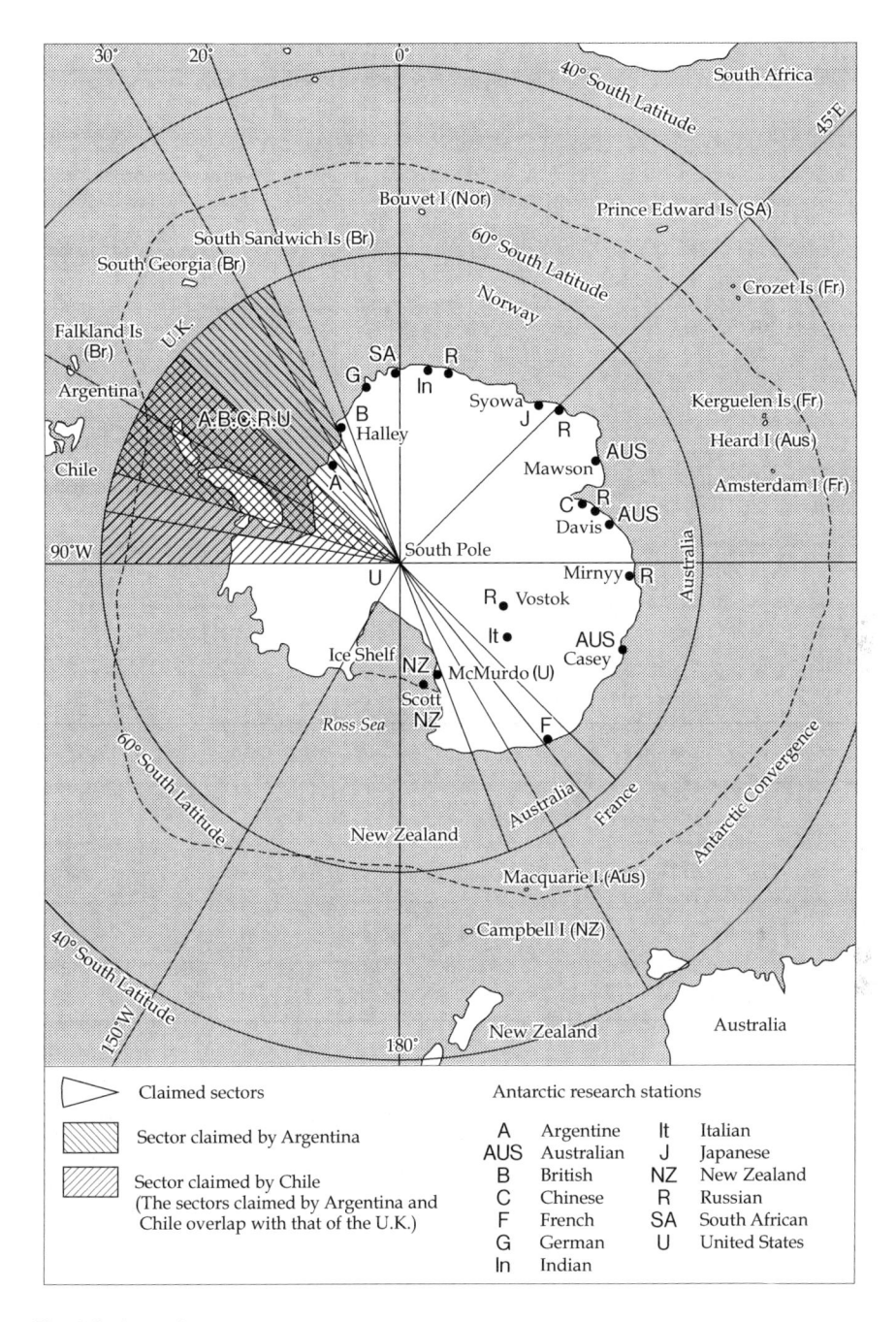

Fig. 1.3 Antarctica

had renounced all claim to any part of the Antarctic area, and the Japanese stated the following in response to a question posed during Diet deliberations over the treaty.

> *Regarding 'any part of the Antarctic' as stated in paragraph (e), in January 1912, Lieutenant Shirase Nobu carried out an exploration to the Antarctic, marking the location at 156 degrees west longitude and 80 degrees south latitude, after which the Japanese government addressed a demarche to the U.S. Department of State in 1938 requesting the preservation of the title to decide the jurisdiction of these areas. In light of these circumstances, Japan has a strong right to express its views on these areas of the Antarctic. Under the aforementioned paragraph, Japan will renounce these claims.*[28]

The paragraph was not actually in the Seven Principles of Peace with Japan issued by the US Department of State in November 1950 and was originally included in the Treaty of Peace with Japan upon the strong urging of Australia, New Zealand, and the UK. The UK government had pushed for making Japan renounce current and future claims in the Antarctic but was unable to gain the agreement of the US, and so the parties settled on the current wording. As such, what Japan renounced was claims based on activities leading up to the conclusion of the peace treaty, in other words those before World War II, and this does not involve any benefits accruing to Japan from its subsequent activities. In fact, in the latter half of the 1970s, amid growing international interest in the harvesting of mineral resources in the Antarctic, the Japanese government stated the following in response to a question on the matter.

> *What Japan has renounced under Article 2 of the Treaty of Peace with Japan is any right, title to or interest in the Antarctic area at the time of the entry into force of said treaty. We do not consider that these provisions mean that Japan has renounced all claim to any right, title to or interest in connection with any part of the Antarctic area whether deriving from the activities of Japanese nationals or otherwise, following the entry into force of the treaty, in other words that Japan has renounced its position from the time of the treaty and into the future.*[29]

In practice as well, Japan is one of the original parties to the Antarctic Treaty, and it has continued to the present to exercise its right to comment on a variety of related issues, including territorial sovereignty. Japan's basic stance on the issue of territorial rights is that, as a party to the Antarctic Treaty, it is possible for Japan to make territorial claims on an equal footing with the other parties to the treaty, but, outwardly, Japan has declared itself to be a non-claimant, in contrast to the claimants in the Antarctic. This policy is likely to remain unchanged.

The Antarctic Treaty includes provisions pertaining to the preservation and conservation of living resources in connection with research activities. However, if issues over the commercial use of resources were to arise, the territorial issues would become highly sensitive. Setting aside the issue of whaling that has taken place since before World War II, the Convention for the Conservation of Antarctic Seals was concluded in London in 1972. Additionally, in the latter half of the 1970s, Japan, the

---

[28] House of Councillors Special Committee on the Peace Treaty and the Japan-US Security Treaty, November 6, 1951.

[29] House of Representatives Committee on Foreign Affairs, April 5, 1978.

former Soviet Union, Poland, and the ROK operated a large-scale trial operation for the production of krill over an area spanning 200,000 km^2, and it was decided that regulations similar to those in conventional fisheries conventions would be established for the conservation of such zooplankton. At the time, the issue of 200 nautical miles became a major point of contention. Ultimately, the Convention on the Conservation of Antarctic Marine Living Resources was concluded in 1980, which extended the applicable area to the Antarctic Convergence and included regulations based on the flag State doctrine.

However, matters become more complicated when issues of petroleum and natural gas deposits or mineral resources on the continental shelf are involved. Discussions on the subject are ongoing among the members countries of the Antarctic Treaty, while even the UN has tried to address such issues since 1983, giving rise to the argument that the Antarctic should be managed internationally as the "common heritage of mankind," as described in the principles governing the deep ocean floor stipulated in the United Nations Convention on the Law of the Sea. Eventually, the Convention on the Regulation of Antarctic Mineral Resource Activities was adopted in June 1988 and was released for signing in November. Additionally, the Protocol on Environmental Protection to the Antarctic Treaty was adopted in October 1991.[30]

---

[30]For more comprehensive research on the various issues related to the Antarctic Treaty, see Ikeshima, Taisaku. 2000. *Nankyoku jōyaku taisei to kokusaihō* (The Antarctic Treaty Regime and International Law). Tokyo: Keio University Press.

Chapter 2
The Northern Territories (Kunashiri Island, Etorofu Island, the Habomai Islands, and Shikotan Island)

As discussed in Chapter 1, Japan delineated its peripheral territories between itself and Russia, China, and the Korean Peninsula in a process from the mid-1800s to early 1900s. In the chapters that follow, I would like to examine each situation in greater detail. Japan has demanded the return of the Northern Territories, comprising the Habomai Islands, Shikotan Island, Etorofu Island, and Kunashiri Island, which are occupied by Russia, while China has claimed sovereignty over the Senkaku Islands (also known as the Diaoyu Islands in Chinese), which are validly controlled by Japan, and Japan has claimed sovereignty over Takeshima (also known as Dokdo in Korean), which is occupied by the Republic of Korea (ROK).

The Northern Territories are inhabited, unlike the Senkaku Islands and Takeshima; there are related treaties and international documents, including the Treaty of Commerce, Navigation and Delimitation between Japan and Russia in 1855, the Treaty for the Exchange of Sakhalin for the Kurile Islands in 1875, the Portsmouth Peace Treaty in 1905, and the San Francisco Peace Treaty in 1951, among others, making the nature of the issue as well as the diplomatic approach quite different from the other territorial issues. Changes in Japan's territories through the establishment of Japan's peripheral regions at the end of the Edo period and beginning of the Meiji period as well as Japan's later expansion have already been covered in the previous chapter.

Background of the Issue

The Joint Compendium of Documents on the History of the Territorial Issue was completed in September 1992 with the cooperation of the ministries of foreign affairs of Japan and Russia. The ministries jointly created this compendium in order to aid in the correct understanding between the peoples of both countries with regard to the territorial issue between Japan and Russia. It includes basic documents issued by Japan, the Soviet Union, and Russia concerning the

© Kreab K.K. 2023
K. Serita, *The Territory of Japan*, https://doi.org/10.1007/978-981-99-3013-5_2

demarcation of territories between the two countries as well as a series of documents and materials about the territorial issue. The preface is written as follows and the background and current status of negotiations with regard to this dispute appear as agreed upon by both foreign ministries (Fig. 2.1).

As a result of the Japanese advance from the South onto the Kurile Islands and the Russian advance from the North by the middle of the 19th century, a Japanese-Russian border emerged between the islands of Etorofu and Uruppu. This border was legally established by the Treaty of Commerce, Navigation and Delimitation between Japan and Russia of February 7, 1855. The treaty peacefully established that the islands of Etorofu, Kunashiri, Shikotan and Habomai were Japanese territory, and that the islands to the north or Uruppu were Russian territory.

According to the Treaty for the Exchange of Sakhalin for the Kurile Islands of May 7, 1875, the islands from Uruppu to [Shumshu] were peacefully ceded by Russia to Japan in exchange for the concession of Japanese rights to the island of Sakhalin.

With the signing of the Treaty on Commerce and Navigation between Japan and Russia on June 8, 1895, the Treaty of 1855 became invalid, but at the same time, the validity of the Treaty of 1875 was reaffirmed.

According to the Portsmouth Peace Treaty between Japan and Russia of September 5, 1905, Russia ceded that part of the island of Sakhalin south of the 50th parallel North to Japan. In light of Japanese and Russian documents from this period, it is obvious that from the time that Japanese-Russian diplomatic relations were established in 1855, the title to the islands of Etorofu, Kunashiri, Shikotan and Habomai was never held in doubt by Russia.

In the Convention on Fundamental Principles for Relations between Japan and the USSR [Union of Soviet Socialist Republics] of January 20, 1925, that announced the establishment of diplomatic relations between Japan and the Soviet Union, the Soviet Union agreed that the Portsmouth Peace Treaty of 1905 would remain in force.

The Joint Declaration of the US [United States] and the UK [United Kingdom] of August 14, 1941 (the Atlantic Charter), which the Soviet Union acceded to on September 24, 1941, stated that the US and Great Britain "seek no aggrandizement, territorial or other" and that "they desire to see no territorial changes that do not accord with the freely expressed wishes of the peoples concerned."

The Cairo Declaration of the US, UK and China of November 27, 1943, which the Soviet Union acceded to on August 8, 1945, stated that the "Allies covet no gains for themselves and have no thought of territorial expansion." At the same time the Declaration stated that the Allies' goal was particularly to drive Japan from "the territories which she has taken by violence and greed."

The Yalta Agreement of the Three Great Powers (the USSR, the US and the UK) of February 11, 1945, stipulated as one of the conditions for the USSR's entry into the war against Japan: "the Kurile Islands shall be handed over to the Soviet Union." The Soviet Union maintained that the Yalta Agreement provided legal confirmation of the transfer of the Kurile Islands to the USSR, including the islands of Etorofu, Kunashiri, Shikotan and Habomai. Japan's position is that the Yalta Agreement is not the final determination on the territorial issue and that Japan, which is not party to this Agreement, is nei[t]her legally nor politically bound by its provisions.

The Potsdam Declaration of July 26, 1945, which the Soviet Union acceded to on August 8, 1945, stated that "the terms of the Cairo Declaration be carried out" and that "Japanese sovereignty be limited to the islands of Honshu, Hokkaido, Kyushu, Shikoku and such minor islands as the Allies would determine." On August 15, 1945, Japan accepted the terms of the Potsdam Declaration and surrendered.

In the Neutrality Pact between Japan and the USSR of April 13, 1941, the parties had an obligation to mutually respect each other's territorial integrity and inviolability. The Pact also stated that it would remain in force for five years and that if neither of the contracting

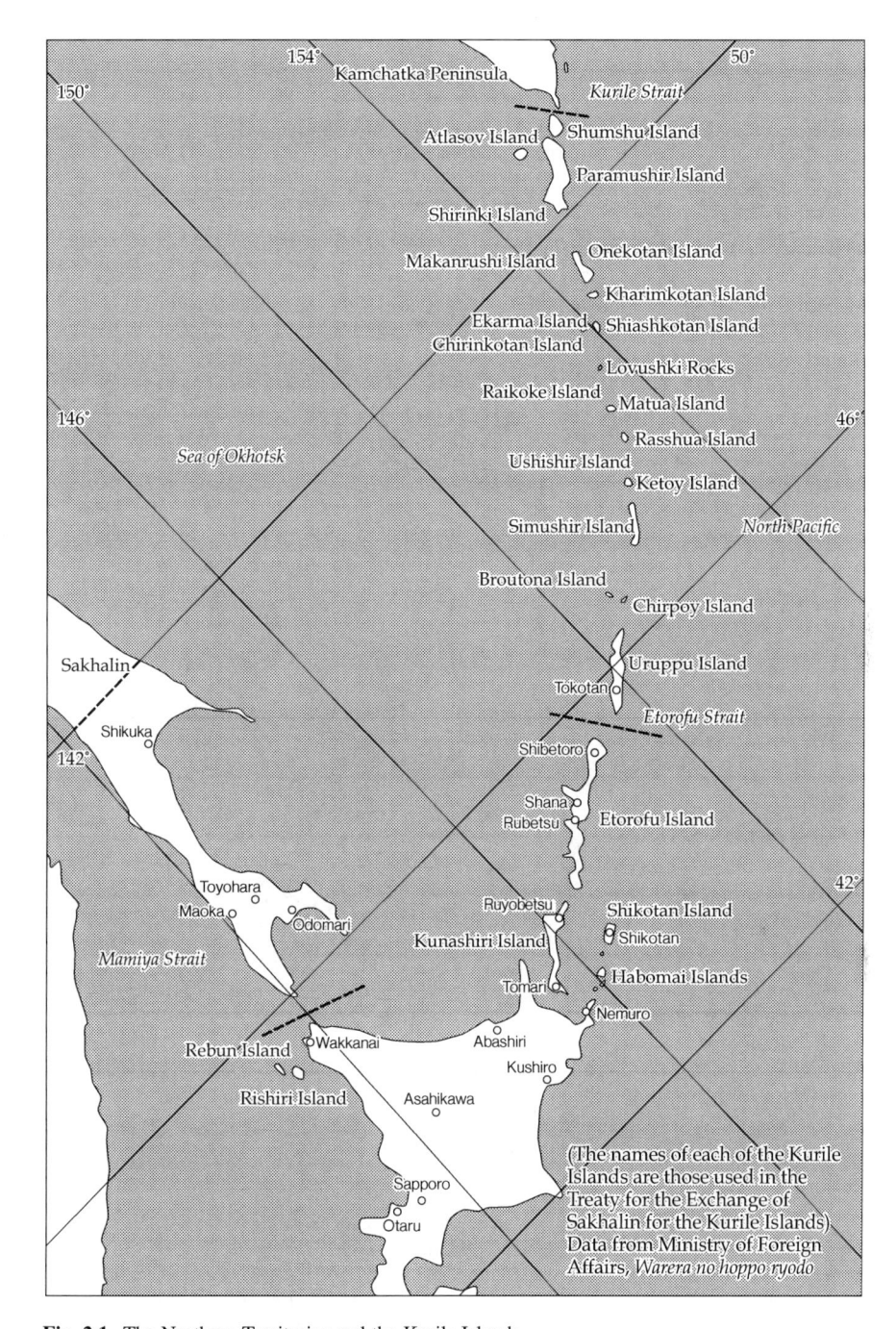

Fig. 2.1 The Northern Territories and the Kurile Islands

parties denounced it a year before its date of expiration, it be considered to be automatically extended for the next five years.

After the Soviet Union announced its intention to denounce the Japanese-Soviet Neutrality Pact on April 5, 1945, the Pact was to have become invalid on April 25, 1946. The Soviet Union declared war on Japan on August 9, 1945.

From late August to early September 1945, the Soviet Union occupied the islands of Etorofu, Kunashiri, Shikotan and Habomai. After that, by the Decree of the Presidium of the USSR Supreme Soviet of February 2, 1946, these islands were incorporated into the then Russian Soviet Federal Socialist Republic.

The San Francisco Peace Treaty with Japan of September 8, 1951 provides for Japan's renunciation of rights, titles and claims to the Kurile Islands and South Sakhalin. However, the Treaty did not determine to which state these territories belong. The Soviet Union did not sign this treaty.

The question of the limits of the Kurile Islands that were renounced by Japan in the San Francisco Peace Treaty was mentioned, for example, in a statement by K[umao] Nishimura, Director of the Treaties Bureau of the Ministry of Foreign Affairs of Japan, in the Japanese Parliament on October 19, 1951, and in a statement by Mr. K[unio] Morishita, Parliamentary Vice-Minister for Foreign Affairs of Japan, in the Japanese Parliament on February 11, 1956, as well as in an Aide-Mémoire from the Department of State of the US, which was one of the drafters of the Treaty, to the Government of Japan dated September 7, 1956.

As the Soviet Union did not sign the San Francisco Peace Treaty, separate negotiations on the conclusion of a peace treaty were conducted between Japan and the Soviet Union. However, because of differences in the positions of the two sides over the territorial clause of the treaty, an agreement was not reached.

An exchange of letters between Mr. S[hunichi] Matsumoto, Plenipotentiary Representative of the Government of Japan, and Mr. A[ndrei] A. Gromyko, USSR First Deputy Minister of Foreign Affairs, on September 29, 1956, showed that the two sides agreed to continue negotiations on the conclusion of a peace treaty, which would also include the territorial issue, after the reestablishment of diplomatic relations between the two countries. This exchange of letters also paved the way for the reestablishment of Japanese-Soviet diplomatic relations and the signing of the Joint Declaration by Japan and the USSR.

The Joint Declaration by Japan and the USSR of October 19, 1956 ended the state of war and reestablished diplomatic and consular relations between the two countries. In the Joint Declaration, Japan and the USSR agreed to continue negotiations on the conclusion of a peace treaty after the reestablishment of normal diplomatic relations, and the USSR also agreed to hand over the islands of Habomai and Shikotan to Japan after the signing of a peace treaty. The Joint Declaration by Japan and the USSR was ratified by the Japanese Parliament on December 5, 1956, and by the Presidium of the Supreme Soviet of the USSR on December 8, 1956. Instruments of ratification were exchanged in Tokyo on December 12, 1956.

In 1960, in connection with the conclusion of the new Japanese-US Security Treaty, the Soviet Union stated that the return of the islands of Habomai and Shikotan to Japan would be conditional upon the withdrawal of all foreign troops from Japanese territory. In response, the Government of Japan raised the objection that the terms of the Joint Declaration between Japan and the USSR could not be changed unilaterally, because it was an international agreement that had been ratified by the Parliaments of both countries.

The Soviet side later asserted that the territorial issue in Japanese-Soviet relations had been resolved as a result of World War II and such an issue did not exist.

The Japanese-Soviet Joint Communiqué of October 10, 1973, issued at the conclusion of the summit in Moscow, noted that "the settlement of unresolved problems left over since World War II and the conclusion of a peace treaty will contribute to the establishment of truly good-neighborly and friendly relations between the two countries."

> *The Japanese-Soviet Joint Communiqué of April 18, 1991, issued at the conclusion of the summit in Tokyo, stated that both sides had conducted negotiations "on a whole range of issues pertaining to the preparation and the signing of a peace treaty between Japan and the USSR, including the problem of territorial demarcation, taking into consideration the positions of both sides on the issue as to where the islands of Habomai, Shikotan, Kunashiri and Etorofu belong." The Communiqué also stressed the importance of accelerating the work on the conclusion of a peace treaty.*
>
> *After the creation of the Commonwealth of Independent States in December 1991 and Japan's recognition of the Russian Federation as the State with the continuity from the USSR, the negotiations on a peace treaty which were conducted between Japan and the USSR have been continuing between Japan and the Russian Federation.*
>
> *Both sides are firmly committed to a common understanding of the need to resolve the territorial issue on the basis of "law and justice."*
>
> *In November 1991 Mr. B[oris] N. Yeltsin, President of the Russian Federation, in his letter to the Russian people, indicated the need to reach a final postwar settlement in relations with Japan and noted that attention would be paid to the interests of the inhabitants of the said islands. The Government of Japan has also declared its intention to respect fully the human rights, interests and wishes of the Russians who now live on the islands, in the course of the resolution of the territorial issue.* [1]

The above represents the preface to the Joint Compendium of Documents on the History of the Territorial Issue. This indicates there is a need to address the unresolved issues that have persisted since World War II. The issue for Japan is the return of these islands. "From the time that Japanese-Russian diplomatic relations were established in 1855, the title to the islands of Etorofu, Kunashiri, Shikotan and Habomai was never held in doubt by Russia," and yet "From late August to early September 1945, the Soviet Union (after Japan agreed to the Potsdam Declaration and surrendered on August 15, 1945) occupied the islands of Etorofu, Kunashiri, Shikotan and Habomai. After that, by the Decree of the Presidium of the USSR Supreme Soviet of February 2, 1946, these islands were incorporated into the then Russian Soviet Federal Socialist Republic."

Documents issued since 1993, including the Tokyo Declaration on Japan-Russia Relations of October 1993, were published in January 2001 as an expanded and revised version of the Joint Compendium of Documents on the History of the Territorial Issue, and transcribed therein. This chapter will touch upon recent trends below.

Japan-USSR Peace Treaty Negotiations, Restoration of Japan-USSR Diplomatic Relations, and the Japan-Soviet Joint Declaration.

---

[1] "Preface," *Joint Compendium of Documents on the History of Territorial Issue between Japan and Russia.* 1992. https://www.mofa.go.jp/region/europe/russia/territory/edition92/preface.html. Accessed on December 6, 2022.

Speech by the USSR Representative to the Peace Conference

Andrei Gromyko, representative of the USSR side, gave a speech on September 5, 1951, at the San Francisco Peace Conference (refer to the Joint Compendium of Documents on the History of the Territorial Issue).[2]

> ... *The peace treaty with Japan should, naturally, resolve a number of territorial questions connected with the peace settlement with Japan. It is known that in this respect as well the United States, Great Britain, China and the Soviet Union undertook specific obligations. These obligations are outlined in the Cairo Declaration, in the Potsdam Declaration, and in the Yalta Agreement.*
>
> *These agreements recognize the absolutely indisputable rights of China, now the Chinese People's Republic, to territories severed from it. It is an indisputable fact that original Chinese territories which were severed from it, such as Taiwan (Formosa), the Pescadores, the Paracel Islands and other Chinese territories, should be returned to the Chinese People's Republic.*
>
> *The rights of the Soviet Union to the southern part of the Sakhalin Island and all the islands adjacent to it, as well as to the Kurile Islands, which are at present under the sovereignty of the Soviet Union, are equally indisputable.*
>
> *Thus, while resolving the territorial questions in connection with the preparation of a peace treaty with Japan, there should not be any lack of clarity if we are to proceed from the indisputable rights of States to territories which Japan got hold of by the force of arms.*
>
> *(abridged)*
>
> *Similarly, by attempting to violate grossly the sovereign rights of the Soviet Union regarding Southern Sakhalin and the islands adjacent to it, as well as the Kurile Islands already under the sovereignty of the Soviet Union, the draft also confines itself to a mere mention of the renunciation by Japan of rights, title and claims to these territories and makes no mention of the historic appurtenance of these territories and the indisputable obligation on the part of Japan to recognize the sovereignty of the Soviet Union over these parts of the territory of the USSR.*
>
> *(abridged)*
>
> *...To sum up, the following conclusions regarding the American-British draft peace treaty can be drawn:*
>
> *(abridged)*
>
> *The draft treaty is in contradiction to the obligations undertaken by the United States and Great Britain under the Yalta Agreement regarding the return of Sakhalin and the transfer of the Kurile Islands to the Soviet Union. ...*

In other words, the USSR was not satisfied with the territorial conditions of the San Francisco Treaty. It did not sign the treaty because "it was not a treaty of peace, but rather a treaty for preparing for a new war in the Far East." Accordingly, it became essential to conclude a peace treaty between Japan and the USSR.

---

[2] "Statement of the First Deputy Minister of Foreign Affairs of the USSR, A. A. Gromyko, at the Conference in San Francisco (1951)," *Joint Compendium of Documents on the History of Territorial Issue between Japan and Russia.* 1992. https://www.mofa.go.jp/region/europe/russia/territory/edition92/period4.html. Accessed on December 6, 2022.

Khrushchev's Peaceful Coexistence Policy

A variety of politicians have come and gone during more than 40 years of history involving Russo-Japanese negotiations. On the Russian side, this includes Stalin who concluded the Yalta Agreement, followed by First Secretaries Khrushchev and Brezhnev, then Presidents Gorbachev, Yeltsin, and Putin.

Khrushchev changed the direction of diplomacy from the Stalin-led Cold War to peaceful coexistence, and he commenced measures in 1955 to approach Japan in an effort to normalize diplomatic relations. The move for USSR-Japan negotiations that began with the Domnitsky document of January 1955 took concrete form in June with the London negotiations involving Matsumoto Shun'ichi, plenipotentiary representative of the Japanese government, and Yakov Malik, Soviet ambassador to the United Kingdom, which involved lengthy discussions about the repatriation of Japanese nationals detained in Siberia and the territorial issue. Negotiations, however, reached an impasse; while they restarted in London in January of the following year, negotiations were eventually cancelled in March. The Japanese side's demands included the return of Kunashiri Island and Etorofu Island as well as the Habomai Islands and Shikotan Island to Japan, and referral of Southern Sakhalin Island and other matters to an international conference. The USSR side asserted that all territorial issues were resolved within the Yalta Agreement, Potsdam Declaration, and the territorial clause of the San Francisco Peace Treaty. This resulted in an impasse between both sides. However, Khrushchev is said to have implied during the second half of the London negotiations that the Habomai Islands and Shikotan Island could be returned conditionally.

The day after the London negotiations were cancelled, the USSR unilaterally announced restrictive measures on salmon fishing in the North Pacific against the Japanese. As a result, Japan was forced to negotiate fishing rights, and while negotiations in Moscow between Kōno Ichirō, minister of agriculture, and Aleksandr Ishkov, minister of fisheries, wrapped up in May 1955, the condition was the conclusion of a peace treaty or the restoration of diplomatic relations. In July, Foreign Minister Shigemitsu Mamoru and Foreign Minister Dmitri Shepilov held negotiations in Moscow, and an agreement was nearly reached with the exception of the territorial issue, but no breakthrough was made with regard to this issue, and in September the following exchange of notes was agreed between Matsumoto Shun'ichi, plenipotentiary representative of the Japanese government, and Andrei Gromyko, first deputy minister of foreign affairs.[3]

---

[3] "1. Letter from the Plenipotentiary Representative of the Japanese Government, S. Matsumoto, to the USSR First Deputy Minister of Foreign Affairs, A.A. Gromyko (1956)," and "2. Letter from the USSR First Deputy Minister of Foreign Affairs, A. A. Gromyko, to the Plenipotentiary Representative of the Government of Japan, S. Matsumoto (1956)," *Joint Compendium of Documents on the History of Territorial Issue between Japan and Russia.* 1992. https://www.mofa.go.jp/region/europe/russia/territory/edition92/period5.html. Accessed on December 6, 2022.

... At the same time the Japanese Government thinks that after the reestablishment of diplomatic relations as a result of these negotiations, it is quite desirable that Japanese-Soviet relations develop even further on the basis of a formal peace treaty, which would also include the territorial issue. (Matsumoto letter)

I have further the honor to inform you on behalf of the Government of the Union of Soviet Socialist Republics that the Soviet Government accepts the view of the Japanese Government referred to above and announces its agreement to continue negotiations on the conclusion of a peace treaty, which would also include the territorial issue, after the reestablishment of normal diplomatic relations. (Gromyko letter)

In October, Prime Minister Hatoyama Ichirō traveled to Moscow despite health problems and on October 19 signed the Joint Declaration by Japan and the USSR. According to this declaration, the state of war would end and diplomatic relations be restored, but the territorial issue was not resolved and the conclusion of a peace treaty was postponed. Paragraph 9 of the Joint Declaration stated the following[4]:

9. Japan and the Union of Soviet Socialist Republics agree to continue, after the restoration of normal diplomatic relations between the Union of Soviet Socialist Republics and Japan, negotiations for the conclusion of a Peace Treaty.
 The Union of Soviet Socialist Republics, desiring to meet the wishes of Japan and taking into consideration the interests of the Japanese State, agrees to hand over to Japan the Habomai Islands and the island of Shikotan. However, the actual handing over of these islands to Japan shall take place after the conclusion of a peace treaty between Japan and the Union of Soviet Socialist Republics.

During the drafting of the declaration, the Japanese side strongly demanded the insertion of the words "including the territorial issue" in the part of the declaration concerning the peace treaty instead of simply stating that they agreed to continue negotiations for a peace treaty. However, this was not included in the finalized declaration.

The Era of the New Japan-US Security Treaty and the USSR's Claim That "Territorial Issues Have Already Been Settled"

Khrushchev Document

The Japan-Soviet Joint Declaration represents the most important fundamental document defining the relations between Japan and USSR following World War II. The following were agreed in accordance with this declaration[5]:

---

[4]"3. Paragraph 9 of the Joint Declaration of Japan and the USSR (1956)," *Joint Compendium of Documents on the History of Territorial Issue between Japan and Russia.* 1992. https://www.mofa.go.jp/region/europe/russia/territory/edition92/period5.html. Accessed on December 6, 2022.

[5]For the original texts, please see, "No. 3768. Union of Soviet Socialist Republics and Japan: Joint Declaration. Signed at Moscow, on 19 October 1956," 263 UNTS 99, pp. 112–116. https://treaties.un.org/doc/Publication/UNTS/Volume%20263/v263.pdf. Accessed on December 6, 2022.

1. The state of war would cease, and peace, friendship and good-neighborly relations would be restored.
2. Diplomatic and consular relations would be restored, and each side would establish its embassy in the territory of the other.
3. Japanese nationals detained in the Soviet Union would be repatriated to Japan.
4. The bilateral agreements including the fisheries convention signed in May 1956 would come into effect.
5. The Soviet Union would support Japan's application for membership in the United Nations.[6]

They also affirmed that in their mutual relations they would be guided by the principles under the United Nations Charter, in particular those set forth in Article 2. It was also promised that a trade, navigation, and other commercial agreements would be concluded on a firm and friendly basis.

The USSR renounced all war reparations, and both countries agreed to forgo their claims against each other arising from the result of the war.

"Since diplomatic relations between Japan and the USSR were restored through the Joint Declaration, bilateral relations showed steady developments in various fields including business, trade and culture, among others."[7] However, Prime Minister Kishi Nobusuke signed the new Japan-US Security Treaty on January 19, 1960 and on January 27, Soviet Foreign Minister Andrei Gromyko handed the following memorandum to Kadowaki Suemitsu, Japanese ambassador to the USSR, unilaterally adding the new condition that all foreign military forces had to withdraw from Japanese territories as a requirement for the return of the Habomai Islands and Shikotan Island agreed upon in the Joint Declaration by Japan and the USSR.[8]

But the Soviet Union certainly cannot ignore such a step as Japan's conclusion of a new military treaty which undermines the basis for peace in the Far East and creates obstacles to the development of Soviet-Japanese relations. A new situation has formed in relation to the fact that this treaty actually deprives Japan of independence and that foreign troops stationed in Japan as a result of Japan's surrender remain on Japanese territory. This

---

[6]The original members of the United Nations (UN) signed the Declaration by United Nations in January 1942 and included countries that had declared war against the Axis countries of Japan and Germany. Members included Axis countries and neutral countries in World War II, as well as newly independent former colonies. Of the defeated countries, the Allies promised to support UN membership for Italy, Finland, Bulgaria, Hungary, and Romania per the 1947 peace treaty, but they could not obtain the necessary votes of approval in the UN Security Council regarding communist countries, so the USSR vetoed Italy and Finland's memberships. Japan obtained the approval for membership from signatory countries under the peace treaty, but the USSR stood in the way of its membership with its veto power, giving as its reason the absence of a peace treaty and Japan's hostile attitude.

[7]Ministry of Foreign Affairs of Japan. 2001. *Warera no hoppō ryōdo* (Our Northern Territories).

[8]"4. Memorandum from the Soviet Government to the Government of Japan (1960)," *Joint Compendium of Documents on the History of Territorial Issue between Japan and Russia*. 1992. https://www.mofa.go.jp/region/europe/russia/territory/edition92/period5.html. Accessed on December 6, 2022.

situation makes it impossible for the Soviet Government to fulfill its promises to return the islands of Habomai and Shikotan to Japan.

(abridged)

But since the new military treaty signed by the Japanese Government is directed against the Soviet Union and the People's Republic of China, the Soviet Government cannot contribute to extending the territory available to foreign troops by handing over such islands to Japan.

Thus, the Soviet Government finds it necessary to declare that the islands of Habomai and Shikotan will be handed over to Japan, as was stated in the Joint Declaration by Japan and the USSR of October 19, 1956, only if all foreign troops are withdrawn from Japan and a Soviet-Japanese peace treaty is signed.

The above memorandum from the Government of the USSR made new assertions by invoking the principle of *clausula rebus sic stantibus* in international law. The Japanese side responded as follows on February 5.[9]

... It is extremely incomprehensible that in its latest memorandum, the Soviet Government is connecting the issue of the revised Japan-US Security Treaty with the issue of handing over the islands of Habomai and Shikotan. ...

(abridged)

This Joint Declaration is an international agreement regulating the foundations of the relationship between Japan and the Soviet Union. It is an official international document which has been ratified by the highest organs of both countries. It is needless to say that the contents of this solemn international undertaking cannot be changed unilaterally. Moreover, since the current Japan-U.S. Security Treaty[10] which is valid indefinitely already existed and foreign troops were present in Japan when the Japan-Soviet Joint Declaration was signed, it must be said that the Declaration was signed on the basis of these facts. Consequently, there is no reason that the agreements in the Joint Declaration should be affected in any way.

The Government of Japan cannot approve of the Soviet attempt to attach new conditions for the provisions of the Joint Declaration on the territorial issue and thereby to change the contents of the Declaration. Our country will keep insisting on the reversion not only of the islands of Habomai and Shikotan, but also of the other islands which are inherent parts of Japanese territory. ...

The USSR was persistent in sending similar memoranda, but finally Premier Khrushchev conveyed in writing to Prime Minister Ikeda Hayato in September 1961 that "territorial issues have already been solved in the series of international agreements concluded some time ago." As a result, the Soviet Union's stance toward the Northern Territories issue took a further step backward. The Government of Japan, however, maintained its consistent point of view in February 1956 that "Kunashiri and Etorofu islands were not included as part of the Kurile Islands in the Treaty of Peace with Japan." During the Budget Committee meeting of the House of Representatives of October 1961, in response to questions on the testimony of Treaties

---

[9]"5. Memorandum from the Japanese Government to the Soviet Government (1960)." Ibid.

[10]Current version of Japan-US Security Treaty (Treaty of Mutual Cooperation and Security Between Japan and the United States of America) was later concluded in 1960.

Bureau Director-General Nishimura Kumao about discussions of a peace treaty, Ikeda replied, "I believe the words of the government committee member[11] are incorrect."

Following this, the USSR continued to assert its belief that "territorial issues have already been settled" until the Tanaka-Brezhnev meetings in October 1973.

Tanaka-Brezhnev Meetings

The Hatoyama Cabinet was followed by: the Ishibashi Cabinet, which was in power only for a short while; the Kishi Cabinet, which focused on revisions to the Japan-US Security Treaty; the Ikeda Cabinet, which planned the path to economic growth; and the Satō Cabinet, which engaged in negotiations for the return of Okinawa. The Okinawa Reversion Treaty entered into force on May 15, 1972, and Prime Minister Satō Eisaku resigned in June. On July 5, Tanaka Kakuei won a fierce four-way battle against rival party leaders (Miki Takeo, Ōhira Masayoshi, and Fukuda Takeo)[12] to be elected head of the Liberal Democratic Party as Satō's successor, and Tanaka was subsequently elected prime minister. He announced on July 7 that he would urgently move forward with the normalization of diplomatic relations with the People's Republic of China. On September 25, Tanaka visited China with Ōhira, minister for foreign affairs, and the Japan-China Joint Communiqué was announced on September 29, officially normalizing relations. Following this, Ōhira visited the Soviet Union in October and began the first negotiations on a peace treaty with Russia with his counterpart, Foreign Minister Andrei Gromyko.

Tanaka sent a letter to Brezhnev in March 1973, and in his response Brezhnev invited the prime minister to visit Moscow. From October 7 to 10, 1973, Tanaka paid an official visit to the Soviet Union, the first by a Japanese prime minister in 17 years. Based on discussions between both leaders, the Japanese-Soviet Joint Communiqué was issued on October 10. This Communiqué stipulated the following about the territorial issue.

> 1. *Recognizing that the settlement of unresolved problems left over from WWII and conclusion of a peace treaty would contribute to the establishment of truly good-neighborly and friendly relations between the two countries, both sides held negotiations on issues pertaining to the contents of a peace treaty. Both sides agreed to continue negotiations on the conclusion of a peace treaty between the two countries at an appropriate time in 1974.*[13]

In response to Tanaka stating that he wished to confirm that the four islands were included in "unresolved issues," it is said that Brezhnev confirmed that that was

---

[11] The director-general of the Treaties Bureau.

[12] Known in Japanese as the "San-Kaku-Dai-Fuku" battle.

[13] "6. Japanese-Soviet Joint Communique (1973)," *Joint Compendium of Documents on the History of Territorial Issue between Japan and Russia*. 1992. https://www.mofa.go.jp/region/europe/russia/territory/edition92/period5.html. Accessed on December 6, 2022.

precisely the case.[14] At any rate, 17 years after normalizing relations with the Soviet Union, which had stated repeatedly that "territorial issues were already settled," an agreement was reached to continue negotiations on territorial issues at the highest level involving both countries' leaders.

However, time passed without clear progress being made. Although former residents had been allowed visits to their relatives' graves on the four islands on and off with only identification cards and without a passport or visa for humanitarian purposes since 1964, in September 1976 the Soviet Union announced its definitive decision to require a Japanese passport and Soviet visa for such visits. As a result, these visits had to be suspended (and remained suspended until August 1986). This was because, for Japan, such measures appeared to be the Soviet Union's attempt to legitimatize that these four islands belonged to the Soviet Union, and such a view could not possibly be accepted.

The Soviet Union established fishing grounds 200 nautical miles off its coast on December 10, 1976 by Decree of the Presidium of the Supreme Soviet, and announced rules for its implementation, including the sea area applicable based on a decision by the Council of Ministers of the USSR in February 1977. The seas around the Four Northern Islands were included. Japan stated emphatically that such a unilateral measure by the Soviet Union was regrettable and could not be accepted, protesting immediately through diplomatic channels. The USSR-Japanese provisional fisheries agreement signed in May 1977 after USSR-Japanese fisheries negotiations began in March the same year contained the clause, "Nothing in this Agreement shall be deemed to prejudice the positions or views of the two Governments ... with regard to matters concerning the relations between them" (Article 8). As a result, Japan's stance toward the territorial issue was clearly reserved. During these negotiations, it is said that the USSR strongly pursued the clear demarcation of the international border determined in the Nemuro Strait between Hokkaidō and Kunashiri Island by the Council of Ministers of the USSR in February and in the Goyōmai Channel between Hokkaidō and the Habomai Islands within the provisional fisheries agreement. This effectively stalled negotiations. Japan established the Act on Temporary Measures Concerning Fishery Waters in July the same year and established a 200 nautical mile zone of its own that also included the seas surrounding the Four Northern Islands (see Chapter 6).

Foreign Minister Sonoda Sunao visited the Soviet Union in January 1978 and held discussions with his counterpart Gromyko, without any progress made. Gromyko did not reciprocate with a visit to Japan, and so the talks were suspended until January 1986.

---

[14]Ministry of Foreign Affairs, *Warera no hoppō ryōdo*.

Improvements in Soviet-Japanese and Russia-Japan Relations

New Thinking Diplomacy Under Gorbachev: Japan's Expanding Equilibrium Policy

Mikhail Gorbachev was appointed the General Secretary of the Soviet Union in March 1985. He embarked on the path of democratization, *glasnost* (openness) and *perestroika* (reform). Diplomatically, he advanced the concept of New Thinking diplomacy. Specifically, Gorbachev was concerned whether the Soviet Union could withstand the economic pressure of competing with US President Ronald Reagan's military expansion, so he strived to restore relations between the United States and the Soviet Union by proposing the Intermediate-Range Nuclear Forces Treaty (INF), the Strategic Arms Reduction Treaty (START), the withdrawal of Soviet troops from Afghanistan, and a unilateral reduction in conventional weapons. As for Soviet-Japanese relations, he highly praised Japan's economic growth and attempted to improve relations through changes in awareness. Subsequently, Foreign Minister Gromyko was dismissed after 30 years in office, with Eduard Shevardnadze appointed in his place. Regular Soviet-Japan foreign ministers' meetings were restored and resumed in January 1986, when Shevardnadze visited Japan; Foreign Minister Abe Shintarō visited Russia that May. A Soviet-Japanese cultural agreement was signed; talks were held about grave visits to the Northern Territories, as well, and a *note verbale* was exchanged that July, with visits resuming in August.

Thus, although its stance toward the territorial dispute remained rigid, there is no denying that the Soviet Union did come to the table to talk. As a result, dialogue between Japan and the Soviet Union gradually expanded. Gorbachev's thinking was highlighted during his speech in Vladivostok in July 1986 and his speech in Krasnoyarsk in September 1987.

Thereafter, the occurrence of the Toshiba Machine matter and Soviet Union spy incident signaled a cooling of Soviet-Japanese relations. However, Shevardnadze visited Japan once again in 1988 and a vice foreign ministerial working group on a peace treaty was formed (meetings were held eight times with the Soviet Union and seven times with Russia; and the Joint Compendium of Documents on the History of the Territorial Issue between Japan and Russia was published in 1992 with the cooperation of both foreign ministries).

Foreign Minister Uno Sōsuke visited the Soviet Union in 1989, where he presented Japan's "expanding equilibrium policy" whereby overall Soviet-Japanese relations would expand while giving priority to the conclusion of a peace treaty and resolution of territorial issues. The policy gained the basic understanding of the Soviet side. This expanding equilibrium policy marked a change in the principle of inseparability between political and economic matters. The Soviet Union's stance remained rigid, however. At the time of Shevardnadze's visit to Japan in 1990, Gorbachev's intention to visit Japan in April 1991 was announced. That visit proceeded as planned, marking the first ever visit by a Soviet head of state to

Japan, and the first Soviet-Japanese summit meeting held in 18 years. While there was no breakthrough on the territorial issue at this meeting, the following Japanese-Soviet Joint Communiqué was signed on April 18.[15]

4. Prime Minister Toshiki Kaifu of Japan and President M[ikhail] S. Gorbachev of the Union of Soviet Socialist Republics held in-depth and thorough negotiations on a whole range of issues relating to the preparation and conclusion of a peace treaty between Japan and the Union of Soviet Socialist Republic, including the issue of territorial demarcation, taking into consideration the positions of both sides on the attribution of the islands of Habomai, Shikotan, Kunashiri, and Etorofu.

The joint work done previously–particularly the negotiations at the highest level–has made it possible to confirm a series of conceptual understandings: that the peace treaty should be the document marking the final resolution of war-related issues, including the territorial issue, that it should pave the way for long-term Japan-USSR relations on the basis of friendship, and that it should not infringe on either side's security.

The Soviet side proposed that measures be taken in the near future to expand exchanges between residents of Japan and residents of the aforementioned islands, to establish a simplified visa-free framework for visits by the Japanese to these islands, to initiate joint, mutually beneficial economic activities in that region, and to reduce the Soviet military forces stationed on these islands. The Japanese side stated its intention to consult on these questions in the future.

As well as emphasizing the primary importance of accelerating work to conclude the preparation for a peace treaty, the Prime Minister and the President expressed their firm resolve to make constructive and vigorous efforts to this end taking advantage of all positive elements that have been built up in bilateral negotiations in the year since Japan and the Union of Soviet Socialist Republic jointly proclaimed an end to the state of war and the restoration of diplomatic relations in 1956.

According to the Japanese side, this Communiqué "...clearly marked the first time in writing without doubt that the four islands of Habomai, Shikotan, Kunashiri, and Etorofu were included in the territorial issue to be resolved in a peace treaty."[16]

This communiqué resulted in the beginning of new efforts. But the domestic situation in the Soviet Union changed rapidly that summer, with a failed coup attempt in August and the end of Communist Party rule. This was followed by the collapse of the Soviet Union in December.[17]

Gorbachev contributed greatly to improved relations with Japan in areas other than the territorial dispute. *Perestroika* was welcomed by developed countries and Gorbachev's personal style of traveling with his wife helped to ease distrust of the Soviet Union among the Japanese people and could be credited with changing the way it was viewed by the Japanese people.

---

[15] "1. Japanese-Soviet Joint Communique (1991)," *Joint Compendium of Documents on the History of Territorial Issue between Japan and Russia*. 1992. https://www.mofa.go.jp/region/europe/russia/territory/edition92/period6.html. Accessed on December 6, 2022.

[16] Ministry of Foreign Affairs, *Warera no hoppō ryōdo*.

[17] See "Sobieto renpō no kaitai (The Break-up of the Soviet Union)" in Serita, Kentarō. 1996. *Fuhenteki kokusai shakai no seiritsu to kokusaihō* (Building on the Global Community and International Law). Tokyo: Yūhikaku.

Collapse of the Soviet Union, and President Yeltsin's Law and Justice: Japan's Multilayered Approach

The Russian Republic, which was part of the Soviet Union, declared its sovereignty in June 1990, followed by Ukraine and Belarus in July. Amidst confrontation with Soviet President Gorbachev, Chairman of the Presidium of the Russian Supreme Soviet Boris Yeltsin signed a basic treaty between Russia and Ukraine in November 1990, and he launched a policy that prioritized equal relations without the assumption of the existence of the Soviet Union as a point of departure for both countries' declaration of sovereignty. In the chaos caused by the attempted coup by the conservative faction of the Soviet Union on August 19, 1991, Yeltsin won a decisive victory. Ukraine and Belarus declared their independence immediately after the failed coup attempt. On December 8 of that year, Russia, Ukraine, and Belarus signed the agreement to create the Commonwealth of Independent States (CIS) in Minsk, the capital of Belarus, declaring the end of the Soviet Union. The leaders of these three countries and other republics excluding the Baltic States met on December 21 in the Kazakh capital of Alma Ata where they adopted a protocol on the agreement in Minsk, officially declaring the creation of the CIS. The Alma Ata Declaration proclaimed: "With the formation of the Commonwealth of Independent States, the USSR ceases to exist."[18]

Japanese Prime Minister Miyazawa Kiichi sent a letter to Yeltsin on December 27, in which he conveyed that the Russian Federation is the state retaining continuing identity with the Soviet Union and that all treaties and other international agreements between Japan and the Soviet Union would continue to be applied between Japan and the Russian Federation.

In other words, Japan recognized the Government of Russia. Japan also explicitly recognized the 10 countries of the CIS, including Ukraine and Belarus, on December 28, when its minister for foreign affairs sent letters to the foreign ministers of each of these countries.[19] The European Community clearly stated on December 23 prior to Japan that it deemed Russia as the successor State of the Soviet Union.

Acting Chairman of the Presidium of the Supreme Soviet Ruslan Khasbulatov visited Japan in September 1991 and delivered a letter from President Yeltsin to Prime Minister Kaifu Toshiki that expressed that he would eliminate the distinction between victor and defeated country of World War II, that the territorial dispute would be resolved based on law and justice, and the resolution of the territorial issue would not be further delayed.

---

[18] "Agreements establishing the Commonwealth of Independent States [Done at Minsk, December 8, 1991, and done at Alma Ata, December 21,1991]," Council of Europe, CDL 94(54), 1994, p. 149. https://www.venice.coe.int/webforms/documents/?pdf=CDL(1994)054-e Accessed 1 March 2023.

[19] Official Telegram No. 815, January 8, 1992, Ministry of Foreign Affairs Bulletin No. 9. For more details about the independence of the three Baltic countries and the independence of the 11 countries including Ukraine, see Serita, 1996 op. cit.

Prime Minister Miyazawa met with Yeltsin in New York in January 1992. During the meeting, Yeltsin stated that he would visit Japan later that year in September. Preparations were made energetically for this visit by both Japan and Russia. During this process, Japan stated that, based on Russia's new approach indicated since September 1991, it would fully respect the human rights, interests, and hopes of the Russian people living on the four Northern Territories after their return to Japan, and that it would respond flexibly with regard to the timing, format, and conditions for the return if Japan's sovereignty over the four islands were confirmed. Yeltsin's visit to Japan was postponed shortly before his departure, however, owing to the domestic situation in Russia. Nevertheless, in September, the Joint Compendium of Documents on the History of the Territorial Issue between Japan and Russia was completed with the cooperation of the Ministries of Foreign Affairs of Japan and Russia as noted above.

Yeltsin did eventually visit Japan in October 1993, and the meeting between both leaders resulted in the Tokyo Declaration on Japan-Russia relations, signed on October 13. The preface of the New Edition of the Joint Compendium of Documents on the History of the Territorial Issue between Japan and Russia from January 16, 2001, states: "This was the first comprehensive document signed between Japan and the Russian Federation establishing the principal direction of progress for bilateral relations. The Tokyo Declaration stipulates the necessity for the early conclusion of a peace treaty through the solution of the issue of where the afore-mentioned islands[20] belong, on the basis of historical and legal facts and based on the documents produced subject to the consent between both countries as well as on the principles of law and justice. Consequently, the Tokyo Declaration is especially important."

New Developments in Japan-Russia Relations

Tokyo Declaration and Krasnoyarsk Agreement/Kawana Proposal

The Tokyo Declaration on Japan-Russia Relations, the first of its kind with Russia after the fall of the Soviet Union, stated the following[21]:

> Based upon the recognition that, with the end of the Cold War, the world is moving away from the structure of confrontation towards cooperation which will open new vistas for advances in international cooperation on both global and regional levels as well as in bilateral relations between different countries, and that this is creating favorable conditions for the full normalization of the Japan-Russia bilateral relations;

---

[20] Namely Etorofu Island, Kunashiri Island, Shikotan Island and the Habomai Islands.

[21] https://www.mofa.go.jp/region/n-america/us/q&a/declaration.html. Accessed on December 6, 2022.

(abridged)

Determined that Japan and the Russian Federation should work together on the basis of the spirit of international cooperation, overcoming the legacy of totalitarianism, to build a new international order and to fully normalize their bilateral relations,

Declare the following:

1. (abridged)

2. *The Prime Minister of Japan and the President of the Russian Federation, sharing the recognition that the difficult legacies of the past in the relations between the two countries must be overcome, have undertaken serious negotiations on the issue of where Etorofu, Kunashiri, Shikotan and the Habomai Islands belong. They agree that negotiations towards an early conclusion of a peace treaty through the solution of this issue on the basis of historical and legal facts and based on the documents produced with the two countries' agreement as well as on the principles of law and justice should continue, and that the relations between the two countries should thus be fully normalized. In this regard, the Government of Japan and the Government of the Russian Federation confirm that the Russian Federation is the State retaining continuing identity with the Soviet Union and that all treaties and other internationals [sic] agreements between Japan and the Soviet Union continue to be applied between Japan and the Russian Federation. ...*

Under international law, such as the Vienna Convention on Succession of States in respect of Treaties, it is only natural that the Russian Federation has the obligation to continue to apply all treaties and other international agreements between Japan and the Soviet Union as the State retaining the continuing identity with the Soviet Union. This is guaranteed in Article 12 of the agreement on the establishment of the Commonwealth of Independent States signed at Minsk in December 1991, and was already mentioned at the time Japan recognized the Government of Russia.[22] However, there was a difference in opinion between Japan and the Soviet Union with regard to the Joint Declaration by Japan and the USSR of 1956, so it is particularly noteworthy that President Yeltsin clarified at the joint press conference held on October 13 that the Joint Declaration by Japan and the USSR of 1956 was included in "treaties and other international agreements."

Thus, Yeltsin's visit to Japan marked an important first step in a new era in Japan-Russia relations.

The year 1996 marked the 40th anniversary of the normalization of diplomatic relations and the signing of the Joint Declaration by Japan and the USSR. It was also an election year for the Russian presidency. Although Foreign Minister Ikeda Yukihiko visited Russia, Prime Minister Hashimoto Ryūtarō held a summit meeting in Moscow during his attendance at the Nuclear Security Summit, and a Japan-Russia foreign ministers' meeting was held at the G7 Lyon Summit, no progress was made. The leaders of Japan and Russia exchanged messages in October to commemorate the 40th anniversary of normalizing diplomatic relations, and Russian Foreign Minister Yevgeny Primakov visited Japan the following month,

---

[22] For implementation of the continuation of Japan's treaties, see Kokusaihō Jirei Kenkyūkai. 2001. *Nihon no jirei kenkyū (5): Jōyaku hō* (Study of Practices in Japan, Vol. 5: Law of Treaties). Tokyo: Keio University Press.

confirming once again that progress was being made in bilateral relations under the Tokyo Declaration. At this time, the Japanese side emphasized the need for efforts to be taken to improve the environment for the resolution of the territorial issue in tandem with the territorial negotiations. In response, the Russian side expressed its belief that while efforts to improve the environment should first be made, such efforts should not serve as an alternative to the resolution of the territorial issue or work to hinder it. It also put forward the idea of advancing "joint economic activities" on the four islands.

In 1997, Ikeda visited Russia in May where he held a regular meeting with Primakov, and following a summit meeting between Hashimoto and Yeltsin on the sidelines of the Denver Summit in June, Hashimoto visited Krasnoyarsk in November for informal and open talks with Yeltsin.[23] In particular, with regard to the territorial issue, both agreed "to make utmost efforts to conclude a peace treaty by 2000 based on the Tokyo Declaration." This is the Krasnoyarsk Agreement. They also agreed to conclude negotiations on a framework for fishing by Japanese vessels in the waters around the Northern Territories by the end of the year, with these negotiations effectively concluded by the end of that year. In February 1998, both countries signed the Agreement between the Government of Japan and the Government of the Russian Federation on certain aspects of cooperation in the fishing of marine living resources.[24] Ten days after the summit meeting, Primakov visited Japan and followed up on the summit meeting. It was agreed to set up a group headed by both foreign ministers, in which negotiations would be conducted at the vice-ministerial level. Vice minister level talks were held in January 1998 on negotiations for a peace treaty, and the Japanese-Russian Joint Committee on the Conclusion of a Peace Treaty was launched, jointly chaired by the foreign ministers of both countries.

An informal summit meeting was held in April 1998 in Kawana, Itō City, Shizuoka Prefecture. The Japanese side presented the Kawana Proposal. The details of this proposal have yet to be officially released, but the proposal contained the following elements according to newspaper reports. The government did not comment on these reports.

Japanese newspapers reported simultaneously on April 20 that Hashimoto had proposed the demarcation of the Japan-Russia border at the meeting on April 19. According to these reports, the Japanese side envisioned, *inter alia*, the following:

1. *Clearly demarcate the border on the northern side of the four islands in a treaty and confirm Japanese sovereignty over these islands;*
2. *Subsequently establish a transitional period, during which Japan will recognize Russian control, although the area will be open to free movement between the two sides;*

---

[23] Ministry of Foreign Affairs, *Warera no hoppō ryōdo*.

[24] https://treaties.un.org/doc/Publication/UNTS/Volume%202718/Part/volume-2718-I-48102.pdf. Accessed on March 1, 2023.

3. *Discuss the length of the transitional period with Russia and confirm at the time of the signing of the treaty; and*
4. *Work together with the Russian side during this period to develop infrastructure on the four islands to make them similar to the Japanese mainland, as well as to make preparations for transfer of control to the Japanese side.*[25]

This proposal shared similar characteristics with the "Five-Step Proposal"[26] presented by President Yeltsin in order to solve the territorial issue. It was reported that the Japanese side decided to submit its own proposal based on the view that without explicit reference to the timeline for reversion of control the situation would end up like that of Okinawa prior to reversion, and that even though it may be viewed as a step backward from the Japan-Soviet Joint Declaration, in which the return of two islands was promised, the Japanese public was unlikely to protest fiercely even if such a bold compromise were to be made.[27]

It was reported that Yeltsin responded in the meeting to the proposal by calling it "interesting," and during the press conference, he said "while I cannot respond immediately to the proposal, I feel optimistic about it." Reportedly, Yeltsin was about to say "da" to express his approval but was stopped by his aides. For the Japanese side, the proposal was a gamble.

Hashimoto later resigned and his successor, Obuchi Keizō, made an official visit to Russia in November 1998, the first such visit in 25 years by an incumbent Japanese prime minister, where he signed the Moscow Declaration on Establishing a Creative Partnership between Japan and the Russian Federation. This declaration aimed to further strengthen bilateral cooperation in various fields, and it contained the Russian side's response to the Kawana Proposal with regard to the issue of concluding a peace treaty.

It instructed both governments to accelerate negotiations based on the Tokyo Declaration, Krasnoyarsk Agreement, and Kawana Proposal, form a border confirmation committee and joint economic activities committee, and allow unrestricted visits by former island residents. In June 1999, at the summit meeting held on the sidelines of the G8 Cologne Summit, Obuchi invited Yeltsin to Japan, but Yeltsin resigned suddenly at the end of the year, to be replaced by the Putin administration.

---

[25] *Yomiuri Shimbun*, April 20, 1998, evening edition.

[26] Yeltsin, as a member of the parliament and a reform leader of the Soviet Union, visited Japan in 1990 and proposed a five-step process leading to the resolution of the territorial issue: (1) The Soviet Union acknowledges the territorial issue; (2) Make the four islands a "Free Enterprise Zone" where Japanese companies can easily establish operations; (3) Demilitarize the four islands; (4) Conclude a peace treaty; and (5) Leave the resolution of the territorial issue to the next generation when political culture matures, mutual exchange and mutual understanding advances between the nations, and public opinion changes for the better.

[27] *Asahi Shimbun*, April 21, 1998.

President Putin and the Irkutsk Statement

For Japan, the Kawana Proposal was a carefully timed initiative and a major gamble. The tide changed with Yeltsin's departure, however, and the proposal was thrown into a state of limbo. Acting President Vladimir Putin faced an election in March 2000. After the election, he needed to first review fully the overall relationship with Japan before heading into territorial negotiations.

On the Japanese side, Prime Minister Obuchi suddenly passed away. The Mori Yoshirō administration took over with all previous ministerial appointments intact. It engaged in a series of dialogues with the Putin administration and held a Japan-Russia summit meeting on the sidelines of the G8 Kyūshū/Okinawa Summit in July 2000. President Putin also paid an official visit to Japan in September. Another Japan-Russia summit meeting was held at the time of the APEC Summit in Brunei in November, and Prime Minister Mori visited Irkutsk in March 2001 where he met with Putin and they signed the Irkutsk Statement.

With regard to the Irkutsk Statement, the Government of Japan considered that "Japan and Russia have made collective efforts toward the signing of a peace treaty based on the Krasnoyarsk Agreement and now a new foundation has been formed for future peace treaty negotiations."[28] In particular, the Statement was well regarded by Japan as "affirming that a basic legal document is in place which forms a departure point for negotiation processes based on the Japan-Soviet Joint Declaration." The Irkutsk Statement reaffirms that the issue of attribution of the four islands must be resolved based on the Tokyo Declaration of 1993 before a peace treaty can be signed.

As was often the case, however, there was a difference in interpretation between the Japanese and Russian sides concerning Paragraph 9 of the Japan-Soviet Joint Declaration. In an interview with *Reuters* on April 4, immediately after the issuance of the Irkutsk Statement, the Russian vice foreign minister stated that the extreme stance on the Japanese side was that of "two islands plus two islands" while the extreme stance on the Russia side was that all four islands were Russian territory. When asked "What happened in Irkutsk? Did Russia make a concession?" he responded, "A statement about the effectiveness of the 1956 Joint Declaration cannot be called 'a concession.' This document is a mark of progress given that the Joint Declaration was the basis for our relationship and yet for the longest time it was not mentioned." Later, *Jiji Press* reported on July 17 that the Soviet minutes of the 1956 negotiations revealed that Khrushchev had imposed his position on the Japanese side that "the reversion of the two islands is our final response." It also reported that "The joint statement made at the Irkutsk meeting in March this year clearly referred to it as a fundamental legal document. At this time, the President pointed out that there were differences of interpretation on the Joint Declaration, and that if it were to make maximum concessions in future negotiations, the Russian side would remain adamant about its stance vis-à-vis the final decision regarding the two

---

[28] Ministry of Foreign Affairs, *Warera no hoppō ryōdo.*

islands."[29] This speculation by *Jiji Press* differed slightly from the nuance of the Russian vice foreign minister's response, demonstrating that *Jiji Press*'s understanding of the course of Japan-Russia negotiations to date was slightly problematic. Nevertheless, it is worthwhile pointing out that such a view did exist.

Background of Japan-Russia Negotiations and Measures for Achieving a Solution

Developments in Japan-Russia Negotiations and Their Significance in the Contemporary Context

Developments in negotiations between Japan and Russia as seen from the Japanese side are as follows. As was explained in Chapter 1, Southern Sakhalin, the Kurile Islands, and the Northern Territories were occupied by the Soviet Union during World War II. The postwar settlement process started with the San Francisco Peace Treaty; Japan then began peace treaty negotiations with the Soviet Union, which had not participated in that treaty.

The San Francisco Peace Treaty did not include a definition of "the Kurile Islands." During territorial negotiations, Khrushchev said he would return the Habomai Islands and Shikotan Island but was firmly against returning Kunashiri Island and Etorofu Island, whereas Japan demanded that Kunashiri Island and Etorofu Island be returned as well. The negotiations thus reached an impasse, and no peace treaty was signed; in its place, the Japan-Soviet Joint Declaration was concluded. Next for the Japanese side, the Soviet Union persisted in its stance that the "territorial issue had already been settled," despite the fact that Kunashiri Island and Etorofu Island were included in the scope of negotiations. So, the time came for the Japanese side to seek confirmation that the four islands were included among the unresolved issues between Japan and the Soviet Union, and Japan focused its efforts to have the Soviet Union confirm that Kunashiri Island and Etorofu Island were included in the scope of negotiations. This was confirmed verbally during the Tanaka-Brezhnev meeting of 1973, but not confirmed in writing.

After the end of the Cold War, this was confirmed in writing in 1991 with Gorbachev's visit to Japan and, following the collapse of the Soviet Union and establishment of Russia, in the Tokyo Declaration of 1993, in which resolving the issue of the Four Northern Islands and concluding a peace treaty was clearly mentioned in writing. The Kawana Proposal was made during this time, and with Putin taking power, a fresh start was made with the Irkutsk Statement.

To sum up, Japan has continually called for the return of the Habomai Islands, Shikotan Island, Kunashiri Island and Etorofu Island. The basis for this claim is "The Northern Territories, which consist of Etorofu Island, Kunashiri Island, Shikotan

---

[29] *Kōbe Shimbun*, July 18, 2001.

Island, and the Habomai Islands, have been handed down from generation to generation by Japanese people, and are inherent territories of Japan which have never been part of a foreign country."[30] The Soviet and Russian sides, for their part, asserted that the territorial issue had already been resolved through the Yalta Agreement, Potsdam Declaration, and surrender documents, and that subsequent peace treaty negotiations and the Japan-Soviet Joint Declaration had only served to confirm this fact. In other words, their position has changed from two islands (1956 Declaration) to "already settled" (since the new Japan-US Security Treaty) and then back to two islands (Irkutsk Statement). Currently, according to the statements the Russian vice foreign minister made during the interview post-Irkutsk Meeting, the idea of "two islands plus two islands" represents the extreme stance of the Japanese side, while the extreme stance on the Russian side is that "all four islands belong to Russia." The Russian stance is not clear. The Irkutsk Meeting gave both leaders the opportunity to send a message to each other's people. Putin gave an interview to NHK in which he said, "Regarding the Declaration of 1956, I recall that it states the following: the (then) Soviet Union agreed to return two islands to the Japanese side under the condition that a peace treaty be signed. This Declaration was ratified by the Presidium of the Supreme Soviets. In other words, this Declaration is binding on us."[31] The true intent of Putin's remarks, however, was likely to lay the groundwork for asserting that although the Declaration bound Russia to return the two islands, it was unable to do so because Japan continued to hold out for the four islands and would not conclude a peace treaty.

Legal discussions at the time are addressed in Takano Yūichi's *Nihon no ryōdo* [Japan's Territory] (University of Tokyo Press, 1962), and afterwards in his *Kokusaihō kara mita hoppō ryōdo* [The Northern Territories from the Perspective of International Law] (Iwanami Shoten, 1986), which was published as part of Iwanami Shoten's booklet series. Also, Taijudō Kanae's "Ryōdo mondai—hoppō ryōdo, Takeshima, Senkaku shotō no kizoku [The Attribution of the Northern Territories, Takeshima, and the Senkaku Islands]," *Jurist* 647, (1977) is recorded in *Ryōdo kizoku no kokusaihō*. Furthermore, it is worthwhile reading historian Wada Haruki's *Hoppō ryōdo mondai o kangaeru* [Considering the Northern Territories Issue] (Iwanami Shoten, 1990), which examines the scope of "the Kurile Islands" from a linguistic perspective and offers realistic proposals for improving Soviet-Japanese relations. Each of these was written during the Cold War era, so discussions and a new perspective that take into account the 10 years of relations with the newly-formed Russia are needed.

In this sense, it is important to point to the opening words of the Tokyo Declaration of 1993: "Based upon the recognition that, with the end of the Cold

---

[30] "The Government of Japan's Position and Basic Policy on the Northern Territories Issue." https://www.cas.go.jp/jp/ryodo_eg/taiou/index.html. Accessed on December 6, 2022.

[31] Presentation entitled "Irukutsuku shunō kaidan go no nichiro kankei (Japan-Russia Relations following the Irkutsk Summit Meeting)" by Togo Kazuhiko, director-general of the European Affairs Bureau, Ministry of Foreign Affairs, at the 36th research presentation session of the Japan Cultural Association on April 19, 2000.

War, the world is moving away from the structure of confrontation towards cooperation which will open new vistas for advances in international cooperation on both global and regional levels as well as in bilateral relations between different countries, and that this is creating favorable conditions for the full normalization of the Japan-Russia bilateral relations; (abridged) Determined that Japan and the Russian Federation should work together on the basis of the spirit of international cooperation, overcoming the legacy of totalitarianism, to build a new international order and to fully normalize their bilateral relations." For this reason, expectations are for a resolution to be reached based on the principles of "law and justice."

The shift from Stalin's Cold War to Khrushchev's Peaceful Coexistence brought about the Japan-Soviet Joint Declaration. Yet, this occurred within the confines of the Cold War, nevertheless. As such, this era was different from the Yeltsin/Putin era of the post-Cold War. The cornerstone of Japanese diplomacy is the Japan-US Alliance. Until the end of the Cold War, Japan-USSR relations were at times tossed about or disrupted altogether by developments in US-Soviet relations. In that sense, there was a limit to what could be achieved in the territorial negotiations. In the early post-Cold War era, however, it was viewed that Japan shared the same fundamental values with Russia, which was undergoing democratization and pursuing a market economy. The territorial issue must be resolved in the context of the overall relationship with our neighbor, Russia.

When viewed over the long span of history, the debate about the scope of the "Kurile Islands," apart from the important facts pointed out by Wada Haruki, has left resentment on the Japanese side, and likely will not contribute to stable bilateral relations between Japan and the Russian Federation. This is because the US side reminded the Japanese side that it could not reopen discussions on the peace treaty proposal during a meeting between Prime Minister Yoshida Shigeru, Secretary of State Dean Acheson, and John Foster Dulles, a special envoy, held 2 days before the San Francisco Peace Conference. Yoshida mentioned the four islands by name during his acceptance speech, but only to call attention to the issue. The Soviet Union accepted the principle of no territorial aggrandizement through its participation in the Potsdam Declaration, and during the peace conference the Soviet representative criticized the United States for violating this very principle with regard to the proposal to place Okinawa under UN Trusteeship. Based on the principle of no territorial aggrandizement advocated by the Allies, the "Kurile Islands" defined in peaceful diplomatic negotiations between Japan and Russia was not included in the areas "taken by violence and greed" as referred to in the Cairo Declaration. It is therefore not the case that Japan was forced to promise to give up the Kurile Islands, if not Southern Sakhalin.

Regardless, from the perspective of stable bilateral relations, there is no better resolution than the border drawn in the Treaty of Commerce, Navigation and Delimitation between Japan and Russia of 1855, which both parties entered into voluntarily. This is because, although the Treaty for the Exchange of Sakhalin for the Kurile Islands of 1875 was concluded peacefully after the Treaty of Commerce, Navigation and Delimitation, it was a source of dissatisfaction among the people of Japan at the time and eventually led to the Russo-Japanese War and the Portsmouth

Peace Treaty of 1905, which required the cession of Southern Sakhalin. This caused indignation among the people of Russia and resulted in the recapture of Southern Sakhalin through World War II and its unspeakable hardships.

We need to put this unfortunate history behind us.

Although there is no denying that the numerous interactions between Japan and Russia in the 50 years after World War II carry weight, from the standpoint of "law and justice" it would be best to bury the past and return to the line drawn by the Treaty of Commerce, Navigation and Delimitation, which is free of resentment and bitterness on both sides.

Steps to be Taken for a Resolution

According to the director-general of the Ministry of Foreign Affairs' European Affairs Bureau, there were 2000 Russians living on Shikotan Island at the time of the Irkutsk Meeting. Yet, not once had the fate of these 2000 Russian nationals been discussed in the territorial negotiations until then.

In April 1989, a reporter for *Hokkaidō Shimbun* became the first journalist to visit Kunashiri Island and cover the lives of the 7500 people living there. He reported the words of the chairman of the Yuzhno-Kurilsk regional executive committee who said, "Some of us are already members of the third generation. We have nowhere else to go." Some experts on the matter were of the view that it was possible to return the two islands if three conditions were met. Namely, guaranteeing the livelihood of the 6500 people living on Shikotan Island and the island's economic development by establishing a fisheries factory after the reduction of US military forces in Okinawa and its reversion to Japan.[32] In other words, they called on Japan to allow the Russian population to continue living there and to permit a Soviet factory to operate there indefinitely. A dozen years later, a reporter allowed to travel to the island without a visa in August 2001 as part of an exchange program found that a new company, Gidrostroy, was supporting the economy of the Northern Territories, which operated three plants on Etorofu Island and one plant on Shikotan Island as part of its hatcheries operation, an integrated business covering fishing, processing, and transport, with sales from the previous year amounting to 2.14 billion yen.

Additionally, humanitarian assistance from Japan helped to support the lives of islanders in the wake of the earthquake that struck off the eastern coast of Hokkaidō in 1994. Furthermore, a thermal power plant and a barge (planned for donation by the Government of Japan) were being used (or were to be used) to power the island's fisheries processing plant, and it was reported that a regular transportation service to Kunashiri Island was being considered. This report also conveyed the voices of

---

[32] 49. See Wada Haruki. 1990. *Hoppō ryōdo mondai o kangaeru* (Considering the Northern Territories Issue). Tokyo: Iwanami Shoten.

former islanders who said they were "worried how people's feelings would change if their lives improved."[33] As for the visa-free exchange program, a male resident of Shikotan Island had a positive view: "We will be able to get to know each other better and foster awareness about the issues."

I mention these examples because they indicate that the framework for crossings that has been established up to now, including exchanges with the four islands and grave visits to the Northern Territories, as well as the freedom of passage, has played a very important role in promoting the understanding and cooperation between the peoples of both Japan and Russia. In order to dispel the concerns of the population, there is a need to put forward a realistic approach regarding guarantees of the human rights of islanders. Individual issues must be discussed carefully and thoroughly, including whether to grant current islanders permanent resident status or allow them their choice of nationality, whether to guarantee business rights, and how to address specific issues in daily life. In this regard, the 25 measures proposed in the report "Hoppō yontō fukki ni tomonau shomondai (Problems Accompanying the Return of the Northern Territories)," prepared by the Research Society on Issues Posed by the Return of the Northern Territories in March 1999, contain useful suggestions.[34] As basic principles for addressing the return of the four islands, this report proposed that first, people residing on the islands for a certain period be granted permanent resident status if they so desire; second, appropriate assistance be provided to Russians who wish to repatriate; and third, development of the four islands should take full account of preserving the natural environment. In accordance with these principles, the report also called for the human rights of Russians wishing to continue to reside on the Four Northern Islands to be respected and various provisions be made to preserve their lifestyles, with the freedom of residence, schooling, and occupation guaranteed, and measures implemented to ensure that the interests of residents of Russian descent are not unjustly violated as a result of problems that might arise from the co-habitation of Japanese and Russian residents. These issues should be discussed widely and awareness of these issues fostered among the public.

---

[33] *Hokkaidō Shimbun*, September 4, 2001; et al.

[34] A private-sector research society whose members included former Japanese Ambassadors to the Soviet Union, Katori Yasue and Nakagawa Tōru, as well as Suetsugu Ichirō, chairman of the Council on National Security Problems.

Chapter 3
The Senkaku Islands

China's Claim Prompted by Potential Oil Reserves

The Senkaku Islands are a group of small islands located 160 km north of the Yaeyama Islands, Okinawa Prefecture. "The Senkaku Islands" is the collective term that refers to Uotsuri Island, Kitakojima Island, Minamikojima Island, Kuba Island (Kōbisho), Taishō Island (Sekibisho), Okinokitaiwa, Okinominamiiwa, and Tobise. Their total land area is approximately 6.3 km^2. The largest island, Uotsuri Island, covers about 3.6 km^2. Apart from the period when Japanese people inhabited them, the Senkaku Islands were, and are still, uninhabited. The islands were thought to have no valuable natural resources, and therefore escaped the world's attention (Fig. 3.1).

This changed in the autumn of 1968, when the United Nations Economic Commission for Asia and the Far East (ECAFE; now the United Nations Economic and Social Commission for Asia and the Pacific) released a report of a geophysical survey led by Japanese, Korean, and Taiwanese scientists of a vast area of the East China Sea. The ECAFE report concluded that there is a possibility of prolific oil reserves on the seafloor of roughly 200,000 km^2 northeast of Taiwan. This drew the attention of the international community to the Senkaku Islands. By late 1970, China began making territorial claims over the islands.[1]

Chapter 6 of this book discusses how negotiations between Japan and China over fishing rights around the Senkaku Islands have been handled. The Chinese government first began to officially assert sovereignty over the Senkaku Islands in a Statement of the Ministry of Foreign Affairs, dated December 1971. On March 8 of the following year, Japan released a document entitled "The Basic View on the Sovereignty over the Senkaku Islands, Ministry of Foreign Affairs." This work will primarily analyze these two documents.

---

[1]For more on issues concerning petroleum, see Takahashi, Shōgorō. 1979. *Senkaku rettō nōto* (Notes on the Senkaku Islands). Tokyo: Seinen Publishing.

© Kreab K.K. 2023
K. Serita, *The Territory of Japan*, https://doi.org/10.1007/978-981-99-3013-5_3

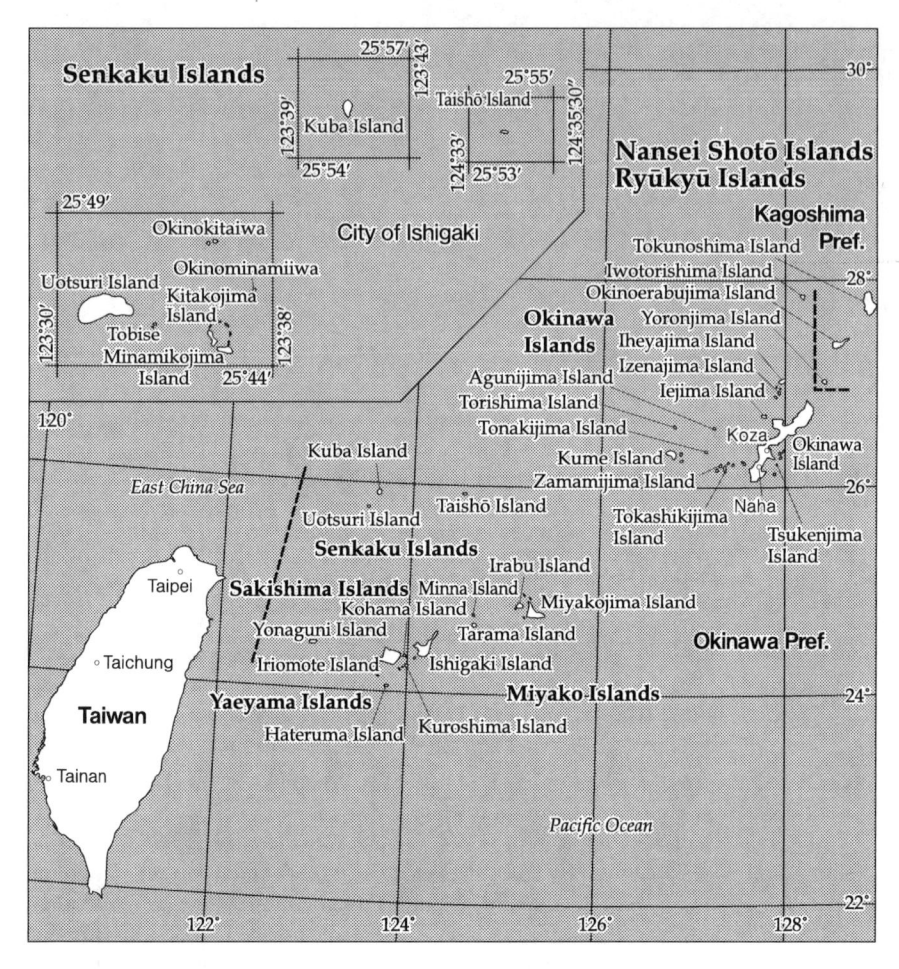

Fig. 3.1 Location of the Senkaku Islands

Examination of China's Argument and Its Basis

Examination of the Argument Asserting the Illegality of the Inclusion of the Senkaku Islands into the "Reversed Areas" of the Okinawa Reversion Treaty.

The Statement of the Ministry of Foreign Affairs of the People's Republic of China dated December 30, 1971 begins as follows:[2]

> *In the past few years, the Japanese Sato government, ignoring the historical facts and the strong opposition of the Chinese people, has repeatedly claimed that Japan has the so-called*

---

[2]"Statement of the Ministry of Foreign Affairs of the People's Republic of China," December 30, 1971. English translation in *Peking Review*, January 7, 1972, p. 12. http://www.massline.org/PekingReview/PR1972/PR1972-01.pdf. Accessed on November 30, 2022.

'title' to China's territory of the Diaoyu[3] *and other islands and, in collusion with U.-S. imperialism, has engaged in all kinds of activities to invade and annex the above-mentioned islands. Not long ago, the U.S. Congress and the Japanese Diet one after the other approved the agreement on the 'reversion' of Okinawa. In this agreement, the Governments of the United States and Japan flagrantly included the Diaoyu and other islands in the 'area of reversion.' This is a gross encroachment upon China's territorial integrity and sovereignty. The Chinese people absolutely will not tolerate this!*

The same statement elaborated on the point as follows:

After World War II, the Japanese government illicitly handed over to the United States the Diaoyu and other islands appertaining to Taiwan, and the United States Government unilaterally declared that it enjoyed the so-called 'administrative rights' over these islands. This in itself was illegal. . . . Now the U.S. and Japanese Governments have once again made an illicit transfer between themselves of China's Diaoyu and other islands. This encroachment upon China's territorial integrity and sovereignty cannot but arouse the utmost indignation of the Chinese people.

The premise of this Chinese argument can be summarized in connection with the San Francisco Peace Treaty as follows. In this argument, the Chinese insist that the Senkaku Islands were part of the region including Taiwan (Article 2) that was eventually separated from the territory of Japan under the terms of the San Francisco Peace Treaty. They were not included in the region that, while remaining part of Japanese territory, would be placed under US administration for the time being, like the Nansei Shotō Islands (Article 3). Furthermore, the argument goes that the Senkaku Islands continued to be under Chinese sovereignty even when the Okinawa Reversion Treaty was signed on June 17, 1971 and entered into force on May 15, 1972.

Indeed, with regard to such areas as Taiwan and other territories, China began the process of "reversion" of "Taiwan and the Pescadores Islands" to China, as provided for in the territorial clause of the Potsdam Declaration soon after Japan accepted the Declaration on August 14, 1945. On August 29, it had already appointed the governor-general of the Taiwan Provincial Administrative Executive Office and the Garrison Command. The Taiwan Provincial Administrative Executive Office Organization Regulation was promulgated on September 20, shortly after Japan signed the Instrument of Surrender on September 2. Specific steps were taken towards the seizure of Taiwan beginning in October. Taiwan was formally restored to China as its territory on October 25, through the formal procedures for the transfer called the "surrender ceremony." China introduced the same administration system in Taiwan as in its other territories. In this manner, such areas as Taiwan were incorporated into China through a purely domestic procedure based on the territorial clause of the Potsdam Declaration, prior to the signing of the peace treaty.[4] Taking these developments into account, the San Francisco Peace Treaty had Japan renounce Taiwan and other territories. From the viewpoint of China, which did

---

[3] The citations from *Peking Review* used "Tiaoyu" following an older style of romanization.

[4] Irie, Keishirō. 1951. *Nihon kōwa jōyaku no kenkyū* (Study of the Treaty of Peace with Japan). Tokyo: Itagaki Shoten, pp. 61–64.

not attend the deliberations on the San Francisco Peace Treaty, the acceptance of the Sino-Japanese Peace Treaty of 1952 and the Joint Statement between Japan and China of 1972, in which Japan maintained its position based on Article 8 of the Potsdam Declaration, gave final legal standing to China on the reversion of Taiwan and the Pescadores Islands to China. Thus, closely examining the Chinese argument from a legal perspective, it can be said that China's exact legal claim is that the Senkaku Islands were already part of Chinese territory at the time the San Francisco Peace Treaty was signed. This interpretation can be deduced from a message delivered on *Radio Peking* on December 30, 1971:

> *It is even more absurd for the United States to want to include China's territory Diaoyu and other islands it has occupied into the 'area of reversion' in accordance with the Okinawa 'reversion' agreement. After World War II, Japanese imperialism returned Taiwan and the Penghu Islands[5] to China. It was illegal in itself that Japan handed over the Diaoyu and other islands appertaining to Taiwan to the United States. There were no legal grounds for this action.[6]*

With respect to the occupation of Okinawa, US forces landed on the Kerama Islands on March 26, 1945, then on the main island of Okinawa on April 1. Following Japan's surrender, the US Navy military government promulgated Proclamation No. 1-A "To the People of the Nansei Shotō Islands and Adjacent Waters" on November 26, 1945 for the Miyako Islands, the Yaeyama Islands and the Amami Islands. Shortly afterward, US forces began to occupy the Miyako Islands and the Yaeyama Islands in March and the Amami Ōshima Islands the following January. Actual military rule was enforced in the Miyako Islands on December 8 and in the Yaeyama Islands on December 28.

During the military occupation of Okinawa, the United States kept the administrative areas of the former Okinawa Prefecture in place as they had been before. When the Supreme Commander for the Allied Powers (SCAP), the General Headquarters (GHQ), issued a memorandum entitled "Governmental and Administrative Separation of Certain Outlying Areas from Japan" on January 29, 1946, the Ministry of Foreign Affairs of Japan informally submitted to GHQ a list of the islands comprising the Nansei Shotō Islands. The list named Sekibisho, Kōbisho, Kitajima Island, Minamijima Island, and Uotsuri Island as comprising the "Senkaku Islands" and included the islands within Okinawa Prefecture. This series of events all took place after China's incorporation of Taiwan and other areas into its territory.

However, there is no evidence that China lodged protests of any kind against these events, despite being fully aware of them as a member of the Allied powers. On April 20, 1971, Wei Yu-sun, spokesperson for Taiwan's Ministry of Foreign Affairs, explained that "the islands were occupied by the U.S. military, but our government

---

[5] More commonly known as the Pescadores Islands.

[6] English translation from "Tiaoyu and Other Islands Have Been China's Territory Since Ancient (U.S.-Japanese Reactionaries' Vain Efforts)" in *Peking Review*, January 7, 1972, pp. 13–14. http://www.massline.org/PekingReview/PR1972/PR1972-01.pdf. Accessed on November 30, 2022.

believed this was a necessary step at the time out of consideration for the safety of the joint defense zone," but he did not provide any evidence to support this.[7]

Furthermore, China responded to "The Basic View of the Ministry of Foreign Affairs," a March 8, 1972 document outlining Japan's position on the Senkaku Islands, with a statement in *Peking Review* on April 7 of that year. It stated, "As is well known, after World War II, the Japanese Government handed over to the United States the Diaoyu and other islands appertaining to Taiwan and the U.S. Government unilaterally declared that it had so-called 'administrative rights' over them. This is illegal in the first place, and the Chinese Government and people have never recognized it."[8] Even here, however, there is no evidence that any objections were lodged against the Senkaku Islands being within the US "area of occupation" or its "area of administration," nor is there any evidence whatsoever that China disapproved of these actions.

Of course, the inclusion of the Senkaku Islands "within the administered reversed areas" does not in and of itself provide the basis for Japan possessing sovereignty over these islands. That is because if they had been arbitrarily included within Japanese territory when the Okinawa Reversion Treaty was signed, then the Chinese objections would be legitimate.

However, were the Senkaku Islands actually continuously part of Chinese territory until the signing of the Okinawa Reversion Treaty after World War II, as China asserts?

The biggest hole in the Chinese argument is that on October 25, 1945, about 2 months before the US occupation began on the Yaeyama Islands of Okinawa Prefecture, which had been under the prefecture's administration prior to the war, China had completed its incorporation of territories including Taiwan. Furthermore, documents compiled by Taiwan Province after World War II identified that Pengjia Islet, situated slightly north of the main island of Taiwan, constitutes the northern end of Taiwan Province. Maps published in Taiwan and Beijing excluded the Senkaku Islands from Chinese territory and marked them as a part of the Ryūkyū Islands. These facts not only show that China did not recognize the Senkaku Islands as its own territory, but that it clearly considered them to be a part of Japan. That is because if China had thought of the Senkaku Islands as Chinese territory and that they were included in the reference in the Cairo Declaration to "the territories stolen from China by Japan—including Manchuria, the island of Taiwan and the Pescadores Islands," then it is unthinkable that China, a victor in the war, would face any difficulties or obstacles in incorporating the Senkaku Islands into its territory as it did immediately after the war's end with islands like Taiwan.

---

[7] The same reference, without supporting evidence, is also made in a book written by a former vice chairman of the Taiwan-Japan Relations Association: Lin Chin-ching. 1987. *Sengo no nikka kankei to kokusaihō* (Postwar Japan-Republic of China Relations). Tokyo: Yūhikaku Publishing, p. 182.

[8] English translation from "Sato Government Tries to Annex China's Tiaoyu And Other Islands (So-Called 'Administrative Rights' Illegal)" in *Peking Review*, April 7, 1972, p. 14. http://www.massline.org/PekingReview/PR1972/PR1972-14.pdf. Accessed on November 30, 2022.

In contrast, even under the US Civil Administration following US military occupation, Japan undertook numerous significant initiatives in the form of actions taken by the US Civil Administration of the Ryūkyū Islands and the Government of the Ryūkyū Islands.

First, the Law Concerning the Organization of the Gunto Governments (Military Government Ordinance No. 22), the Provisions of the Government of the Ryukyu Islands (Civil Administration Ordinance No. 68) and the geographical boundaries of the Ryukyu Islands (Civil Administration Proclamation No. 27) defined areas under the jurisdiction of authorities, including the US Civil Administration of the Ryūkyū Islands and the Government of the Ryūkyū Islands, by indicating latitude and longitude coordinates, and naturally included the Senkaku Islands in these areas.

Secondly, in 1951 the US Navy set up maritime areas for aerial bombing training exercises on Kōbisho and Sekibisho, with the former designated as a special exercise area. Taishō Island (Sekibisho), which was State-owned land, was designated as an exercise area after April 16, 1956. For the privately-owned land of Kuba Island (Kōbisho), the US Civil Administration concluded Basic Lease GRI Nr. 183-1 on July 1, 1958 between its agent, the Ryūkyū government, and the landowner, Koga Zenji. Accordingly, a lease was paid to Mr. Koga. The Ryūkyū government had been levying a fixed asset tax[9] on the four islands he owned, and after the Basic Lease was concluded, it began to withhold taxes from the revenue earned from the utilization of military land on Kuba Island. According to an understanding reached between the Japanese and US governments during the Okinawa reversion negotiations, the Japanese government would provide firing ranges on Taishō Island and Kuba Island to the US forces in Japan as facilities and areas under the Japan-US Security Treaty, and under the Japan-US Status of Forces Agreement after the islands were restored to Japan.

Thirdly, Japan took measures against the dismantlement of submerged ships on Minamikojima Island by Taiwanese people in August 1968. On August 12, an officer of the Immigration Agency of the Ryūkyū government's Legal Department discovered that Xingnan Engineering, a Taiwanese salvage company, had set up a tent workshop and cranes for the dismantlement of submerged ships. As the company did not have a permit to enter the area, the agency ordered the intruders to immediately leave and recommended that the company apply for entry onto the islands. The Taiwanese workers soon exited and applied for entry to Minamikojima Island. On August 30, 1968 and on April 21, 1969, the company received a permit to enter the area with the approval of the High Commissioner of the Ryūkyū Islands. The High Commissioner issued a permit retroactively to allow Taiwanese workers to

---

[9]The fixed asset tax was described as follows in an interview conducted by the author with the city of Ishigaki's financial affairs section on March 3, 1983. Taishō Island (Sekibisho: Block 2394, Tonoshiro, Ishigaki) is State-owned land. Koga Zenji, who was residing in the city of Naha at the time, sold Uotsuri Island (Block 2392, Tonoshiro, Ishigaki), Kitakojima Island (Block 2391), and Minamikojima Island (Block 2390) on June 21, 1974 to Kurihara Kunioki, a resident of Ōmiya, Saitama Prefecture. Therefore, Koga paid a fixed asset tax of 90,000 yen for Kuba Island (Kōbisho: Block 2393), while Kurihara paid a fixed asset tax of 450,000 yen for the other three islands.

enter the area from August 1, 1968 to October 31, 1969, and permission was also issued for them to bring some equipment and facilities into the area as well. No nation protested this matter. Incidentally, the head of the salvage company had licenses including a dismantlement license issued by the Taiwanese Ministry of Communications, as well as an exit permit issued by the Taiwanese garrison head office. This, along with the absence of protests, provides sufficient grounds to presume that Taiwanese authorities did not consider Minamikojima Island as their territory.

From July 8 to 13, 1970, the Ryūkyū government erected a territorial signboard on the Senkaku Islands. (*Radio Peking* criticized these moves on December 30, 1971, calling them the government's "attempt to make Japan's 'possession' of these islands a *fait accompli*.") China claimed title to the Senkaku Islands for the first time, albeit informally, on December 4 of that year, as the *Xinhua News Agency* criticized the joint development of resources on the continental shelf in the East China Sea by Japan, Taiwan, and the Republic of Korea (ROK). The *People's Daily* also reported on December 29 that "Japan is also trying to incorporate into its territory even some islands and waters that belong to China, including Diaoyu" and that "islands, including Diaoyu, Huangwei, Chiwei, Nanhsiao, and Peihsiao, have, as has Taiwan, been the territories of China since ancient times." In other words, China never made territorial claims and never lodged effective protests from 1945 to 1970. To put it differently, Japan exercised State control over the Senkaku Islands in a peaceful and continuous manner for 25 years after World War II. However, the Government of the Republic of China (ROC), with which Japan had diplomatic relations until 1972, granted a permit to an American oil company to explore for oil along the continental shelf including the Senkaku Islands. At the House of Councillors' Special Committee on Okinawa and Northern Problems on August 10, 1970, the Japanese government reported that it had issued a statement to the ROC government that "these kinds of unilateral measures are invalid under international law."[10] In addition, in testimony during a secret meeting at the Legislative Yuan on September 4, Taiwanese Foreign Minister Wei Tao-ming said for the first time that the Senkaku Islands "are five islands that belong to the national government." His remarks were reported the following day. However, the basis for this statement is unknown.

In light of the foregoing, one cannot but conclude that the Chinese argument that the Senkaku Islands have always been part of Chinese territory, or that at the least they were already Chinese territory at the time of the conclusion of the San Francisco Peace Treaty as well as the Okinawa Reversion Treaty, is made on very weak grounds.

---

[10] *Asahi Shimbun*, August 11, 1970.

Analysis of the Arguments that the Senkaku Islands Appertain to Taiwan

The Statement of the Ministry of Foreign Affairs of the People's Republic of China dated December 30, 1971 reads as follows:

> *The Diaoyu and other islands have been China's territory since ancient times. Back in the Ming Dynasty, these islands were already within China's sea defence areas; they were islands appertaining to China's Taiwan but not to Ryukyu, which is now known as Okinawa. The boundary between China and Ryukyu in this area lies between Chiwei Yu and Kume Island and fishermen from China's Taiwan have all along carried out productive activities on the Diaoyu and other islands. During the 1894 Sino-Japanese War, the Japanese Government stole these islands and in April 1895 it forced the government of the Ching [Qing] Dynasty to conclude the unequal "Treaty of Shimonoseki" by which "Taiwan, together with all islands appertaining to Taiwan" and the Penghu Islands were ceded.* [11]

The December 30, 1971 broadcast by *Radio Peking* provided more details:

> *To resist harassment by Japanese invaders, China's Ming Dynasty in 1556 appointed Hu Tsung-hsien [Hu Zongxian] commander of the punitive force in charge of military action against the Japanese invaders in the coastal provinces. The islands such as Diaoyu Island, Huangwei Yu and Chiwei Yu were then within the scope of China's coastal defence. It was more specifically stated in the records of missions sent to the Ryukyu Islands by China's Ming and Ching [Qing] Dynasties and in geography and history books that these islands belong to China and that the demarcation line between China and the Ryukyu Islands lies between Chiwei Yu and Kome Island, namely, present-day Kume Island.*
>
> *In 1879, when Li Hung-chang [Li Hongzhang], Minister Superintendent of Trade for the Northern Ports of China of the Ching [Qing] Dynasty, held negotiations with Japan on the title to the Ryukyus, both the Chinese and Japanese sides held that the Ryukyus comprised 36 islands. Diaoyu and the other islands were not among those 36 islands at all.*
>
> *The Diaoyu and other islands were under China's jurisdiction for several centuries, and it was only in 1884 that the Japanese "discovered" them. The Japanese Government immediately plotted to annex them, but dared not lay hands on them then. It was in 1895 when the defeat of the government of the Ching [Qing] Dynasty in the [First] Sino-Japanese War had become inevitable that these islands were grabbed by Japan. The Japanese Government then compelled the Ching [Qing] Dynasty government to sign the "Treaty of Shimonoseki" which ceded "Taiwan, together with all islands appertaining to Taiwan" and the Penghu Islands to Japan.* [12]

These statements by the Chinese Ministry of Foreign Affairs and *Radio Peking* can be summarized in the following four points; each of them shall be examined individually.

1. The Senkaku Islands were within China's coastal defense zone as early as the Ming period, and the islands appertained to the Chinese territory of Taiwan.

---

[11] "Statement of the Ministry of Foreign Affairs of the People's Republic of China," December 30, 1971. Op. cit.

[12] "Tiaoyu and Other Islands Have Been China's Territory Since Ancient (U.S.-Japanese Reactionaries' Vain Efforts)", op. cit.

2. As historical sources such as the records of investiture missions make clear, the border between China and the Ryūkyū Kingdom lay between Sekibisho and Kume Island (modern-day Kuba Island).
3. In the Sino-Japanese negotiations regarding the so-called Ryūkyū issue, both sides recognized that the Senkaku Islands were not included in the "36 islands of Ryūkyū."
4. The Japanese discovered the Senkaku Islands in 1884, only after they had already become part of China hundreds of years before. When the defeat of the Qing dynasty government became certain during the First Sino-Japanese War of 1895, Japan "stole" the Islands. Soon afterward, the Japanese government forced the Qing administration to sign the Treaty of Shimonoseki, under the terms of which Taiwan and all its affiliated islands, along with the Pescadores Islands, were ceded to Japan.

Detailed Examinations of Each of China's Arguments

1. While the statements from China's Ministry of Foreign Affairs did not cite Ming documents proving that the Senkaku Islands were within China's coastal defense zone, it can be surmised from various studies that the source they are referring to is *Chou Hai Tu Bian* (*An Illustrated Compendium on Maritime Security*), edited by Hu Zongxian in the mid-sixteenth century.[13]

   According to Inoue Kiyoshi, in the first volume, "Map of Coastal Mountains," the maps "Fujian 7" and "Fujian 8" show the coastal seas of Luoyuan and Ningde counties, with the following islands running from west to east: Jilong Shan ("*shan*" literally means "mountain" but used in reference to an island), Pengjia Shan, Diaoyu Yu, Huaping Shan, Huangwei Shan, Ganlan Shan, and finally Chi Yu. These islands start off the coast of Keelung, Taiwan, which is located in the seas of southern Fuzhou Province. The line along which the islands are situated heads eastward, and they "undoubtedly include the Diaoyu Islands." "These maps show that the Diaoyu Islands were added to the islands in Chinese territory in the coastal waters of Fujian. Volume 1 of *Chou Hai Tu Bian* shows maps, starting in the southwest and moving northeast, of not only Fujian, but also all the Chinese coastal waters that Japanese pirates would raid. None of these maps include any areas outside of Chinese territory, so there is no basis for only excluding the Diaoyu Islands from Chinese territory."[14]

[13] See sources such as: Inoue, Kiyoshi. 1972. *Senkaku rettō* (The Senkaku Islands). Tokyo: Gendai hyōronsha, p. 32; Ozaki, Shigeyoshi. "Senkaku shotō no kizoku ni tsuite (Territorial Sovereignty over the Senkaku Islands) (Part 3-2)," *Reference* 263, p. 158. Ozaki wrote further on the historical examination section of his paper: Ozaki, Shigeyoshi. 1995. "Senkaku shotō no kokusaihō-jō no chii (The Status of the Senkaku Islands in International Law)," *Tsukuba hōsei* (Tsukuba Law and Policy) 18(1), March.

[14] Inoue, op. cit. 32.

Incidentally, does Inoue's argument stand up to scrutiny? According to Ozaki Shigeyoshi, Volume IV of *Chou Hai Tu Bian* contains a "Map of the Coast of Fujian Province." While the map contains the Pescadores Islands, it does not mark Taiwan, Keelung Islet northeast of Taiwan, Pengjia Islet, nor the Senkaku Islands. "This is based more on the true situation at the time." Other more recent sources, including the *Luoyuan County Annal* (1614, during the Ming dynasty) and the *Ningde County Annal* (1718, Qing dynasty), both official local publications, indicate that at the time the Senkaku Islands were not included in the administrative control of these counties in Fujian Province. Further still, the Senkaku Islands are not charted in the "Map of Fujian's Coastal Defenses" in Volume I of another government publication called *Chongzuan Fujian Tongzhi* (*Recompiled General Annals of Fujian*; 1838, Qing dynasty). Moreover, according to Okuhara Toshio, if *Chou Hai Tu Bian* is cited as a source, "it would be appropriate to say that 'Borders of Fujian,' the seventeenth map of Volume I, shows the borders of Fujian Province at the time."[15] While this map does mark the Pescadores Islands, Taiwan and the Senkaku Islands are not drawn on it. In other words, the Senkaku Islands did not belong to Fujian Province.

Hu Zongxian was appointed as supreme commander in charge of repelling the Japanese pirates in 1556, several years before *Chou Hai Tu Bian* was written. In any case, at the time that the Japanese pirates were most violent, between 1553 and 1559, China had to primarily focus on defending the coastal areas of its mainland. Consequently, the Ming dynasty could not even extend its defensive capabilities to the Pescadores Islands. While the pirates travelled quite freely between mainland China and the Ryūkyū Kingdom, particularly between the Miyako and Yaeyama Islands, it has not been confirmed in either Chinese or Ryūkyū historical records whether Ming military ships reached as far as the Ryūkyūs in pursuit of the pirates.

Wang Zhi, who had mustered several dozen Japanese pirate groups in 1553, was a Chinese man from the same town as Hu Zongxian. The pirate leader was lured to his hometown and was executed in 1560. Considering this, the fact that the Senkaku Islands are depicted only in "Map of Coastal Mountains" means simply that these islands either lay along the routes the Japanese pirates used in their raids or were in the vicinity of waters infested by the pirates. Therefore, this would merely indicate that the area was one warranting attention for the sake of defending the mainland. The text of *Chou Hai Tu Bian* does not make any mention that the Senkaku Islands were inside the Japanese pirate defense zone at the time, but even if there are any other sources unnoticed by the studies conducted thus far that indicate that the Senkaku Islands were within China's coastal defense zone as early as the Ming period, the aforementioned facts make it inconceivable that Chinese control did in fact extend to the Senkaku Islands in any form.

---

[15] Okuhara, Toshio. 1978. "Senkaku shotō ryōyūken no konkyō (Evidence for the Territorial Rights over the Senkaku Islands)." *Chūōkōron* (Central Review), July.

Then were the Senkaku Islands appertaining to the Chinese territory of Taiwan during the Ming period? In *History of Ming*, an official Chinese historical record, Taiwan was included in the "Biographies of Foreign Countries" as a foreign territory of the east, while Jilong Shan of northern Taiwan (modern-day Keelung) was also included in the "Biographies of Foreign Countries." Thus, during the Ming period, Chinese control did not extend to northern Taiwan (Keelung), nor to islands northeast of Taiwan such as Pengjia Islet, Huaping Shan, or Mianhua Yu. In addition, China did not consider these places as its territory. Although Taiwan was conquered by the Sui and the Yuan dynasties of China, the land remained undeveloped. Taiwan became a base for Japanese pirates during the Ming period, and by the end of the dynasty's rule in the beginning of the seventeenth century, the Dutch had constructed outposts like Fort Zeelandia where the present-day city of Tainan is located. The Spanish came from Manila to establish trading outposts in such locations as Keelung in northern Taiwan. The Dutch soon drove them off, however, and Taiwan was under the continuous rule of the Netherlands for about 40 years.

The Ming dynasty collapsed in 1644 when the Qing dynasty entered Beijing. The Qing later conquered southern China as well by 1681. However, Zheng Chenggong, who led a resistance movement against the Qing, crossed over to Taiwan in 1661 and drove out the Dutch. He made his base there to continue the resistance, but in 1683 surrendered to the Qing armies dispatched to Taiwan. This is when the Qing first added Taiwan to its territory. The island became Taiwan Prefecture, a part of Fujian Province. Accordingly, it would be proper to say that the Senkaku Islands did not in fact appertain to the Chinese territory of Taiwan during the Ming period.

Zheng Shungong wrote *Riben Yijian* (*A Chronicle on Japan*) in 1556 based on materials he had accumulated after returning from an investigation of Japan's state of affairs and its geography under the orders of Hu Zongxian's predecessor. In a section of the book, "Wanli Chang-ge (Ballad of 10,000 Li)," Zheng makes mention of "small islands of Xiaodong." This shows that Zheng thought of the Diaoyu Islands as being small islands affiliated with, or near to, Xiaodong (Taiwan). Although the information presented thus far indicates that the Senkaku Islands were not included within the territory incorporated into the Qing dynasty's territory together with Taiwan, this does not provide a definitive answer to the question. In any case, Zheng was merely an individual person acting in an unofficial capacity.

2. China argues that, as historical sources such as the records of investiture missions make clear, the border between China and the Ryūkyū Kingdom lay between Sekibisho and Kume Island.

The first formal negotiation between China and the Ryūkyū Kingdom took place in 1372. Soon after, Emperor Taizu of the Ming dynasty (personal name Zhu Yuanzhang) overthrew the Yuan dynasty and acceded to the throne. He dispatched a mission to the Ryūkyū Kingdom to provide notification on the unification of China and to urge the kingdom's submission to the Ming court. Responding to and accepting this notice of the emperor, called a *zhao yu* (invitation), the Ryūkyū King of Chūzan dispatched an envoy to the Ming court in the same year. (Emissaries were also sent that year to the Muromachi shogunate in Japan. As the Ryūkyū Kingdom did, Shogun Ashikaga Yoshimitsu accepted the *zhao yu* and pledged his loyalty as "the King of Japan, by your grace.")

When small neighboring States dispatched envoys to the Ming court and pledged their allegiance as a response to the invitation, the Ming court called this act *ru gong* or *chao gong*. The gifts presented to the Ming court at the time of *ru gong* were called *gong wu* or *fang wu* (meaning "tribute"). The diplomatic missions and the ships that carried them to the court were called by such names as *chao gong*, *ru gong*, or *jin gong chuan* (this last literally meaning "tribute ship"). The Ming emperor, in return for the tributes, issued an imperial decree that conferred the title of "kings of tributary States" on the kings of their nations by granting *chi shu* (investiture). As this tribute-investiture relationship[16] between Ryūkyū and China became formalized incrementally, the preparations for and the formality of the tribute and investiture ceremonies were considered highly important national events in Ryūkyū. Customarily, Ryūkyū sent envoys called *qing feng shi* for the entreaty for investiture to China 2 years after the demise of the previous Ryūkyū king. There were two major ceremonies necessary to mark an investiture: the funeral for the previous king (*yu zhai*) and the conferment of the title of the new king (the aforementioned *qing feng shi*). China dispatched investiture missions to Ryūkyū 23 times during the 500-year period spanning from 1372 to 1879, the year that the Meiji government abolished the domain of Ryūkyū, established Okinawa Prefecture, and prohibited its tributary relations with China. Of these 23 instances, 15 took place during the Ming dynasty and eight took place during the Qing dynasty. For its part, Ryūkyū dispatched ships for various purposes to China other than tribute ships, particularly during the Ming period. For example, Ryūkyū dispatched ships called *jie feng chuan* to Fuzhou, the capital of Fujian Province, to escort Chinese investiture ships prior to their departure from Fuzhou City. Ryūkyū also dispatched ships called *xie en chuan* to escort Chinese investiture missions on their return voyages from Ryūkyū to China in order to express its appreciation, as well as *qing he chuan* (celebratory ships) for some celebratory events. During the Ming dynasty, Ryūkyū dispatched ships on as many as 171 instances. As this number indicates, Ryūkyū ships travelled to China far more often than Chinese ships to Ryūkyū. During the Ming dynasty, Ryūkyū also conducted trade with Korea and South Pacific countries. As a result, Ryūkyū flourished as a trading hub, making its people well acquainted with the sea routes in surrounding waters, particularly the sea routes between Ryūkyū and China.

Chinese investiture missions not only absorbed knowledge of the Ryūkyū Kingdom, but also customarily kept records of all their experiences and

---

[16]For more on the significance of the *chao gong* system in East Asia, see Hamashita, Takeshi. 1997. *Chōkō shisutemu to kindai ajia* (The Tributary System and Modern Asia). Tokyo: Iwanami Shoten.

knowledge, such as matters relating to navigation, all ceremonial customs, as well as the state of affairs in the Ryūkyū Kingdom. These records served as guidelines for subsequent missions.[17] According to Taira Kazuhiko, the earliest record of the investiture missions in existence is Chen Kan's *Shi Liuqiu Lu* (The Records of the Imperial Title—Conferring Envoys to Ryūkyū) of 1535, in which the descriptions of islands such as Diaoyu Yu [Uotsuri Island], Huangwei Yu [Kōbisho], and Chiwei Yu [Sekibisho] can be seen for the first time. Today there exist 13 such records including *Shi Liuqiu Lu*, ranging up to the last mission conducted by Zhao Xin for the investiture of Shō Tai, the last king of Ryūkyū.[18]

(a) Chen Kan's *Shi Liuqiu Lu* (Records of the Imperial Missions to Ryūkyū): journeyed to Ryūkyū in 1534.

(b) Guo Rulin's *Chongke Shi Liuqiu Lu* (Supplementary Records of the Imperial Missions to Ryūkyū): journeyed to Ryūkyū in 1561.

(c) Xiao Chongye's and Xie Jie's *Shi Liuqiu Lu* (Records of the Imperial Missions to Ryūkyū): journeyed to Ryūkyū in 1579.

(d) Xia Ziyang's and Wang Shizhen's *Shi Liuqiu Lu* (Records of the Imperial Missions to Ryūkyū): journeyed to Ryūkyū in 1606.

(e) Hu Jing's *Dutianshi Cefeng Liuqiu Zhenji Qiguan* (A Report on Ryūkyū, Written by the Chinese Envoy Du Tian): senior envoy Du Sance, deputy envoy Yang Lun, and their subordinate Hu Jing journeyed to Ryūkyū in 1633.

(f) Zhang Xuezha's *Shi Liuqiu Ji* (Report of the Imperial Missions to Ryūkyū): journeyed to Ryūkyū in 1663.

(g) Wang Ji's *Shi Liuqiu Zalu* (Miscellaneous Records of the Imperial Missions to Ryūkyū): journeyed to Ryūkyū in 1683.

(h) Xu Baoguang's *Zhongshan Chuanxin Lu* (Missives to Zhongshan): senior envoy Hai Bao, deputy envoy Xu Baoguang journeyed to Ryūkyū in 1719.

(i) Zhou Huang, *Liuqiuguo Zhilue* (Brief Gazetteer of Ryūkyū): senior envoy Quan Kui, deputy envoy Zhou Huang journeyed to Ryūkyū in 1756.

(j) Ji Dingyuan's *Shi Liuqiu Ji* (Report of the Imperial Missions to Ryūkyū), senior envoy Zhao Wenjie, deputy envoy Ji Dingyuan journeyed to Ryūkyū in 1800.

(k) Qi Kun's and Fei Cizhang's *Xu Liuqiuguo Zhilue* (Supplement to Brief Gazetteer of Ryūkyū): journeyed to Ryūkyū in 1808.

(l) Senior envoy Lin Hongnian and deputy envoy Gao Renjian journeyed to Ryūkyū in 1838, but as the records are currently unavailable their course must be elucidated from the following source.

---

[17] Kishaba, Kazutaka. "Senkaku shotō to sakuhōshi roku (The Senkaku Islands and Chinese Envoys)." *Kikan Okinawa* (Okinawa Quarterly) 63.

[18] Taira, Kazuhiko. "Chūgoku shiseki ni arawaretaru Senkaku (Chōgyo) shotō (The Senkaku [Diaoyu] Islands in Chinese Historical Records)." *Ajia/Afurika shiryō tsūhō* (Asia and Africa Document Bulletin) 10, No. 4 & 6.

(m) Zhao Xin's and Qian Guangjia's *Xu Liuqiuguo Zhilue* (Supplement to Brief Gazetteer of Ryūkyū): journeyed to Ryūkyū in 1866.

Of all of the records, the following two are particularly important in terms of the influence they had on other records and the frequency of reference. The first is *Shi Liuqiu Lu*, written by Chen Kan during the Ming dynasty. As the oldest record in existence, it was highly valued as a primary source and served as a guideline of sorts to the succeeding missions and records. The second is *Zhongshan Chuanxin Lu* (Missives to Zhongshan) by Xu Baoguang. This record serves as a representative example of the mission records during Japan's Edo period (1603–1867) and as a guideline for many scholars and intellectuals.[19]

Inoue Kiyoshi, whose article was translated wholesale into Chinese, and introduced in the *Guangming Daily* and the *People's Daily* published in Beijing on May 4, 1972, attaches importance to the following passages of these mission records. In Chen Kan's records it is written, "On the evening of the 11th, Gumi Shan (now called Kume Island) was in sight. It belongs to Ryukyu." Guo Rulin's records state that "Chi Yu is a hill bordering on Ryukyu territory." Wang Ji, who travelled to Ryūkyū in the Qing dynasty era, writes, "An island came into sight on the morning of the 25th. Although Huangwei should come first, followed by Chi Yu later, we somehow arrived at Chi Yu without having sighted Huangwei Yu. On the evening of that day, we passed through the *jiao*. The winds and waves were very rough. ... I inquired as to the meaning of the *jiao* and was informed that it was the boundary between inside and outside. I asked how one can identify the boundary, to which I was told one only estimates its location." In his records Xu Baoguang writes such entries as, "Gumi Shan is a garrison hill on the southwest border of Ryūkyū ..."[20]

Considering that a full translation of Inoue's article was introduced in the *People's Daily*, perhaps it contains the basis for the assertions made in the statement by China's Ministry of Foreign Affairs.

Judging only from the passages reviewed above, the only thing that is certain is that Kume Island was within Ryūkyū territory. This would make one think at first that the Senkaku Islands are outside Ryūkyū territory. However, in order to fully understand these writings, one must also note the condition of the sea routes at the time and what the authors wrote on their return journeys, not only on their way to Ryūkyū. That is the careful scrutiny that these records warrant as historical documents. When doing so, one finds that not all the writings are necessarily supportive of China's territorial claim over the islands.

Navigating from Fuzhou to Ryūkyū at the time, all of the islands on the route to Kume Island were uninhabited after passing the island currently known as Taiwan. There was absolutely no activity of substantial utility on these islands.

---

[19] Kishaba, op. cit.

[20] Inoue, op. cit.; Taira, op. cit.; Kishaba, op. cit. See an English version at "The Tiaoyu Islands (Senkaku Islands) and Other Islands Are China's Territory" in *Peking Review*, May 12, 1972, pp. 18–22. http://www.massline.org/PekingReview/PR1972/PR1972-19.pdf. Accessed on December 1, 2022.

Kume Island was the first inhabited island on the sea route from Fuzhou. Moreover, it was recognized that along the Fuzhou-Ryūkyū sea route, Kume Island was the southwest boundary of lands inhabited by the people of the Ryūkyū Kingdom. In order to be considered part of the territory of the Ryūkyū Kingdom of the time, i.e., the 36 islands of Ryūkyū, an island had to be inhabited and had a duty to pay tribute to the king's court in Shuri, the capital of Ryūkyū. Only those islands that satisfied these conditions were marked as territories under the administration of the king.

In this light, Kume Island was the southwestern boundary of Ryūkyū, and Hateruma Island and Yonaguni Island of the Yaeyama Islands were the most southern areas of Ryūkyū.[21] The Senkaku Islands were not within the territory of the Ryūkyū Kingdom which requires such conditions as human habitation and tribute. Likewise, none of the official local publications from either Fujian Province during the Ming and Qing dynasties, or from Taiwan Province during the Qing dynasty (after Taiwan Prefecture was established upon the island of Taiwan, becoming part of Chinese territory), indicate that the Senkaku Islands were under the administrative control of either Fujian Province or Taiwan Province.[22] In other words, in terms of administration, the fact is that there is no definitive evidence showing that the Senkaku Islands were incorporated into the Ryūkyū Kingdom, Fujian Province, or Taiwan Province. Accordingly, the most natural way to view mentions of such islands as Uotsuri Island in the mission records is as landmarks on the sea routes then running between Fujian and Ryūkyū.

Navigation records of return journeys to China further underscore these views. Investiture ships that left Naha Port, after passing the Baji and Gumi "mountains" (islands), took a sea route north of islands of Huangwei, Chiwei, Diaoyu, and Xiaoliuqiu, and then south of the "mountains" of Nanba, Fengwei, Yu, Tai, and Lima as they entered Dinghaisuo in Fujian and proceeded to Geanzhen An. Xu Baoguang, in the volume entitled "Zhenlu (Course)" in his *Zhongshan Chuanxin Lu*, refers to the title of the islands for the first time on his journey from Ryūkyū, when Nanba Shan, an island that belongs to Wenzhou, Zhejiang Province, becomes visible in the distance. This style stands in contrast to that of Chen Kan's records, who wrote of Gumi Shan on his way to Ryūkyū: "The island belongs to Ryūkyū." Xu Baoguang's delegation departed for China on February 16, 1720. On February 24, he wrote, "In the morning, steering southwest of the compass for one *geng* (about 60 miles), we arrived at Yu Shan and Fengwei Shan. These two *shan* (mountains) belong to Taizhou. The investiture ship left the compass to the same direction and headed to Nanba Shan in Wenzhou. The Yu and Fengwei mountains are located 500 Chinese miles from Nanba Shan." Xu Baoguang made no reference to the title of the islands comprising the present day Senkaku Islands, which were located on the sea route to the two mountains. On

---

[21] Kishaba, op. cit.

[22] Ozaki, op. cit. (Part 3-2), 160.

the other hand, it is only after touching upon Yu Shan and Fengwei Shan that he wrote that "both mountains belong to Taizhou." This indicates basically the same thing as investiture missions and other envoys, who noted Kume Island as the southwestern boundary of Ryūkyū when they traveled there.

Zhao Xin, on the last investiture mission which arrived at Ryūkyū in 1866, describes in his record the conditions of the return route of the previous investiture mission in 1838. He states that after departing Naha Port on October 12, 1838, and passing Gumi Shan on the following day, "On the 18th a wind blew over the sea from the north-northeast. Therefore, we are using the *jiuxuzhen* method of orientation, following a bearing between west and west-northwest. In the early morning we could see mountains beyond China's realm. In the mid-afternoon we could see Nanba Shan and began using the *weishenzhen* method of orientation, following a bearing between south-southwest and west-southwest. On the 19th we passed Dingmei at around noon and entered the Wuhumen (Five Tiger Passage) in the mid-afternoon."

The record presents, however, no explanations of the islands along the sea route on the way to the mountains beyond China's realm. The records of the return voyage include no references to the Senkaku Islands, except for islands near present-day Taiwan. As historian Kishaba Kazutaka says, descriptions such as "Nanba Shan (mountain) in Wenzhou" and "*shan* (mountains) beyond China's realm" are equivalent in meaning to the descriptions "the island belongs to Ryūkyū," "a garrison hill on the southwest border of Ryūkyū" and "a mountain that marks the border of Ryūkyū Region." They are inextricably linked. Thus, in the end these islands near both points of departure and arrival were for mariners nothing more than markers that they needed to confirm along their route. Accordingly, it would be improper to see these passages from the mission records as definitive indicators of territory. Moreover, as Kishaba has examined in detail, upon examining the use of terminology such as *jiao* and *gou* (i.e., "boundary between inside and outside")[23] in the mission records, keeping in mind such matters as how ships navigated at the time, the presence of the Kuroshio Current that flows across the sea routes, and religious beliefs associated with the ocean in that era, one comes to the conclusion that these words do not hold territorial meaning as a border separating inside and outside, but are rather merely intended to describe "pathways on the waters."

The examination thus far has shown that China's argument that historical sources such as the records of investiture missions show that the border between China and the Ryūkyū Kingdom lay between Sekibisho and Kume Island rests on weak grounds, and that the assertion is not necessarily clear.

---

[23] Kishaba, op. cit. p. 71 *ad passim.*

3. China argues that during the Sino-Japanese negotiations regarding the Ryūkyū issue,[24] both sides affirmed that the Senkaku Islands were not included in the "36 islands of Ryūkyū."

However, as noted earlier, the so-called 36 islands of Ryūkyū refers to inhabited islands within the territorial extent of the Ryūkyū Kingdom at the time. These islands were obligated to pay tribute to the king's court in Shuri. Therefore, it must be remembered that these islands, and only such islands, were cited as the territories of Ryūkyū in the Ryūkyū's historical records and in records of imperial missions. As far as what is evident in the local annals of Fujian Province and Taiwan Province during the Ming and Qing dynasties, the Senkaku Islands were not included within the administrative area of either Fujian Province or Taiwan Province. Equally, it can be said that the Senkaku Islands were not under the administrative area of Ryūkyū, in that they were not included among the 36 islands of Ryūkyū that satisfy the criteria that such an island must be inhabited and obligated to pay tribute. Accordingly, the fact that the Senkaku Islands were not included among the "36 islands of Ryūkyū" cannot be supposed to have any legal meaning whatsoever with regard to territorial sovereignty of the Senkaku Islands. This does not provide conclusive evidence supporting the argument that the Senkaku Islands were Chinese territory.

4. China also makes the following argument. The Japanese discovered the Senkaku Islands in 1884, hundreds of years after they had already become part of China. When the defeat of the Qing dynasty government became certain during the First Sino-Japanese War of 1895, Japan "stole" the Islands. Immediately afterward, the Japanese government forced the Qing government to sign the Treaty of Shimonoseki, under the terms of which Formosa (Taiwan) and all islands appertaining or belonging to the said island of Formosa, along with the Pescadores Islands, were ceded to Japan.

It is unclear what exactly the Chinese mean when they say that the Japanese "discovered" the Senkaku Islands in 1884. However, Governor of Okinawa Nishimura Sutezō submitted a written report to Minister of Home Affairs Yamagata Aritomo by September 22, 1885 that stated:[25]

Under secret orders recently received by chief secretary Morimoto, currently stationed in Tokyo, we have conducted a survey of the uninhabited islands lying between Okinawa Prefecture and Fuzhou of the Qing Dynasty. As outlined in the appended documentation,

---

[24] For more on the Sino-Japanese negotiations concerning the sovereignty over Ryūkyū see Hanabusa, Nagamichi. 1955. "Okinawa kizoku no enkaku (A History of the Attribution of Okinawa)," in *Japanese Society of International Law. Okinawa no chii* (The Position of Okinawa). Tokyo: Yūhikaku, pp. 20–40.

[25] Existing primary document on territorial incorporation of the Senkaku Islands in Ministry of Foreign Affairs of Japan, *Teikoku hanto kankei zakken* (Miscellaneous Records Related to Imperial Territory). Quotation included in *Kikan Okinawa* 56. Also see Okuhara, Toshio, "Senkaku rettō no ryōdo hennyū keii (The Circumstances Leading to Territorial Incorporation of the Senkaku Islands)," *Kokushikan daigaku seikei gakkaishi (Journal of the Politics and Economics Society of Kokushikan University)* 4.

the islands have long been referred to within the prefecture as Kumeaka Island, Kuba Island, and Uotsuri Island. Furthermore, they are uninhabited islands that are located near islands under the jurisdiction of the prefecture, such as Kume Island, the Miyako Islands, and the Yaeyama Islands. Therefore, there are no objections to considering these islands as being under the jurisdiction of Okinawa Prefecture. However, their terrain does differ from that of the Daitō Islands, which were reported earlier, and there are doubts over whether the islands may be the same as those mentioned in Zhongshan Chuanxin Lu *(Records of the Messages from Zhongshan): Chogyo-dai [Uotsuri Island], Kōbisho, and Sekibisho. If they were the same, then clearly the Qing would have already known the islands in detail from investiture missions to the former King of Chūzan, have already given names to each of them, and have used them as markers for navigation to and from Ryūkyū. Therefore, we are hereby requesting permission to conduct an on-site survey and erect a national marker thereat as was done on the Daitō Islands. The hired steamship* Izumo-maru *is scheduled to depart in mid-October for the Sakishima Islands. On its return we intend to conduct the survey. I would like to receive orders concerning the survey and the erection of national markers.*

After receiving this report, Home Minister Yamagata wrote the following recommendation that proposed to the Grand Council of State (Dajōkan, equivalent to today's Cabinet) the "erection of national markers on Kumeaka Island and two other uninhabited islands":

With regard to the survey of Kumeaka Island and the two other uninhabited islands lying between Okinawa Prefecture and Fuzhou Province of the Qing Dynasty, as explained in the appended documents, the islands reported upon by the prefecture's governor seem to be the same islands mentioned in Zhongshan Chuanxin Lu *(Records of the Messages from Zhongshan). However, the islands were merely used as course markers by the Qing and no evidence can be confirmed that they belong to the Qing. In addition, the names of the islands vary between what we and they call them, and they are uninhabited islands located near the Miyako Islands and the Yaeyama Islands, both of which are under the jurisdiction of Okinawa. Therefore, I believe that there is no problem with Okinawa Prefecture erecting national markers upon conducting a survey. Accordingly, I ask you to give this matter urgent consideration, along with the content of the appended documents.*

Consequently, these official documents and the actual situation of the investiture relationship between China and Ryūkyū, as described above, demonstrate that there is absolutely no basis for the Chinese argument that the Japanese discovered the Senkaku Islands in 1884. Moreover, if discovery refers to the finding of economic value and utility from the Senkaku Islands, then this sort of discovery by the Japanese occurred in 1885 as described in an application to lease State-owned lands that Koga Tatsushirō, a private citizen, submitted on June 10, 1895. Koga wrote, "When I took a boat and landed on Kuba Island in 1885, I unexpectedly discovered a colony of albatrosses, colloquially called *baka-dori*. I have heard that albatross feathers are highly prized by Westerners, so I am certain that these feathers will be of great value as products for overseas export."

Yamagata consulted with Foreign Minister Inoue Kaoru on October 9 and asked his opinion on the 1885 proposal to erect national markers before submitting the issue to a Cabinet meeting. Inoue's response dated October 21 stated:

> *...[Senkaku islands] are in proximity to the national border with the Qing Dynasty, their circumferences appear smaller than those of the Daitō Islands, ... and ... their names are being attached by the Qing Dynasty. There are rumors recently circulated by Qing newspapers and others, including one that say[s] our government is going to occupy the islands in the vicinity of Taiwan that belong to the Qing Dynasty, which are arousing their suspicions towards our country and frequently alerting the Qing government for caution. If we promptly took measures such as publicly erecting national markers, it would result in making the Qing Dynasty suspicious. Therefore, we should have the islands surveyed and details—such as the configuration of harbors and the prospect of land development and local production—reported and stop there. We should deal with the erection of national markers, land development, and other undertakings some other day.[26]*

This demonstrates the diplomatic deference that Japan, the smaller power, gave toward the Qing dynasty, the larger power. It is alleged that Japanese private citizens, including Koga, had landed on the islands after 1885 and that the warships *Kongo* and *Kaimon* conducted field surveys on the Senkaku Islands in 1887 and 1892, respectively. The Qing did not protest these activities. Despite the critical opinion of Japan in Qing newspapers, the Qing government appears not to have taken any action, as can be seen from Inoue's response. Compared to the Clipperton Island case, in which Mexico dispatched the gunboat *La Democrata* and France immediately lodged a protest upon realizing this, it is sufficient to infer from these facts that the Qing did not recognize the Senkaku Islands as its own territory. It was no earlier than in 1971 that China objected that Japan "stole" the islands, an objection that carries no legal weight.

Lastly, the issue of the "names" of the island, which Inoue Kaoru mentioned in his response, should be briefly touched upon.

The names of the islands comprising Okinawa, not only those included among the "Oki," are clearly Japanese names: Iejima Island, Minna Island, Sezoko Island, Yonaguni Island, Iriomote Island, Kuruma Island and Kudaka Island. When the Meiji government carried out the Ryūkyū Disposition[27] in 1879, the King of the Ryūkyū Kingdom asked the Qing dynasty for aid. In response, He Ruzhang, the Chinese ambassador to Japan, argued that Ryūkyū was China's.[28] At that time, however, Higashionna Kanjun, a historian from Okinawa, addressed the naming of the islands in a counterargument in which he pointed out that the individual names of the islands are in fact Japanese, not Chinese. Takahashi Shōgorō, executive director of the Association for the Promotion of International Trade, takes a similar approach in his counterargument asserting that the names of

---

[26] English from "Reference 1: A letter dated October 21, 1885, sent by Foreign Minister Inoue to Interior Minister Yamagata." https://www.mofa.go.jp/region/asia-paci/senkaku/qa_1010.html. Accessed on December 20, 2022.

[27] See Chapter 1 for more on the Ryūkyū Disposition.

[28] For more on the argument's relationship with the Ryūkyū Disposition see Ōyama Azusa. "Ryūkyū kizoku to nissei fungi (Attribution of the Ryūkyūs and Japan-Qing Dynasty Dispute)" in Ōyama Azusa (ed). 1980. *Nihon gaikōshi kenkyū* (Studies in Japanese Diplomatic History). Tokyo: Ryōsho fukyūkai, pp. 107–151.

Huangwei Yu, Chiwei Yu, and Diaoyu Yu,[29] which are Chinese, clearly indicate that these three islands are part of the Taiwanese chain of islands including Huaping Yu, Mianhua Yu, and Pengjia Yu and that they are Chinese territory.[30] However, research conducted before and after World War II by Higashionna Kanjun, Fujita Motoharu, and other scholars has found that the people of Okinawa had names for these islands long before, such as "Igun Kubajima," "Yukun Kubajima," and "Yukun Kuba." Additionally, it is quite conceivable that such names as "Igun (or Yukun)," which had been passed down in Ryūkyū, were transcribed during investiture missions by Ryūkyūan sailors who accompanied the delegations and that the names became established as Chinese words,[31] taking into consideration the research Miyanaga Masamori conducted for his *Yaeyama gōi* before the war,[32] as well as the situation in Ryūkyū at the time written by Chen Kan during an investiture mission ("The people of Ryūkyū do not study Chinese characters. There are no relevant records. No Chinese people go there [i.e., to the Senkaku Islands].")

Regardless, although the names of the islands are of great significance for identifying the islands in dispute, under international law, names alone are not decisive factors for determining possession of territory. Let us review some related cases. Clipperton Island, claimed by both France and Mexico (the dispute was later settled through arbitration in France's favor) is believed to have been named after a British adventurer who used the island as a refuge in the early eighteenth century. The Island of Palmas (today a part of Indonesia) was contested by the Netherlands and the US (eventually awarded to the former after arbitration). Although Palmas was discovered by Spain, it was given a Portuguese name. Furthermore, the name of islands claimed at the heart of the Minquiers and Ecrehos case (concerning small islands lying between the mainland of France and the British-held Channel Islands, settled by the International Court of Justice (ICJ) in the United Kingdom's favor) clearly have French-oriented names. Although the language currently spoken on the Channel Islands is English, French is used for rituals. Nonetheless, these names had no major significance in terms of determining sovereignty over the territory at issue. Accordingly, even if the names of Kōbisho and Sekibisho originate from Chinese, this fact alone does not give greater credence to China's claim.

---

[29] In Japanese, Kōbisho and Sekibisho are written with the same characters as used in Chinese, while the Japanese name of the third island, Uotsuri Island, inverts the first two of the three characters.

[30] Takahashi, op. cit.

[31] See Ozaki, op. cit. (Part 2-1).

[32] Miyanaga, Masamori. 1930. *Yaeyama gōi* (Lexicon of the Yaeyama Islands). Tokyo: Tōyō Bunko.

Examination of Japan's Argument

The basic view on the sovereignty over the Senkaku Islands of the Ministry of Foreign Affairs of Japan released on March 8, 1972 states the following; it seems that Japan's argument rests solely on the occupation of *terra nullius*:[33]

> From 1885 on, surveys of the Senkaku Islands had been thoroughly conducted by the Government of Japan through the agencies of Okinawa Prefecture and through other means. Through these surveys, it was confirmed that the Senkaku Islands had been not only uninhabited but also showed no trace of having been under the control of the Qing dynasty of China. Based on this confirmation, the Government of Japan made a Cabinet Decision on January 14, 1895, to erect markers on the islands to formally incorporate the Senkaku Islands into the territory of Japan.

"The Senkaku Islands," a Ministry of Foreign Affairs document dated January 1978, largely contains the same content as a pamphlet of the same title that was published by the Ministry's Public Information Bureau in 1972. The 1978 document contains the following on the Islands' incorporation into Japanese territory:

> 1. Deliberate process of incorporation
>
> In 1879, the Meiji government abolished the domain of Ryukyu and set up Okinawa Prefecture. Afterward, from 1885 onward the Japanese government conducted surveys of the Senkaku Islands through the agencies of Okinawa Prefecture and through other means, taking as long as ten years. After having carefully ascertained that there had been no trace of control over the Senkaku Islands by the Qing Dynasty, under the cabinet decision on January 14, 1895, the Japanese government decided to place the Senkaku Islands under the jurisdiction of Okinawa Prefecture and erect national markers on the islands.
>
> Thus, the Senkaku Islands were incorporated into Japanese territory. (This incorporation occurred before April 17, 1895, the day of the signing of the Treaty of Shimonoseki that provided for the cession of Taiwan to Japan as a result of the [First] Sino-Japanese War. Therefore, the Senkaku Islands have never been treated as part of Taiwan) . . .

The Governor of Okinawa Prefecture submitted proposals on three occasions: the aforementioned first proposal in 1885; the second on January 13, 1890 entitled "Inquiry Concerning the Matter of the Uninhabited Islands: Kuba and Uotsuri Islands"; and the third on November 2, 1893. As a result, the Cabinet decision on January 14, 1895 was adopted as follows: "Regarding the matter submitted by the Home Minister for deliberation: In recent years, certain persons have sailed in the direction of the uninhabited islands known as Kuba Island and Uotsuri Island situated northwest of the Yaeyama Islands of Okinawa Prefecture with the intent to engage in fishing and other activities. Given the need to control such activities, there is no hindrance to determining that the said islands come under the jurisdiction of Okinawa Prefecture and permitting the erection of jurisdictional markers as requested in the petition of the Okinawa Prefectural Governor." An order dated January 21 was issued to the governor of Okinawa Prefecture which stated: "Approved the proposal concerning the erection of markers as requested." Although it remains unconfirmed whether Okinawa Prefecture erected the markers on the

---

[33] See the section on occupation in Chapter 1.

Senkaku Islands under this order, this was how the Islands were incorporated into Japan.

However, in addition to Uotsuri Island and Kuba Island (Kōbisho), which were mentioned in the Cabinet decision, the Senkaku Islands include Sekibisho (known as Kumeaka Island in Okinawa), as well as two small islands north and south of Uotsuri Island and reefs. Since Minamikojima Island and Kitakojima Island, along with the reefs of Tobise, Okinominamiiwa, and Okinokitaiwa, are a part of the same island chain with Uotsuri Island and Kuba Island (Kōbisho), these small islands and reefs were also considered within the scope of the territorial incorporation, even without explicit mention in the Cabinet decision. A district system was introduced in Okinawa Prefecture based on the imperial edict of April 1, 1896. Under the system, both Uotsuri Island and Kuba Island were incorporated into Yaeyama District shortly afterwards and were designated as State-owned land along with Minamikojima Island and Kitakojima Island. However, it was only on July 25, 1921 that Kumeaka Island (Sekibisho) was designated as State-owned land, listed in the national land register, and renamed Taishō Island.

Does this show that Kumeaka Island was incorporated into Japanese territory in 1921, as some people argue? To reach that conclusion from these events in 1921 is unnatural. The Cabinet decision of 1895 was based on the proposals submitted by the governor of Okinawa Prefecture. Given that the governor's proposals in 1885 and 1890 include Sekibisho by referring to "Uotsuri Island and two other islands," there is no particular reason to distinguish and exclude Sekibisho from the scope of the Cabinet decision (although the 1893 proposal by the governor of Okinawa Prefecture is not necessarily clear). After the decision, Koga Tatsushirō started developing Kuba Island (Kōbisho), and in May 1900 he went to Sekibisho and erected wooden markers there. The waters around Sekibisho have strong currents of two to three knots from the Kuroshio Current that turn turbulent as they envelop the isle. This makes it difficult for ships to land on the island, even on calm, sunny days. Moreover, the island did not have much appeal in terms of exploitation since it did not seem to have valuable resources and its entire area is a rugged mountain, making it unsuitable for development. These factors explain the delay in Sekibisho's designation as State-owned land.

However, the territorial incorporation of the Senkaku Islands would seem to be irregular as this measure was not accompanied by the notifications, announcements or edicts Japan used when incorporating other islands into the territory, and because it is not possible to verify whether the markers were actually erected.[34]

As is well known, for occupation to be legitimate under international law, the territory in question must be *terra nullius* and effectively occupied by a State with the intention of possessing said territory. In other words, the problem is about the State indicating intention to possess the territory as the subjective requirement of occupation, and its effective occupation as the objective requirement. Typically,

---

[34]See Kokusaihō Jirei Kenkyūkai. 1990. *Nihon no kokusaihō jirei kenkyū (3): Ryōdo* (Study of Practices in Japan, Vol. 3: Territory). Tokyo: Keio University Press.

intention to take possession of land is indicated by declaring the State's intent to incorporate the area into its territory, or to incorporate it through legislative or administrative means, or by notifications delivered to other countries. Some argue that, as provided by Chapter VI, Article 34 of the General Act of the Berlin Conference of 1885 on the partition of Africa, notification is a required condition in order to complete occupation. But only the signatories to the Act were obliged to obey its provisions, so this is not part of general international law. Furthermore, as can be seen from the decisions made in the cases of Palmas Island and of Clipperton Island,[35] the prevailing theory denies such an argument.[36] According to the prevailing theory, even if no notification is made, it is sufficient if intention to possess the territory is expressed by other means. It is possible to confirm that Japan's intention to possess the Senkaku Islands fulfills the criteria of international judgments and the prevailing theory.

There are two views on the definition of effective occupation. One is that it means physical occupation in the form of actually utilizing the land or establishing a settlement there. The other defines effective occupation as social occupation via the establishment of control over the land. All international judicial precedents support the social occupation theory, as exemplified by the rulings in such cases as those concerning the Palmas, Eastern Greenland, as well as Minquiers and Ecrehos. This means that in the case of an uninhabited island, simply discovering the island and hoisting one's national flag upon it in a symbolic act of territorial incorporation does not constitute an effective occupation. As demonstrated in the judgment of the Palmas case, the prevailing theory does accept the inchoate title of discovery, but acquisition of territory is incomplete if effective occupation does not follow. This norm has been part of international law since the nineteenth century. Accordingly, even if markers had been erected, this alone would not complete Japan's occupation of the Senkaku Islands. According to the international law of the nineteenth century, the occupation of an uninhabited island is not effective unless the functions of the State extend to the said island, such as through regular patrols by warships or other government vessels.

As explained earlier, the Senkaku Islands were incorporated into Japanese territory via a Cabinet decision of January 14, 1895. Koga Tatsushirō submitted an application to lease State-owned lands on June 10 of that year, and the Japanese government granted Koga permission in September 1896 to lease four islands, namely Uotsuri Island, Kōbisho, Kitakojima Island, and Minamikojima Island, for 30 years free of charge for the purpose of promoting their development. During this time, however, the peace treaty that ended the First Sino-Japanese War was signed on April 17, 1895, its instrument of ratification was exchanged on May 8, and the cession of Taiwan was completed on June 2. Clearly Japan exerted valid control over

---

[35] For details on these rulings, see Serita, Kentarō. 1999. *Shima no ryōyū to keizai suiiki no kyōkai kakutei* (Sovereignty over Islands and the Delimitation of Economic Zones). Tokyo: Yūshindo Kōbunsha.

[36] This point is addressed further in Chapter 4, "Takeshima."

the Senkaku Islands, but this was mostly during Japan's administration of Taiwan, after the island had been ceded. Therefore, despite the lack of objections from China, it may not necessarily be possible to distinguish between whether Japan controlled islands that were *terra nullius* prior to occupation, or whether the control was over islands that were ceded. In this sense, it might be possible that the actions taken by Japan up until its defeat on August 14, 1945 may be frozen, and that only the actions taken after the war may be counted as effective occupation. However, for good or bad, it was in 1971 that China began lodging objections and claiming the Senkaku Islands as its own territory. This means that the "critical date"[37] can be set as June 17, 1971, the date on which the Okinawa Reversion Treaty was signed.[38]

So, were the Senkaku Islands *terra nullius* prior to occupation in 1895, which can be subject to occupation? China argues that the islands were Chinese territory, using historical records from diplomatic missions as evidence. As addressed earlier in our examination of China's argument and its basis, China asserts that the border between it and Ryūkyū lay between Sekibisho and Kume Island. However, in investiture mission records, their return journey described the islands known by the Chinese as Yu Shan and Fengwei Shan with the phrase "both *shan* (mountains) belong to Taizhou." This, along with phrases like "Nanba Shan in Wenzhou" and "outlying *shan* (mountains) of China," indicates that it is natural to consider that the Senkaku Islands, which lay upon the sea route between Fuzhou and Ryūkyū, were noted in these historical mission records as navigational markers. In addition, China did not take any sort of measures to improve safety along the route. However, even if there were evidence that it had taken some measures, this would still be insufficient. In the Minquiers and Ecrehos case,[39] France made its argument by citing facts, regarding Minquiers, showing it had conducted field investigations for hydrographic surveys, installed lights and buoys, and established temporary markers for conducting field research. But in its judgment, the ICJ stated, "The Court does not find that the facts, invoked by the French Government, are sufficient to show that France has a valid title to the Minquiers. . . . such acts can hardly be considered as sufficient evidence of the intention of that Government to act as sovereign over the islets . . ."[40] In many cases, actions by a State for the sake of safety of ships are taken irrespective of the intention to possess an island as territory, and it is difficult for such actions to be direct evidence of title to sovereignty. Therefore, it can be inferred that the Senkaku Islands were *terra nullius*.

---

[37] This can be interpreted as a deadline for permissible evidence, as any facts arising after this date will not be accepted for examination as evidence in an international court.

[38] Matsui Yoshirō believes that the most appropriate and equitable date is mid-February 1971, when China or Taiwan lodged its first objection and claim. See Matsui, Yoshiro, "International Law of Territorial Acquisition and the Dispute over the Senkaku (Diaoyu) Islands," *The Japanese Annual of International Law* 40 (1997): 8.

[39] A case filed and lost by France.

[40] International Court of Justice, *The Minquiers and Ecrehos Case (France/United Kingdom) Judgment of 17 November 1953*, p. 71.

Next, assuming from the copious Chinese documents available, even if new ones were discovered that provide clear proof of the Senkaku Islands being Chinese territory, a distinction must be made between the "creation of rights" and the "existence of rights," as the judgment in the Palmas case makes clear. With regard to this point, neither the Ming nor the Qing dynasties utilized the Senkaku Islands for economic purposes, and even if China acquired original title to the islands arising as a result of their discovery and that the title remained in China's possession in inchoate form until 1895, such inchoate title must give way to continuous and peaceful display of sovereignty by another state.

Accordingly, the basis of Japan's position on sovereignty over the Senkaku Islands is first of all, occupation of *terra nullius*, which seems favorable according to private sector research, even if the critical date is set as 1895. However, by setting the critical date as June 17, 1971, when the Okinawa Reversion Treaty was signed, the actions taken by Japan between 1895 and 1970, facts that show valid control by Japan, can be considered permissible evidence. Therefore, in addition to the occupation of *terra nullius*, the title arising from the "continuous and peaceful display of sovereignty"[41] should also be insisted upon. At least, so long as China denounces the Okinawa Reversion Treaty's inclusion of the Senkaku Islands in the "reversed areas" and asserts that it has retained continuous sovereignty over the Islands, it would be logical to set the critical date to the time when the Okinawa Reversion Treaty was signed.

In that case, it can be noted that Japan exerted "continuous" control for 75 years beginning in 1895, while there were no objections lodged by China; in other words, this is more than sufficient to prove that Japan exercised State authority over the Islands in a "peaceful" manner. However, even if the Senkaku Islands are not considered as having been *terra nullius*, there is no room to argue the permanent title, which Judge Max Huber called the "continuous and peaceful display of sovereignty," if the islands were ceded, along with Taiwan, to Japan in accordance with the Treaty of Shimonoseki. That is because this cession constitutes a clearer source of title. But were the Senkaku Islands actually included as islands appertaining or belonging to Taiwan under the terms of the Treaty of Shimonoseki?

The fact that, according to local government publications from Fujian Province and Taiwan Province during the Ming and Qing dynasties, the Senkaku Islands were not considered within the administrative control of either province has been addressed above. The instrument of ratification for the Treaty of Shimonoseki was exchanged on May 8, 1895. Pursuant to Article 5 of the Treaty, plenipotentiary Kabayama Sukenori of the Japanese delegation and plenipotentiary Li Jingfang of the Qing delegation signed the "Note on the delivery of Taiwan" on June 2. On this occasion, the following conversation took place between plenipotentiary Li and

---

[41] A precedent set by the Palmas case.

Minister Resident Mizuno Jun of Japan regarding the scope of the islands appertaining or belonging to Taiwan:[42]

> Li: "Is it not necessary to list in the index the names of the islands described as islands appertaining or belonging to Taiwan? In the Treaty of Peace, the area of the Pescadores Group is clearly demarcated with latitude and longitude coordinates. However, the Treaty does not specify the area of the islands appertaining or belonging to Taiwan. I worry that it may bring a dispute if Japan, at a later time, will point to the islands near Fujian Province and assert that they are islands appertaining or belonging to Taiwan."
>
> Mizuno: "If we list the names of the islands as you say, there may be islands that are omitted from the list, or islands which do not have any names, in which case this would mean that such islands do not fall under the territory of either government. That is an inconvenient result. In addition, in nautical charts, maps, and other sources, it has been recognized officially, referring to the islands near Taiwan, that these islands belong to Taiwan. The Japanese government will never claim that the islands near Fujian Province are appertaining or belonging to Taiwan. I will surely explain this point to Governor-General Kabayama on the return ship. This is more true when considering the fact that the Pescadores Group lies between Fujian Province and Taiwan. Your concern will be proved unfounded, Your Excellency."
>
> Li: "Agreed."

The maps and nautical charts of Taiwan published in Japan before 1896 identified without exception that Taiwan extended up to Pengjia Islet. Both Japan and the Qing dynasty seemed to share the view that the Senkaku Islands were not included in the "islands appertaining or belonging to Taiwan as recognized officially in nautical charts, maps, and other materials," i.e., the islands over which an issue was raised at the time of Taiwan's delivery.

Approaches to a Final Settlement

The way to pursue the settlement of a dispute differs depending on which side actually holds the disputed island. In the case of the Senkaku Islands, they are under Japan's control, and thus, until a final settlement is reached, Japan should simply maintain control and there is no particular need to strengthen it.

Twenty years ago, in the early morning of April 12, 1978, the date on which the negotiation concerning the Treaty of Peace and Friendship between Japan and the People's Republic of China was conducted, a large number of Chinese fishing vessels appeared in the territorial waters around the Senkaku Islands. The Japan-China negotiations on the Treaty, which had just resumed, were temporarily suspended. On April 15, Vice Premier Geng Biao stated, "The [Senkaku] incident was incidental. The settlement of this issue of small islands should be left to the future." After the statement, all Chinese fishing vessels were cleared from the territorial waters around the Senkaku Islands.

---

[42]Inō, Kanori. 1965. *Taiwan bunkashi (3)* (Cultural History of Taiwan [Vol. 3]). Tokyo: Tōkō Shoin. Reprint, pp. 936–937.

The negotiations later resumed in Beijing, and Foreign Minister Sonoda Sunao arrived in Beijing on August 8. After his talks with Foreign Minister Huang Hua on August 9 and with Vice Premier Deng Xiaoping on August 10, the Treaty of Peace and Friendship between Japan and the People's Republic of China was signed on August 12. At a press conference following the signing, Sonoda stated in his opening remarks, "I explained the position of the Japanese government regarding the Senkaku Islands during my talks with Vice Premier Deng Xiaoping on the afternoon of the 10th. The Vice Premier responded that the Chinese government would never repeat confrontations like the recent incident." Deng's comment was repeatedly brought up during the treaty deliberations at the Diet in Japan. During a session of the Committee on Foreign Affairs of the House of Representatives on October 13, Sonoda stated, "I explained the position of Japan regarding the Senkaku Islands. I said that we feel disturbed by incidents like the previous one, and strongly requested the Chinese government to prevent such incidents. Vice Premier Deng Xiaoping responded that the incident was incidental and that they would never engage in such an incident again."[43] On the following day, October 14, Sonoda stated, "Vice Premier Deng Xiaoping stated clearly at an official meeting that the previous incident was incidental and that they would never engage in such incidents again. This is in the record of discussion. I believe these incidents will not occur in the future."[44]

Deng visited Japan from October 22 to 29 for the exchange of the instruments of ratification of the Treaty of Peace and Friendship between Japan and the People's Republic of China. He held a press conference at the Japan Press Center on October 25 and commented on territorial title over the Senkaku Islands: "When we normalized diplomatic relations between our two countries, both parties promised to leave the issue aside. At this time of negotiation on the Treaty of Peace and Friendship, we agreed to leave the issue aside in much the same way ... I think it is better to avoid the issue when our countries have negotiations. Even if this means the issue is temporarily shelved, I don't think I mind. I don't mind if it's shelved for 10 years." This Chinese decision to place the territorial issue on the shelf was beneficial to Japan.

Minister of Transport Moriyama Kinji stated at a press conference on January 16, 1979 that "In order to build facilities on the Senkaku Islands of Okinawa Prefecture, where issues with China have not been ultimately addressed, the Okinawa Development Agency will start conducting surveys in fiscal 1979. To support this survey, the Japan Coast Guard will consult with the Okinawa Development Agency to build a temporary heliport on Uotsuri Island (an uninhabited island) of the Senkaku Islands." As a result, the Senkaku Islands were again on the agenda at the 87th session of the Diet. In connection with the 30-million-yen survey cost and the issue of the heliport's construction, Foreign Minister Sonoda stated, "It is in the

---

[43] Foreign Minister Sonoda, 85th Diet, Meeting of the Committee on Foreign Affairs of the House of Representatives, 1st session.

[44] Ibid., 2nd sess.

interest of Japan to quietly continue its current valid control over the islands. However, if the heliport is going to be constructed as an evacuation area or for the safety of the residents and fishermen in the area, then construction should proceed while provoking China as little as possible. It is problematic if the heliport is being constructed to flaunt our valid control."[45] Sonoda further stated that while the Senkaku Islands were Japanese territory, provocative actions were not desirable.[46] Nonetheless, it led Director Shen Ping of the Department of Asian Affairs of China's Ministry of Foreign Affairs to summon Ban Shōichi, chargé d'affaires ad interim of the Japanese embassy in China, to the ministry to verbally express his regret on May 29. The following is the full text of *Xinhua News Agency*'s article on that date regarding the protest that Shen lodged:[47]

> *This morning, Shen Ping, Director of the Department of Asian Affairs of the Ministry of Foreign Affairs of the People's Republic of China, met with Shoichi Ban, Japanese chargés d'affaires ad interim to China. Discussion took place on the Japanese government's recent dispatch of the patrol vessel Soya for the transport of personnel and equipment to China's Diaoyu Island, the establishment of a temporary heliport and the dispatch of survey missions and vessels.*
>
> *Islands including Diaoyu Island have been part of the territory of China since ancient times. On December 30, 1971, the Chinese Ministry of Foreign Affairs issued a statement to this effect. However, China and Japan have different views regarding the issue of the attribution of island territories, including the Diaoyu Islands. When diplomatic relations were normalized between China and Japan, and when the Treaty of Peace and Friendship was concluded, the two parties agreed to leave this issue aside for the sake of the China-Japan friendship, and to settle the issue in the future.*
>
> *In accordance with this agreement, Director Shen Ping noted, 'The Japanese side is clearly betraying the aforementioned bilateral understanding. We are forced to express regret over the actions of Japan. Moreover, we do not deem that Japan's actions have legal value.'*
>
> *Shen Ping also stated, 'We would like the Japanese government to adopt a broad perspective and respect the understanding that our countries' leaders reached on the issue of Diaoyu Island, and to take measures to refrain from all activities that undermine the bilateral friendship and neighborly cooperative relations.'*

Regarding the above protest, Sonoda responded at the Diet that, "As long as our counterpart has lodged a protest, we are compelled to understand that China interpreted our action as an activity intended to demonstrate our valid control."[48] It would seem that Sonoda's idea was that the government's top policy priority should be for Japan to quietly maintain its current possession of the islands. However, what must be kept in mind is that, as explained earlier, while France argued in the Minquiers and Ecrehos case that it had conducted field investigations for hydrographic surveys, installed lights and buoys, and established temporary

---

[45] Committee on Cabinet, 14th session, 23.

[46] Committee on Foreign Affairs, 13th session, May 30, 30.

[47] For an English summary of the account, see May 29 "Chronicle" item on front page of *Beijing Review*, June 8, 1979. http://www.massline.org/PekingReview/PR1979/PR1979-23.pdf. Accessed on March 25, 2023.

[48] Committee on Foreign Affairs, 13th session, May 30, 30.

markers for conducting field research, the ICJ determined, "The Court did not find that the facts invoked by the French Government were sufficient to show that France has a valid title to the Minquiers." Thus, action taken solely for the safety of ships is insufficient grounds. However, the case of Grisbadarna, in which Norway and Sweden engaged in a dispute over the border between their southern territorial waters, must also not be forgotten. Sweden, which had erected markers, conducted maritime surveys, and installed lights, considered such actions not only as the exercise of its rights, but also as "the fulfillment of duties." Meanwhile, since Norway expressed nearly no interest in the waters with regard to these actions, the court decided that the shoal belongs to Sweden.

Accordingly, as can be seen from the case described above, the reason why Japan should maintain its current control of the Senkaku Islands and why there is no particular need to further strengthen the said control is as follows. Since Japan holds territorial sovereignty over the Islands, rather than taking some sort of action to exercise its rights, Japan should simply continue carrying out the actions it has thus far. To elaborate, since May 15, 1972, when administrative rights over the Nansei Shotō Islands reverted to Japan, Japan Coast Guard patrol vessels and aircraft have continued to monitor the areas around Okinawa in the same manner as before, including the Senkaku Islands. They still regulate intrusion into territorial waters and illegal fishing in such waters. Therefore, it is proper for Japan to warn Chinese civil activists who in recent years have conducted demonstrations at sea and forcibly entered the territory, and request that they leave. It should be noted that the actions taken by States after the critical date are not permissible as evidence of valid control. Thus, such measures as the Law of the People's Republic of China Concerning the Territorial Sea and the Contiguous Zone, which China enacted in 1992 treating the Islands as its own territory, are meaningless under international law.

Chapter 4
Takeshima

The Republic of Korea's Declaration Concerning Maritime Sovereignty: The Origin of the Dispute

Takeshima is located in the Sea of Japan (37°9′30″ north latitude and 131°55′ east longitude), 115 nautical miles from the Japanese mainland, approximately 90 nautical miles from the Oki Islands, and 120 nautical miles from the Republic of Korea (ROK) mainland, approximately 50 nautical miles from Ulleungdo. It comprises two islands, one to the east and one to the west, and numerous reefs connected to these islands. It has a total land area of approximately 0.23 km², making it slightly larger than Hibiya Park in Tokyo. Takeshima is exposed to strong sea winds, and apart from some weeds growing on the islands' southwestern side, it consists of bare rocks that cannot even sustain trees. The east and west islands are separated by a channel of water approximately 150 m wide. The coastline of continuous sheer cliffs is subjected to high waves, and since drinking water is also scarce, Takeshima is unsuited to human habitation. In a Cabinet decision on January 28, 1905, Japan named the islands Takeshima, incorporated it into Japanese territory, and put it under the jurisdiction of the Oki Islands office affiliated to Shimane Prefecture. The governor of Shimane Prefecture was then directed to announce the Cabinet's decision; based on this directive, he made a public announcement to that effect on February 22, 1905 by means of a prefectural notice (Fig. 4.1).

After World War II, the ROK ceased being a Japanese colony and became independent. In September 1951, when the Treaty of Peace with Japan was signed and the restoration of Japan's sovereignty became a certainty, the ROK established fishery protection zones on the Korean coast and ramped up efforts to regulate fishing activities by foreign countries. The ROK issued the Presidential Proclamation of Sovereignty over the Adjacent Seas (the Syngman Rhee Line Declaration) on

© Kreab K.K. 2023
K. Serita, *The Territory of Japan*, https://doi.org/10.1007/978-981-99-3013-5_4

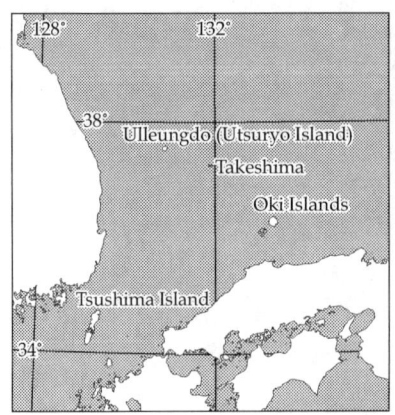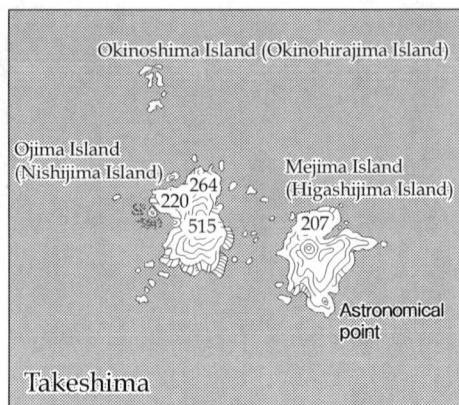

Fig. 4.1 Takeshima

January 18, 1952, unilaterally proclaiming ROK sovereignty over sea areas that included Takeshima.[1]

Japan immediately lodged a protest with the ROK side on January 28, stating with regard to Takeshima that, "in the proclamation the Republic of Korea appears to assume territorial rights over Takeshima (otherwise known as Liancourt Rocks). The Japanese Government does not recognize any such assumption or claim by the Republic of Korea concerning these islets which are without question Japanese territory."[2] The ROK responded on February 12 of the following year, countering that Japan's assertion was unreasonable in light of the instruction note issued by the Supreme Commander for the Allied Powers No. 677 (SCAPIN No. 677). The two countries have continued to trade barbs ever since, right up to the present day.

ROK security personnel (police) have been stationed on Takeshima's Higashijima (Mejima) Island since around July 1954. Higashijima (Mejima) Island is equipped with living quarters, a lighthouse, observation posts, antennas, and other facilities, and the ROK is bolstering this presence year by year.[3]

In essence, the ROK's argument is that, to begin with, Takeshima has been Korean territory since long ago; secondly, that Japan's territorial incorporation of Takeshima in 1905 is invalid; and thirdly, that a series of measures, from the Cairo

---

[1] For details of the problems from the standpoint of the Law of the Sea, see Oda, Shigeru. 1972. *Kaiyōhō no genryū o saguru* (Exploring the Origins of UNCLOS). Tokyo: Japan Fisheries Association; and Kawakami, Kenzō. 1972. *Sengo no kokusai gyogyō seido* (The Postwar International Fisheries System). Tokyo: Japan Fisheries Association.

[2] Ministry of Foreign Affairs. January 28, 1952. https://www.cas.go.jp/jp/ryodo_eg/shiryo/takeshima/detail/t1952012800101.html. Accessed on December 2, 2022.

[3] Rough seas made landing on the island impossible on July 25, 1983, so the ceremony to commemorate the 30th anniversary of the deployment of the Dokdo Volunteer Guard was held by shifting the venue from Dokdo to Ulleungdo. Ahead of a Japan-ROK Ministerial Meeting on August 29 and 30, 1983, the *Asahi Shimbun* raised this issue in the *Shinso* column in its August 28, 1983 edition and published photographs of the islands and the ROK's facilities.

Declaration during World War II through to postwar peace treaties, confirm that Takeshima is Korean territory.

Examining the ROK Side's Arguments and Their Basis

Examining the Argument that Takeshima Has Been Korean Territory since Long Ago

These days Takeshima is known as "Dokdo" in the ROK, but according to the ROK, previously it was called "Usando" or "Sambongdo," and subsequently it was also recorded as "Jasando" and "Usando" (written with slightly different characters). Long ago in Japan, Takeshima was known by the name "Matsushima." It was given the names "Liancourt Rocks" and "Hornet Rocks" as a result of European naval voyages in the nineteenth century. Thus, it was also familiarly known by the name "Ryanko Island," a corruption of "Liancourt." As this shows, Takeshima might have had around ten names. The examination that follows is based largely on Kawakami Kenzō's *Takeshima no rekishi chirigakuteki kenkyū* (A Geographical Study of the History of Takeshima, Tokyo: Kokon Shoin, 1966), along with Hori Kazuo's "1905-nen Nihon no Takeshima ryōdo hennyū (Japan's Incorporation of Takeshima into its Territory in 1905)" in *Chōsenshi kenkyūkai ronbunshū* (*Bulletin of Society for Study in Korean History* 24, March 1987), which is a critical examination of Kawakami's work.

According to the ROK, the first person who discovered Takeshima was a Korean. Takeshima appears in a Korean document, *Sejong sillok jiriji* (Geographical Appendix to the Veritable Records of King Sejong) from 1454 (effectively 1432, according to Hori), which states "Usando and Mureungdo . . . The two islands are not far from each other so that one is visible on a clear day." This predates any mention in Japanese documents by some 200 years. In *notes verbales* from the ROK's diplomatic mission in Japan, the ROK asserts that the Mureungdo mentioned here was another name for Ulleungdo that was used in the Silla period, meaning the document is referring to a separate island to Ulleungdo, that the two islands can be seen from each other on a clear day, and so conceivably, that Usando, Takeshima, and Dokdo are one and the same.[4]

In response to this, Kawakami states that the Usando that appears in ancient Joseon documents is another name for Ulleungdo, and the location of Sambongdo was not confirmed by a survey conducted by a private citizen named Kim Jaju, nor by a number of surveys conducted by the government, and consequently nothing

---

[4]ROK's diplomatic mission in Japan, official notes dated September 9, 1953; September 25, 1954; and January 7, 1959; in Kawakami, Kenzō. 1966. *Takeshima no rekishi chirigakuteki kenkyū* (A Geographical Study of the History of Takeshima). Tokyo: Kokon Shoin, pp. 114–117.

whatsoever can be found to actively substantiate that these references correspond to the Takeshima of today.[5] Hori Kazuo, meanwhile, is thoroughly critical of Kawakami's assertion that Usando does not exist, and attempts to verify that the existence of Usando was widely known in the Korea Peninsula.

Historically, Ulleungdo was an independent State, Usan-guk (the State of Usan), before yielding allegiance to the Silla Kingdom at the beginning of the sixth century. But assuming that Usando is not another name for Ulleungdo, then even if Usan-guk were made up of Ulleungdo and Usando as the ROK claims, to have used Usando (i.e., Takeshima)—uninhabitable rocky hills without water 100 km away from the inhabited Ulleungdo—as the name of the country, while not impossible, is certainly unusual, as Taijudō Kanae points out.[6, 7] Assuming that Usando is Takeshima, then surely the country would have been known as "Ulleung-guk," or by Ulleungdo's other names of Mureung-guk or Ureung-guk, rather than "Usan (i.e., Takeshima)-guk"?

In any event, Hori concludes that "The Joseon government recognized Takeshima/Dokdo as its own territory, Usando, from the fifteenth century, and while periods of confusion did occur, it clarified this territorial awareness once again at the end of the nineteenth century."[8] However, the accounts in the various records also reveal some confusion, making it difficult to believe that the descriptions were undertaken based on a clear awareness at the time. Furthermore, although the ROK's *note verbale* of September 1953 mentions that Kim Jaju saw Sambongdo (which it says Dokdo was called from the early stages of the Joseon Kingdom) from afar, given that he was not actually able to land on the island, even if Takeshima was discovered by the Joseon, this document does not demonstrate that the kingdom actually administered the island.

From the fifteenth century the Joseon government adopted a "vacant island" policy on Ulleungdo, effectively abandoning it. During this period, based on a "Takeshima (today's Ulleungdo) Voyage License" obtained from the shogunate in 1618, the Ōya and Murakawa families developed and utilized Ulleungdo. In the course of making round trips to and from Ulleungdo, they also developed and utilized today's Takeshima (called Matsushima at the time), and the island's indigenous produce was presented to the shogunate also. The two families' management of Ulleungdo continued for around 80 years without interference from the Joseon. A

---

[5] Separate to Kawakami's argument, there is an additional theory that Sambongdo is also another name for Ulleungdo.

[6] Taijudō, Kanae. 1966. "Takeshima funsō (The Takeshima Dispute)," *Kokusaihō gaikō zasshi* (*The Journal of International Law and Diplomacy*) 64, No. 4–5: p. 111.

[7] According to recent reports, Usando is apparently used on Ulleungdo as the historic old name for the island. There is an Usan Culture Festival held on Ulleungdo, and a Jasan Middle School there, for example. See *Sankei Shimbun*, March 19, 1997, *Ringoku e no ashioto* (7).

[8] Kazuo, Hori. 1987. "1905-nen Nihon no Takeshima ryōdo hennyū (Japan's Incorporation of Takeshima into its Territory in 1905)" in *Chōsenshi kenkyūkai ronbunshū* (*Bulletin of Society for Study in Korean History*) 24, March: p. 101.

large number of the Joseon confronted them for the first time in 1692, after which trouble ensued.[9]

This "Takeshima Affair" (*Takeshima Ikken*) at the end of the seventeenth century concluded with the January 1696 decision to ban voyages to Takeshima (today's Ulleungdo) by the Ōya and Murakawa families. Subsequently the Joseon government began dispatching an inspector to Ulleungdo once every 3 years. However, even under the national seclusion of the Edo period, voyages to Takeshima (Matsushima at the time) were not banned. Taijudō Kanae says this is also clear from a verdict reached against ship merchant Imazuya Hachiemon of Hamada in 1836. Imazuya was given the death penalty for violating a ban by traveling to Ulleungdo, but in the wording of said verdict it states that he "[t]raveled to Takeshima (today's Ulleungdo) under the pretense of voyaging to Matsushima (today's Takeshima)." This wording therefore suggests that even after the ban on voyaging to Ulleungdo was in place, voyaging to today's Takeshima (Matsushima at that time) posed no problems whatsoever.

The period of approximately 50 years following that is unknown, but at the very least, from the Meiji period many Japanese citizens were traveling to Ulleungdo, at that time still a vacant island, for logging and fishing. Then, a Joseon inspector's discovery of this activity in 1881 triggered a protest from the Joseon government to the Government of Japan. This resulted in Japan confirming that Ulleungdo was the territory of the Joseon Kingdom and banning Japanese fishermen from traveling to the island. It was at this point that the Joseon government revised the existing vacant island policy and decided to develop Ulleungdo.

With the above in mind, the argument that the Takeshima of today has been Korean territory since ancient times does not necessarily have a sufficient historical basis. What can be said, based on the way the Takeshima Affair of the Edo period and the logging incident of 1881 were dealt with, is that in the respective eras, the Joseon's actual control did not extend to Ulleungdo, and consequently Japanese citizens were visiting and utilizing the island in large numbers. Nevertheless, Ulleungdo was confirmed to be Joseon territory by Japan's handling of these incidents. Regardless of the position of Ulleungdo, however, it would be a stretch to declare that both sides perceive today's Takeshima as "Ulleungdo's territorial island" and that as a territorial island its fate is always shared with that of Ulleungdo. Conversely, it can be surmised that, historically, Korea's control has never extended to today's Takeshima.

---

[9]See Kawakami, 1966, p. 93; and Taijudō, op. cit. 113. However, according to Hori Kazuo, "A major clash occurred on Ulleungdo in 1693, between a party from the Ōya family and An Yong-bok and other Korean fishermen who had gone fishing from Gyeongsang," (Hori, op. cit. 101).

Examining the Argument that Japan's 1905 Territorial Incorporation of Takeshima Is Invalid

The ROK's argument regarding this point can be summarized as follows.[10]

First, Japan's unilateral domestic measure was an act of title by occupation of *terra nullius*, but because Takeshima is Korean territory and not *terra nullius*, the measure is invalid.

Second, Japan's announcement of its intent of territorial acquisition took the form of a notification by Shimane Prefecture, but that notification was undertaken extremely stealthily, and the Korean government was not notified, so it is invalid.

Third, even if the Korean government had known this fact at that time, it was not in a position to raise objections with the Government of Japan as a result of the Protectorate Treaty of 1904, the First Japan-Korea Agreement.

Fourth, with regard to Japan's activities following its territorial incorporation measure, the surveys and other activities undertaken by the Government of Japan were carried out as one part of its activities for invading Korea, and consequently they are not acceptable as ongoing activities of territorial control based on international law.

Now, the first of the ROK's assertions is the same point as the discussion above relating to whether or not today's Takeshima was Korean territory since ancient times. Thus, as has already been revealed in this examination, it is not possible to say unequivocally that Takeshima was Korean territory. Incidentally, the Government of Japan does not recognize this territorial incorporation as an act of title by occupation of *terra nullius*. In its argument regarding this point, Japan expresses the view that international laws did not apply to Japan before the opening of the country, and at that time, Japan actually believed that Takeshima was Japanese territory and treated it as such, and unless another country disputed that, then this was sufficient to constitute possession.

Even so, in terms of the form of the acquisition of territorial title, the measure that Japan adopted took the form of an act of title by occupation, and where this point is concerned there is a need to examine how Japan defined its neighboring territories as a whole towards the end of the Edo period and during the Meiji period.[11] In the case of the Ogasawara (Bonin) Islands, which Japan incorporated into Japanese territory in 1876, the Meiji government argued that it was self-evident that they came under Japan's jurisdiction, but the United States, the United Kingdom, and other countries were not necessarily convinced of this, and the jurisdiction was decided following

---

[10]Minagawa, Takeshi. 1963. "Takeshima funsō to kokusai hanrei (The Takeshima Dispute and International Precedent)" in *Kokusaihōgaku no shomondai: Maehara Mitsuo kyōju kanreki kinen* (Issues of International Law: In Commemoration of Professor Maehara Mitsuo's 60th Birthday). Tokyo: Keio University Press; and Taijudō, op. cit.

[11]See Chapter 1.

complex and difficult diplomatic negotiations.[12] No disputes over Takeshima had arisen with any countries, including Korea. Japan adopted the incorporation measure in order to control the hunting of sea lions, as overhunting took place on a large scale from around 1903.[13] In regard to this point, Korea took no action against the overhunting of sea lions and did not suppress such activities, suggesting that it did not recognize Takeshima as its own territory.

The ROK's second assertion rests on the issue of whether a State's declaration of its territorial intention is required to follow a defined format under international law. The ROK argues that, because no particular notification was made to the Korean government, Japan's declaration was invalid. Recent research by a Korean scholar of international law[14] also argues that this notification duty exists under international law.

However, this research is not necessarily adequate or accurate in the way it interprets the arbitral award in the Clipperton Island case[15] or its in interpretation of theory, for example. In addition to international judicial precedents, the theories advanced by the UK's L. F. L. Oppenheim and Ian Brownlie, France's Charles Rousseau and Paul Reuter, and Japan's Yokota Kisaburō and Taoka Ryōichi, among others, state that where title by occupation is concerned, a definite format such as notification is not required, and conversely the key point is "effectiveness." As Rousseau states, the goal of the rules in the Act of Berlin was also to make "fictitious" occupation into effective occupation.[16] Reuter points out that if the possession is effective it is inconceivable that it could remain a secret,[17] and as Taoka says, notification is only "desirable for the safety of legal communication."[18] Incidentally, the General Act of the Berlin Conference of 1885 considered the establishment of regional authority as well as notification to be obligatory requirements for title by occupation, but the Act of Berlin's validity was regionally limited to the African continent's coast. Moreover, the Treaty of Saint-Germain, which

---

[12] See Ueda, Toshio. 1952. "Ryōdo kizoku kankeishi (History related to Territorial Attribution)," in *Japanese Society of International Law. Heiwa jōyaku no sōgōteki kenkyū* (Comprehensive Studies of the Treaty of Peace with Japan). 1; and Kuribayashi, Tadao. "Ogasawara," in *Kokusaihō Jirei Kenkyūkai.* 1990. *Nihon no kokusaihō jirei kenkyū* (3): *Ryōdo* (Japanese Practices [Vol. 3]: Territory). Tokyo: Keio University Press.

[13] Yokokawa, Arata. "Takeshima," in *Kokusaihō Jirei Kenkyūkai.* 1990. *Nihon no kokusaihō jirei kenkyū* (3): *Ryōdo* (Japanese Practices [Vol. 3]: Territory). Tokyo: Keio University Press.

[14] See the chapter "Nihon no sensen shuchō to tsūkoku gimu (Japan's Assertion of Prior Occupation and Obligation of Notification)," in Kim Myung-ki. 1991. *Dokudo to kokusaihō* (Takeshima and International Law). This book was a privately published Japanese translation of the Korean edition: Kim Myung-ki. 1987. *Dokdo wa gukjebeop* (Takeshima and International Law). Seoul: Hwahaksa.

[15] Serita, Kentarō. 1999. *Shima no ryōyū to keizai suiiki no kyōkai kakutei* (Sovereignty over Islands and the Delimitation of Economic Zones). Tokyo: Yūshindo Kōbunsha; and Kim, op. cit. 149.

[16] Rousseau, Charles. 1970. *Droit International Public* (Public International Law), 5th edition. Paris: Dalloz, pp. 148–149.

[17] Reuter, Paul. 1973. *Droit International Public* (Public International Law), 4th edition. Paris: Presses Universitaires de France, p. 143.

[18] Taoka, Ryōichi. 1955. *Kokusaihō kōgi* (Lecture on International Law). Tokyo: Yūhikaku, p. 338.

annulled the Act of Berlin in 1919, confirmed the duty to maintain regional authority but excluded the duty of notification.

Furthermore, although the ROK states that Japan carried out the territorial incorporation measure "stealthily," in fact the notice was officially announced publicly, and moreover, it was also reported in newspapers.

Thirdly, the ROK says that even if it had known of the matter at the time, Japan had made the Korean government promise to appoint a foreigner recommended by the Government of Japan as a diplomatic advisor, and so Korea was in no position to raise objections with the Government of Japan. Certainly, based on the power relationship between the two countries at the time, there is room to be sympathetic to the ROK's position. The individual who was actually appointed, however, was the American Durham Stevens, and it is doubtful Korean diplomacy was influenced by him. In the verdict reached in the case concerning the Temple of Preah Vihear,[19] considering that the International Court of Justice (ICJ) placed emphasis on the fact that Thailand did not protest against France, then even if assuming the situation that existed was as the ROK claims, it would not make the incorporation measure invalid as the ROK asserts. What is important is that Korea was fully in a position to be able to exercise effective control over Takeshima prior to 1904, yet it did not exercise that authority.

Incidentally, to summarize Hori Kazuo's views on Japan's declaration and the Korean side's response, "The Korean side learned of Japan's territorial incorporation of Takeshima in March 1906, 1 year after the measure was taken."[20] 1906 was the year a delegation led by Shimane Prefecture administrative official Jinzai Yoshitarō undertook an inspection survey of Takeshima, stopping off at Ulleungdo on its way back. On March 28 the delegation visited Shim Heung-taek, the island's magistrate, and notified him of Takeshima's incorporation into Japanese territory. Surprised by this unexpected news, Shim promptly sent a report to his central government the following day and requested instructions. The central government's instructions are not clear in the form of an administrative document, but leading newspapers in Korea of the time picked up the story: "It is certain that many Korean people learned through this newspaper coverage of the Japanese move to incorporate Takeshima/ Dokdo into its territory and must have viewed it as an invasion of Korean territory." In summary:

> Korea's central government, the local Ulleungdo county magistrate, and civilians all considered Japanese incorporation of Takeshima/Dokdo as aggression [invasion] at that time. But, by that time, Japan had virtually started colonial rule over Korea, by establishing the Residency-General in Korea. That is why no further development could be made within the Korean government to cope with the problem of Takeshima/Dokdo. As the entire country was being robbed of its sovereignty and vanishing, it could not afford to pay attention to trifling matters such as a small rocky island. However, that the Korean people clearly raised

---

[19]Cambodia, which had become independent from France, became involved in a dispute with Thailand over the possession of the Preah Vihear Temple on the Cambodia-Thailand border, and the land in the temple's vicinity. Cambodia won the case.

[20]Hori, op. cit., pp. 118–120.

objection to the Japanese action of incorporating Takeshima/Dokdo is a decisively important fact worthy of historical evaluation.[21]

This point that historian Hori raises is very important in terms of understanding how Koreans today feel about Takeshima; it should be listened to empathetically. If one is to calmly analyze international judicial precedents on territorial disputes and view them with the eyes of a lawyer, however, it must be said that, when making a legal assessment, the significant points are that the Korean government did not lodge a protest (the administrative documents outlining the moves made by the central government at that time have not been disclosed), and above all else, that Korea had not been taking any effective measures with regard to Takeshima prior to its incorporation into Japanese territory.

Fourthly, the ROK argues that where Japan's activities following its territorial incorporation were concerned, the surveys and other activities undertaken by the Government of Japan were carried out as part of its activities for invading Korea, and consequently are not acceptable as ongoing activities of territorial control based on international law. As noted earlier, this argument does not constitute a reason unless it can be verified that Takeshima was Korean territory.

With regard to this point, Taijudō Kanae states that "As a result of using the harsh term 'invasion,' Korea appears to have indirectly acknowledged that Japan had effectively occupied Takeshima and acknowledged that Korea itself did not exercise effective control over Takeshima."[22] In other words, Japan's 1905 territorial incorporation can only be described as invalid by verifying that Takeshima had been effectively under Korean possession. Incidentally, in Korea's Imperial Decree No. 41 issued on October 27, 1900, which is titled "The renaming of Ulleungdo to Uldo and the promotion of the post of the Island Chief [dogma] to county magistrate [gunsu]," Article 2 states that "The county office shall be located at Taeha-dong, and as regards its districts, all of Ulleungdo as well as Jukdo and Seokdo shall be placed under the jurisdiction of [Uldo-gun (Uldo county)]," and consequently the ROK claims that Takeshima was already incorporated as Korean territory administratively.[23]

However, the Takeshima of today came to be called "Takeshima" after Japan incorporated it into its territory. It was never called "Takeshima" in Korea at that time. In Korea, today's Takeshima is called "Dokdo," and according to research by a Korean scholar,[24] the origins of the name are not necessarily clear—it is said to have been named to mean distant island, or alternatively it was called Dokdo to mean

---

[21] English adapted from Hori, Kazuo. "Japan's Incorporation of Takeshima into Its Territory in 1905," in *Korea Observer*, Autumn 1997, pp. 520–524. The article was slightly revised from the original in Hori, op. cit.

[22] Taijudō, op. cit.

[23] For example, *Mainichi Shimbun*, April 4, 1996. The English text here follows that found on page 24 in "Dokdo, Beautiful Island of Korea – Pamphlet" at https://dokdo.mofa.go.kr/eng/pds/pdf.jsp. Accessed on March 7, 2023.

[24] Taijudō, op. cit., p. 115.

rocky island because rocks are known as "dok" in the dialect of South Gyeongsang Province. However, "Ulleungdo residents probably gave it that name after Ulleungdo was opened up in 1881." Accordingly, it is not possible to identify which islands are the "Jukdo and Seokdo" referred to in this decree. There are suggestions that it may refer to "Jukdo" adjacent to the east coast of Ulleungdo, but in any event, the lack of clarity means it cannot be said to verify Korea's effective control.

Examining the Argument that in Addition to the Cairo Declaration, a Series of Postwar Measures Confirm Takeshima to be Korean Territory

The Cairo Declaration of November 27, 1943 states that "Japan will be expelled from all other territories which she has taken by violence and greed." Article 8 of the Potsdam Declaration of July 26, 1945 states that "The terms of the Cairo Declaration shall be carried out and Japanese sovereignty shall be limited to the islands of Honshu, Hokkaido, Kyushu, Shikoku and such minor islands as we determine."

Accordingly, the ROK argues that Japan assumed an obligation to fulfil the Cairo Declaration as a result of agreeing to and accepting the Potsdam Declaration, thus determining that Takeshima, which Japan supposedly took from Korea through violence and greed, would be separated from Japan. Additionally, Japan ceased exercising authority over Takeshima after Takeshima was included in the certain regions to be administratively separated from Japan along with Jeju Island and Ulleungdo that were designated as a result of SCAPIN No. 677, "Governmental and Administrative Separation of Certain Outlying Areas from Japan," dated January 29, 1946. In addition, regulations on the passage of mainstream commercial vessels and fishing vessels were eased immediately after Japan's defeat in the war, and the MacArthur Line was established on June 22, 1946, restricting the operating zones of fishing vessels. Takeshima was placed outside the operating zones of Japanese fishing vessels, however.[25] The ROK invokes these facts to assert that Takeshima was separated from Japan and became Korean territory.

The Japanese government refutes these assertions by the ROK as entirely without foundation.

To begin with, Paragraph 6 of SCAPIN No. 677 states: "Nothing in this directive shall be construed as an indication of Allied policy relating to the ultimate determination of the minor islands referred to in Article 8 of the Potsdam Declaration." As such, it was a provisional measure under the Occupation and did not exclude Takeshima from Japan's territory.

---

[25] For information on the MacArthur Line, see Kawakami, 1972, Chapter 1, Paragraph 1, "The MacArthur Line."

Paragraph 5 of SCAPIN 1033/1, which was the note that established the MacArthur Line, clearly states that the note is "not an expression of [A]llied policy relative to [the] ultimate determination of national jurisdiction, international boundaries or fishing rights in the area concerned or any other area."

Japan's territory following its defeat in the war was settled in the Treaty of Peace with Japan signed in San Francisco (San Francisco Peace Treaty), which entered into force on April 28, 1952. The treaty also determined the ownership of Takeshima: Article 2 (a) of that treaty determines that "Japan, recognizing the independence of Korea, renounces all right, title and claim to Korea, including the islands of Quelpart [Jeju Island], Port Hamilton [Geomundo] and Dagelet [Ulleungdo]." It excludes Takeshima from the regions renounced by Japan. The name Takeshima had been clearly stated in SCAPIN No. 677; the fact that it disappeared in the Treaty of Peace with Japan must be considered to be materially significant.[26] Assuming that there was the intention of recognizing Takeshima, a solitary island approximately 90 km away from Ulleungdo, as Korean territory, that fact would no doubt have had to have been clearly stated in the treaty in the same way that the treaty made clear mention of Port Hamilton (Geomundo), which is somewhat separated from the Korean mainland.

Examining the Japanese Side's Arguments

Japan argues that its view is that international laws were not applicable to it before the opening of the country, that at that time Japan actually believed that Takeshima was Japanese territory and treated it as such, and that unless another country disputed that, then it was sufficient to constitute possession. Japan cites the fact that Ōya Jinkichi and Murakawa Ichibei, merchants from Yonago, Hōki Province, received permission in 1618 for passage to Ulleungdo from the shogunate via Matsudaira Shintarō (Ikeda Mitsumasa), a feudal lord. Subsequently, they traveled to Ulleungdo to engage in fishing every year, customarily presenting the abalone they gathered there to the shogunate.

As explained earlier, after the Ōya and Murakawa families obtained a voyage license (the "Takeshima Voyage License" of 1618, for Ulleungdo was known as Takeshima at the time), they administered Takeshima (today's Ulleungdo) for 80 years with no interference. The two families also managed Matsushima (today's Takeshima), which is located on the way to Takeshima (today's Ulleungdo), and they were newly granted around 1661 a voyage license to Matsushima as well. Today's Takeshima first appears in Japanese documents in *Onshū shichō gōki* (Records of Observations in Oki Province) of 1667, written by Saitō Hōsen, an Izumo feudal retainer, where it is cited alongside Takeshima (today's Ulleungdo)

---

[26]For a similar view, see Taijudō, op. cit., p. 130; and Takano, Yūichi. 1962. *Nihon no ryōdo* (Japan's Territory). Tokyo: University of Tokyo Press, p. 69.

using the name Matsushima. There are descriptions in materials cited by Kawakami such as "Matsushima in the vicinity of Takeshima," "Matsushima in the neighborhood of Takeshima," and "a small island in the neighborhood of Takeshima," which very interestingly demonstrate the different usage values assigned to the two islands at the time. However, given the distances between the two islands, it is not possible to declare that today's Takeshima (Matsushima at that time) is a dependent domain of today's Ulleungdo (Takeshima at that time). In any event, compared to the Japanese side, which knew about the form of these two islands in considerable detail, the Korean side had almost no detailed knowledge of Takeshima (then-Matsushima) at that time (which is perhaps only natural, for although Korea supervised today's Ulleungdo by dispatching an inspector there once every 3 years after the aforementioned Takeshima Affair, there is no record that today's Takeshima was inspected).[27] Even after Japanese authorities prohibited the voyaging to today's Ulleungdo, they did not prohibit voyaging to Takeshima. Subsequent records, such as the *Takeshima zusetsu* illustrated work that was compiled in the Hōreki period (1751–1763), contain the expression "Okinokuni Matsushima," while the account *Chōsei Takeshima ki* of 1801 mentions "the westernmost part of Japan," indicating that, either way, Matsushima (today's Takeshima) is Japanese territory. The positional relationship of today's Takeshima is accurately recorded in maps, including Nagakubo Sekisui's *Nihon yochi rotei zenzu* (1773), said to be the first Japanese map to use a graticule.

Nevertheless, Japan's knowledge was extremely disordered as a result of contact with Europe and the United States from the latter part of the Edo period to the early years of the Meiji period. Successive French and British vessels that entered the Sea of Japan at the end of the eighteenth century "discovered" Ulleungdo, and because locational surveying was inaccurate, the island was referred to as two separate islands, Dagelet and Argonaute, and today's Takeshima was given the name "Liancourt." Even on maps, Ulleungdo was depicted as two islands—Takeshima and Matsushima—while today's Takeshima was omitted; the existence of Argonaute was denied; or, in contrast to the Edo period, Ulleungdo was called "Matsushima," and some maps showed only one island in the Sea of Japan.

Unconnected to this, Japanese private forays to Ulleungdo intensified and the government received requests to develop it. In connection with the "Argument for the Development of Matsushima," the warship *Amagi* carried out an on-site survey in July 1880 that established that the Matsushima referred to in the development requests was Ulleungdo, and thus all the development requests were rejected. Nevertheless, Japanese citizens continued to visit Ulleungdo for logging and fishing as usual, and when this was discovered by a Joseon inspector in 1881, the Joseon government promptly referred the incident to the Japanese government and requested that these voyages be banned. The Japanese government acknowledged Ulleungdo to be the territory of the Joseon Kingdom, and it took action in 1883 by

---

[27]Hori, op. cit., p. 101. For the wording in the records of the various documents, see Yokokawa, op. cit., pp. 166–167.

forcibly repatriating all of the 254 Japanese citizens residing on Ulleungdo.[28] No such action whatsoever was taken with today's Takeshima, however.

It appears there were ongoing voyages to Ulleungdo from regions around Japan even after the removal of Japanese citizens en masse in 1883. The administration of Takeshima was also moving ahead. To regulate the excessive hunting of Takeshima's sea lions, it was decided in January 1905 to name the islands Takeshima, incorporate Takeshima into Japanese territory, and put it under the jurisdiction of the Oki Islands branch office attached to the Shimane Prefectural Government. That April, Shimane Prefecture amended its fishing industry control regulations to introduce a licensing system for sea lion hunting at Takeshima, and approved applications by Nakai Yozaburō and other hunters. Sea lion hunting and the harvesting of abalone, seaweed, and other produce from the island ebbed and flowed but nonetheless continued until being suspended in 1941 as a result of the war; license holders continued to pay land usage fees into the national coffers every year. In this way, Japan's effective control over Takeshima continued peacefully until the end of World War II.

Approaches to the Takeshima Issue until a Final Decision is Reached

The process for resolving the dispute will differ depending on which side actually occupies the island while it is under dispute. Takeshima is in fact occupied by the ROK, which will undoubtedly maintain that occupation until a final resolution is arrived at. Consequently, from a legal perspective, in addition to proposing peaceful resolutions, Japan will have to take actions such as lodging effective protests proactively and repeatedly.

The Government of Japan sent a series of *notes verbales* of protest to the Government of the ROK between 1952 and 1960. They comprised five notes in 1953, when an incident occurred in which ROK authorities at Takeshima fired upon a Japan Coast Guard patrol boat; nine notes in 1954, when ROK authorities became permanently stationed on Takeshima; and one note each year in other years.[29] Beginning in 1971, Japan has published its response to Takeshima in its *Diplomatic Bluebook*. There is only one mention in the 1992 edition: "As for the territorial dispute over Takeshima between Japan and the ROK, it is clear on both historical and legal grounds that the islets are a part of Japanese territory. From this standpoint, Japan has made protests against the ROK whenever necessary."[30]

---

[28] Hori, op. cit., p. 107.

[29] For the content of the *note verbale* of December 26, 1961, see Yokokawa, op. cit., p. 177.

[30] "Section 1. Asia-Pacific; 2. The Korean Peninsula; 2-3. The Republic of Korea; (2) Relations with Japan" https://www.mofa.go.jp/policy/other/bluebook/1992/1992-3-1.htm#2.%20The%20Korean. Accessed on December 3, 2022.

In a *note verbale* dated September 12, 1954, Japan proposed to the ROK that the dispute be resolved through the ICJ, but on October 28 of the same year the ROK rejected this proposal in a memorandum, in which it asserted the following: "The proposal of the [Japanese] government [that the dispute be submitted to the International Court of Justice] is nothing but another false attempt disguised in the form of judicial procedures. Korea has the territorial rights *ab initio* over Dokdo and sees no reason why she should seek the verification of such rights before any international court."[31]

Following this, Japan and the ROK started negotiations in 1951 that concluded in June 1965 with the signing of the Treaty on Basic Relations between Japan and the Republic of Korea. No progress whatsoever was made on the Takeshima issue, however, and the matter simply ended with the Exchange of Notes concerning the Settlement of Disputes between Japan and the Republic of Korea.

Certainly, this exchange of notes stipulated that "Unless otherwise agreed on in advance, the two governments are to seek to settle disputes through diplomatic routes. In cases where disputes cannot be settled in this manner, the governments are to attempt to achieve resolution through conciliation as per the procedures agreed by the two countries." The ROK foreign minister told an ROK National Assembly special committee in August 1965 that "Japan's Minister for Foreign Affairs Shiina Etsusaburō and Prime Minister Satō Eisaku accepted that this did not include the Dokdo problem," an assertion that Foreign Minister Shiina and Prime Minister Sato both rejected in their responses at a special committee of the House of Representatives on the Treaty on Basic Relations between Japan and the ROK later that October. As these events show, discrepancies exist between Japan's and the ROK's interpretations of the exchange of notes concerning the settlement of disputes; this exchange of notes is not functioning in terms of resolving the Takeshima issue. It is unclear whether or not the Japanese side has thus far made any proposals aimed at reconciliation. Consequently, the current situation is as stated in the above-mentioned *Diplomatic Bluebook*, namely, that Japan is making protests against the ROK whenever necessary, based on Japan's standpoint.

Therefore, in light of the examination just made of both countries' arguments, it is difficult to detect a legitimate reason why Takeshima should belong to the ROK historically. However, could it not be said that Japan's protest was no more than a "paper protest" as described by Judge Levi Carneiro in his separate opinion in the Minquiers and Ecrehos case mentioned earlier, whereby "The British Government ... continued to exercise its sovereignty [while] the French Government was satisfied to make a 'paper' protest (*protester 'sur le papier'*). Could it not have done anything else? It could have, and it ought to have, unless I am mistaken,

---

[31] "Q&A on Dokdo: What was the Korean government's response to its Japanese counterpart's proposal in 1954 to refer the issue of Dokdo to the International Court of Justice (ICJ)?" https://dokdo.mofa.go.kr/m/eng/dokdo/faq14.jsp. Accessed on December 3, 2022.

proposed arbitration."[32] "The failure to have not made such a proposal deprives the claim of much of its force; it may even render it obsolete."[33] In other words, diplomatic protests are not enough to prevent origin of rights from being obtained based on unlawful occupation. Alongside the legal maxim *"ex injuria non oritur jus"* (unjust acts cannot create law), the normative force also has to be considered. That is because the legal maxim *"ex factis oritur jus,"* in which the existence of facts creates law, also exists.

Naturally, Japan must avoid resorting to the use of force at any cost. But if it maintains a passive attitude, then ultimately third parties are likely to accept that Japan tacitly consents to the ROK's territorial claim to Takeshima. If strictly limiting resolution standards to international law is not considered to be politically desirable, then undoubtedly it would make sense to take equitable factors into consideration.

Certainly, there are also emotive issues that arise from Japan's 36-year colonial rule over Korea, and it has to be acknowledged that difficult circumstances exist, including problems between the two countries that are yet to be resolved even today. Even now in the ROK, comments that reflect a detailed knowledge of Japan—not just pro-Japanese comments—seem to spark fierce attacks from the government and the media. Furthermore, the reality is that in school education, ROK students are taught that Takeshima is ROK territory, and there is even a widely-known song to that effect, yet in Japan not even law students know of Takeshima's existence.

In addition, the existence in Japan of ethnocentric history textbooks and the fact that its prime ministers offer prayers at Yasukuni Shrine, where Class A war criminals are enshrined, are also issues that serve to inflame the sentiments of the Korean people and ignite nationalism. On occasion, ROK politicians can also be seen using these sentiments of the Korean people for political ends. Taking these various circumstances into account, the most important thing for the two countries to do is to decide first and foremost to reform the current approach of one side making dogmatic decisions on the matter. Where resolving the Takeshima issue is concerned, rather than taking the course of blowing up Takeshima, as a certain high-level ROK official is reported to have suggested, the issue should pursue a constructive course.[34]

---

[32] International Court of Justice. 1953. *Reports of Judgments, Advisory Opinions and Orders*, p. 107.

[33] Ibid., 108.

[34] See the proposal by Serita in the April 4, 1996 edition of the *Mainichi Shimbun*, and Chapter 7.

Chapter 5
Territorial Sea and Exclusive Economic Zone

Classification of the Sea: Territorial Sea, High Seas, and Exclusive Economic Zone

The seas that cover the earth are classified as those that are the territory of a nation (territorial sea), those that no nation can lay claim to and that cannot be subject to sovereignty (high seas), and those that lie between the territorial sea and high seas, and that no nation can lay claim to but that can be subject to sovereign rights and jurisdiction (exclusive economic zone (EEZ)).

Territorial Sea

Territorial sea, in a broad sense, includes all the seas that are the territory of a State. This also includes ports, bays, and inland seas, which these days are referred to as internal waters (also used to refer to lakes, rivers, and other such waters within a territory). The baseline is the line that separates internal waters and territorial sea; normally this is the low-water line along the coast, as marked on the large-scale charts officially recognized by a coastal State (the spring tide is the lowest tide, but this is generally understood to be the coastline in nautical charts). However, if the coastline is deeply indented or cut into, or if there is a series of islands along the coast in its immediate vicinity, the straight baseline method may be used to join appropriate points along the coastline.

The sovereignty of a coastal State extends, beyond its land territory and internal waters, to an adjacent belt of the sea, described as the territorial sea, and to the air space over the territorial sea as well as its seabed and subsoil. The coastal State has the right to prohibit foreign nations from fishing in its territorial sea, to restrict coastal transport (also called coastal trade; at present, it generally refers to transport between the ports of that nation) to only its national citizens, and to exercise police

© Kreab K.K. 2023
K. Serita, *The Territory of Japan*, https://doi.org/10.1007/978-981-99-3013-5_5

authority in those seas. Furthermore, if any foreign ship violates the laws of the coastal State while in its territorial sea or internal waters, the nation may engage in continuous pursuit of that foreign ship and arrest it on the high seas (even if the ship itself is on the high seas, when the boats and crew on board are in the territorial sea, the ship on the high seas is also deemed as being in the territorial sea). This is referred to as the right of hot pursuit.[1]

This is how territorial sea is subject to the sovereignty of its coastal State, although, since ancient times, the seas have been used for international transport, and hence the sovereignty of a coastal State over its territorial sea is restricted for the purpose of international transport. As such, a system has been established to allow for innocent passage[2] in the seas that balances the interests of coastal States with the interest of international transport. Accordingly, a coastal State must allow the continuous and expeditious passage of foreign ships in its territorial sea, provided that such passage does not harm the nation's peace, good order, or security. Correspondingly, a foreign ship is naturally prohibited from engaging in military training exercises, as well as fishing, research, communication jamming, and other

---

[1] The right of hot pursuit: This action can only commence once a ship or aircraft of the coastal State has launched a visual or audio stop signal from a distance that the suspicious ship can confirm by sight or sound. The pursuit must continue without interruption, and it is to end if the suspicious ship is no longer in sight or if it enters the territorial sea of its flag State or that of another country. The pursuit is usually carried out by an ordinary ship that issues warnings and intimidations while pursuing the suspicious ship, but pursuit by aircraft may also be used. In that case, the aircraft must pursue the suspicious ship by taking active measures to alert the ship of its presence and pursuit, such as by buzzing, whereby the aircraft repeatedly swoops near the ship, etc. Relay pursuit may also be used, whereby the pursuit alternates between a high-speed ship and ordinary ship, etc.; however, the suspicious ship may not be ambushed during the pursuit. During a March 1999 incident, Japan Coast Guard patrol ships and Japan Maritime Self Defense Force escort ships engaged in pursuit of a suspicious ship detected in the territorial sea of the Noto Peninsula while firing warning shots, and an aircraft was also used in the pursuit. The pursuit ended, however, when the suspicious ship left Japan's Air Defense Identification.

The United Nations Convention on the Law of the Sea (UNCLOS) recognizes the right of hot pursuit of a coastal State, also in the event of the violation of the laws and regulations of the coastal State by a foreign ship in the EEZ and continental shelf—including the safety zone surrounding the equipment in the continental shelf—to which those laws and regulations apply. A suspicious ship, thought to be a remodeled fishing ship, was detected in the EEZ off the coast of Amami Ōshima Island in Kagoshima Prefecture in December 2001. It was pursued by a Japan Coast Guard patrol ship to 4,000 km offshore in China's EEZ of the East China Sea; after an exchange of fire between the suspicious ship and the patrol ship, the suspicious ship sank. See Serita, Kentarō. 2001. "Heiwa ya jinken ni somukanu kokusai kyōchō o (International Cooperation that Does not Infringe upon Peace or Human Rights)," *Kōbe Shimbun*, January 30.

[2] It has long been debated whether warships have the right of innocent passage, but the provisions of UNCLOS can be positively interpreted that they do. If any warship does not comply with the laws and regulations of the coastal State concerning passage through the territorial sea and disregards any request for compliance therewith which is made to it, the coastal State may require it to leave the territorial sea immediately. Refer to the Soviet Nuclear Submarine Incident on August 21, 1980, in which a Soviet nuclear submarine caught fire on the high seas to the east of Okinawa while forcefully passing through the territorial sea (strait) of Japan between Okinoerabu Island and Yoron Island, amid protests by the Japanese government.

such activities in that sea; additionally, it must also not engage in the loading and unloading of any commodity, currency, and person that violates the coastal State's current customs, fiscal, immigration, or sanitary laws and regulations. Furthermore, a coastal State may designate sea lanes and prescribe navigation and traffic separation schemes, and require foreign ships to use them, in order to prevent accidents from occurring in its territorial sea in the event of maritime traffic congestion.

The authority of a coastal State in its inland waters is more exclusive than that in its territorial sea; it is virtually the same as the authority it has in its territory. Accordingly, a coastal State is not subject to any duty similar to that of innocent passage. The Seto Naikai of Japan is an inland sea, and while foreign ships are able to pass through it, it does not mean they have the right of innocent passage.

In the 1958 Convention on Territorial Sea and the Contiguous Zone, innocent passage is permitted for a ship passing through a strait used for international navigation, in other words an international strait being a body of water that is a territorial sea; and unlike in other territorial seas, innocent passage was never suspended in those waters. However, when the breadth of the territorial sea is expanded from 3 to 12 nautical miles, the section of the high seas which foreign ships and aircraft can freely pass through under the existing freedom of the high seas then newly becomes part of the territorial sea of the coastal State bordering the strait. A foreign ship has the right of innocent passage in territorial seas; however, the air space over a territorial sea is territorial air space, and hence a foreign aircraft must obtain permission from a coastal State in order to fly in that air space. This substantially impedes the freedom of movement of not only private aircraft but also carrier-based aircraft, and it requires submarines to navigate on the sea surface. Furthermore, a coastal State can block the passage of non-innocent foreign ships, and this may also interrupt international transport in the seas if there is no other way for the ships to pass.

A regime of passage through straits used for international navigation was newly established in the 1982 United Nations Convention on the Law of the Sea (UNCLOS) to recognize the right of transit passage that is unimpeded by the ship or aircraft of any country. This regime also takes into consideration the military strategy of the United States and the Soviet Union, and it is separate from the regime of innocent passage in territorial seas, insofar as it endeavors to ensure the effective freedom of passage on the high seas. In Japan's case, when its territorial sea was expanded to 12 nautical miles, five of the approximately 70 straits included within this geographic scope (the Sōya Strait, Tsugaru Strait, the East and West Channels of the Tsushima Strait, and the Ōsumi Strait) were stipulated as "the designated areas" based on the fact that they were key points in international transport for connecting major seas, and because they were third State routes through which many foreign ships pass. Limiting the breadth of the territorial sea to 3 nautical miles in these areas opens up a path for securing freedom in international navigation and flight.

High Seas: International Waters

The high seas do not belong to any country (freedom from possession) and are open to the citizens of all nations to be used freely (freedom of use). The typical freedom referred to here is freedom of navigation and fishery on the high seas, and the traditional order of the ocean is precisely this freedom of the high seas. Oceanic States have so far been able to enjoy freedom of the high seas within a narrow 3 nautical mile territorial sea amid the vast ocean. This also applies to Japan. During the era of the 3 nautical mile territorial sea, each State aimed to monopolize its offshore fishery area for its own citizens and shut out foreign fishing vessels from it. This was known as the 12 nautical mile fishery zone.

The 1982 UNCLOS established the system of a 12 nautical mile territorial sea and 200 nautical mile EEZ under the jurisdiction of a coastal State. Subsequently, in the era of the 3 nautical mile territorial sea, there was an overwhelmingly large number of near-coastal voyages navigating the offshore high seas within a distance of 4 or 5 to 10 nautical miles and from which land and the outline of any islands are still visible. As such, ships could freely navigate the high seas then. These days, however, ships navigate these waters under the system of innocent passage. In the past, Japan freely caught most of its fish in waters within a 200 nautical mile range. Now, however, these waters have come under the jurisdiction of a coastal State. So, in that sense, the traditional high seas system has been laid to rest and replaced with a new high seas system that has internationalized the waters. Freedom of fishery is no longer, and other freedoms have been recognized to facilitate international transport, including freedom of navigation and overflight, and the laying of submarine cables and pipelines.

So, what about the seabed of the high seas? The exploitation of offshore petroleum fields was already being debated in the 1930s. In September 1945, immediately after World War II, the US government issued the Truman Proclamation on the Continental Shelf, which declared that the area under the high seas is contiguous with the US coast and the natural resources in its seabed belong to the United States and are under its jurisdiction and regulation. Many other nations followed suit, and countries in Latin America and the Caribbean quickly asserted their claim to the marine resources offshore from their coast. Another example of this is the Syngman Rhee Line (the Presidential Proclamation of Sovereignty over the Adjacent Seas on January 18, 1952) that dominated the fishery negotiations held between Japan and the Republic of Korea (ROK) from February 1952 to June 1965. This is how the continental shelf regime, which recognizes the sovereign rights of a coastal State for the exploration and exploitation of natural resources, was approved in the Convention on the Continental Shelf adopted at the United Nations Conference on the Law of the Sea I in 1958. The Convention is the basis for establishing the current EEZ, and it recognizes the sovereign rights of a coastal State over the seabed and area subjacent to it within 200 nautical miles from its coast; hence, this is of significance for continental shelves that extend beyond 200 nautical miles offshore.

The high seas do not belong to any nation; therefore, to maintain order of the high seas, any ship on the high seas is under the exclusive jurisdiction of the ship's nationality (the ship navigates on the high seas while raising the flag of its country of registration, which is referred to as the flag State). In other words, the laws and regulations of the flag State apply to that ship, and any incident involving it is deliberated at the courts and government ministries and agencies of the flag State. This is known as the flag State doctrine, which rules out interference from any other country, apart from the flag State, in the matters of a ship on the high seas. However, a warship of any nation has the right to board and inspect a ship suspected of engaging in piracy or slave trade.[3]

Expansion of the Territorial Sea Breadth from 3 to 12 Nautical Miles

In the 1960s, Japan, as a pelagic fishery nation looking for fish as far up as offshore the coastline of foreign countries, did not recognize the 12 nautical mile fishery zone system established in international law. In reality, however, in order to ensure trouble-free fishery in the offshore waters of partner countries, Japan concluded "similar circumstances but different objectives" or "shelving-style" fishery agreements with each nation. Then, in 1965, Japan concluded the Agreement on Fisheries Between Japan and the Republic of Korea (Japan-ROK Fishery Agreement), based on the 12 nautical mile fishery zone.[4] This was followed by Japan's adoption of the 1977 Territorial Waters Act stipulating a 12 nautical mile territorial sea, and the Fishery Zone Temporary Measures Act stipulating a 200 nautical mile fishery zone. Subsequently, Japan adopted the Act on the Exclusive Economic Zone and Continental Shelf in 1996.

The Declaration of Neutrality that Japan issued in the Franco-Prussian War on July 28, 1870 states Japan's territorial sea to be "not only within the harbor and inland sea, but also within a distance of 3 nautical miles from the open sea, in which the passage of warships and commercial ships of both countries is to be permitted."[5] Later, on August 29, the Grand Council of State Proclamation No. 546 revised "within a distance of three *ri*" to be "within a distance of three *ri* from any point of land, such that it could be reached by a cannonball." This was the start of prohibiting the combat of warring nations within 3 nautical miles from the coast. Notably, there

---

[3] UNCLOS, Article 110.

[4] On January 23, 1998, the Japanese government announced a Cabinet decision to end the Agreement and duly notified the ROK side of its decision. The Agreement was subsequently terminated one year later, and in this state of no agreement, both Japan and the ROK actively proceeded with negotiations that resulted in the signing of a new Japan-ROK Fishery Agreement on November 28, 1998, which came into effect on January 22, 1999. See Chapter 6.

[5] Grand Council of State Proclamation No. 492.

was no law in existence at that time which stipulated the territorial sea breadth to be 3 nautical miles. Japan's expansion of the territorial sea breadth to 12 nautical miles was triggered by the approach of foreign fishing vessels, particularly from the former Soviet Union, to the coastal waters of Japan.[6] Then-Minister of Agriculture, Forestry and Fisheries Abe Shintarō had already proposed to the Diet in 1975 the necessity of expanding the territorial sea breadth to 12 nautical miles. Subsequently, a Cabinet decision was made in January 1977 to formulate the Territorial Waters Act, and the decision to present the Territorial Waters Draft Bill to the Diet was made at the Cabinet meeting on March 29, 1977.

So why was it considered necessary to formulate a statute law such as the Territorial Waters Act? Prime Minister Miki Takeo, at a plenary session of the House of Representatives on January 26, 1976, indicated the government's policy of a 12 nautical mile territorial sea. Then, at a meeting of the House of Representatives Budget Committee on February 2, he stated his intent to resolve this issue within the year, irrespective of the conclusions reached at UN Conference on the Law of the Sea sessions, and to uphold the three non-nuclear principles of Japan. There, the government outlined its reasoning for requiring a legal basis to expand the territorial sea breadth:[7]

> At present, there is no international law that has set the territorial sea breadth at 12 nautical miles ... so it is only natural that Japan make a decision to this end. Incidentally, the existing territorial sea breadth of 3 nautical miles is an international law that is also recognized as law in Japan. Therefore, our new decision aims to change this standard territorial sea breadth of 3 nautical miles ... we deem that realizing such a change is not the sole domain of the executive branch.
>
> Expanding the territorial sea will also naturally widen the scope covered by Japan's domestic laws; however, the scope of application of these laws is, of course, to be stipulated in the laws themselves, provided there is no express mandate otherwise. Such an expansion of the territorial scope of application of Japan's domestic laws will directly impact the rights and duties of Japanese citizens and as such needs to be referred to the legislative branch. The positive acceptance of the need for a new law to this effect is therefore anticipated.

Put simply, if a 12 nautical mile territorial sea were established in international law, then there would perhaps be no need to formulate a law specifically for it. However, as it is a 3 nautical mile territorial sea that has been established in international law, it is necessary for a State to unilaterally establish a new law for setting its territorial sea breadth at 12 nautical miles. It should be noted that in 1976, there was already a permissible rule in international law for a 12 nautical mile territorial sea, and a State was able to unilaterally expand its territorial sea breadth to 12 nautical miles. Furthermore, although in international law it is acceptable for the executive branch of a State to unilaterally declare the expansion of its territorial sea breadth, widening the application scope of domestic law will impact the rights and duties of its national citizens. As such, it is necessary to formulate a new law. In other words, the existence of a 3 nautical mile territorial sea that is established in international law

---

[6]Mizukami, Chiyuki. 1995. *Nihon to kaiyōhō* (Japan and UNCLOS). Tokyo: Yūshindō Kōbunsha.

[7]House of Representatives Budget Committee, No. 9, February 6, 1976, 10.

requires no further action by a State, as all countries naturally have a 3 nautical mile territorial sea breadth. Conversely, the fact that a 12 nautical mile territorial sea has not been established in international law requires further action by a State in order to establish a 12 nautical mile territorial sea breadth; moreover, a State cannot be denied the right to freely determine its territorial sea breadth up to a maximum of 12 nautical miles. To reiterate, there is a permissible rule in international law for a 12 nautical mile territorial sea. This customary international law is codified in the 1982 UNCLOS as, "Every State has the right to establish the breadth of its territorial sea up to a limit not exceeding 12 nautical miles . . ."

The 1977 Territorial Waters Act established a 12 nautical mile territorial sea breadth; however, the five designated waters of the Sōya Strait, Tsugaru Strait, the East and West Channels of the Tsushima Strait, and the Ōsumi Strait have a territorial sea with a limit of 3 nautical miles. The 12 nautical mile fishery zone stipulated in the 1965 Japan-ROK Fishery Agreement was only relevant to Japan in terms of these designated areas; the ROK did not object otherwise. Incidentally, in 1977, the global trend towards setting a zone of 200 nautical miles also saw Japan enacting the Fishery Zone Temporary Measures Act, which in one sweep stipulated a 200 nautical mile fishery zone that so far had not been recognized as a system in international law. The Act also set the fishery zone to be the whole of the Pacific Ocean and only east of the Sea of Japan from a longitude of 135° east. Furthermore, the Act only applied to the former Soviet Union and its fishing vessels.[8]

Japan ratified UNCLOS in 1996, while also adopting the straight baseline method for its territorial sea and establishing its own EEZ. With these actions, Japan entered the era of a new maritime order.

As for bilateral treaties, in addition to the Japan-ROK Fishery Agreement, there is the Convention on the Continental Shelf, and also the Japan-China Fishery Agreement.[9] In regard to general issues between Japan and the ROK and China, as has already been briefly mentioned, these concern the territories of Takeshima and the Senkaku Islands.

There is also the issue of the status of the 200 nautical mile fishery zone established off the far south Okinotorishima Island.

Unless all of these issues are fully understood and coordinated by all sides, it is difficult to declare the beginning of a new maritime order. Therefore, prior to discussing EEZs, it is perhaps useful to review the background of establishing the EEZ regimes in the international law of the sea, and to clarify the implication of the issues in this area of law.

Furthermore, new fishery agreements and treaties have been concluded between Japan, and the ROK, and China. According to precedent and the prevailing view,

---

[8] For further details see the section on the 1977 Act on Temporary Measures Concerning Fishery Waters in this chapter.

[9] A new Agreement was signed on November 11, 1997, which the Japanese Diet approved in April 1998. However, delays with procedures in China resulted in the Agreement only coming into effect on June 1, 2000. See Chapter 6.

under the duty to observe international law as stipulated in Article 98 (2) of the Japanese Constitution, legal force follows the order of the Constitution, then treaties, and then laws, which would lead to the partial suspension of the binding force of domestic laws such as those on EEZs. In regard to issues in international law, consistency with the following Article 311 (3) of UNCLOS would become a moot point:

> *Two or more States Parties may conclude agreements modifying or suspending the operation of provisions of this Convention, applicable solely to the relations between them, provided that such agreements do not relate to a provision derogation from which is incompatible with the effective execution of the object and purpose of this Convention, and provided further that such agreements shall not affect the application of the basic principles embodied herein, and that the provisions of such agreements do not affect the enjoyment by other States Parties of their rights or the performance of their obligations under this Convention.*

The 200 Nautical Mile Fishery Zone and 1977 Fishery Zone Temporary Measures Act

The International Nature of the Delimitation of Maritime Areas

On December 18, 1951, the International Court of Justice (ICJ) ruled on a dispute between the United Kingdom and Norway, known as the Fisheries Case, concerning the method Norway used to draw a baseline to delimit the fishery zone for its fishermen. The following is an excerpt from the ruling:

> *The delimitation of sea areas has always an international aspect; it cannot be dependent merely upon the will of the coastal State as expressed in its municipal law. Although it is true that the act of delineation is necessarily a unilateral act, because only the coastal State is competent to undertake it, the validity of the delineation with regard to other States depends upon international law.*[10]

Incidentally, the Territorial Waters Act and the Fishery Zone Temporary Measures Act, Japan's two maritime laws that were promulgated on May 2, 1977 and took effect on July 1, were valid until the revision, abolition, and formulation of domestic laws related to UNCLOS of June 1996; each had established the territorial sea and fishery zone of Japan to be from the baseline to a breadth of 12 nautical miles and 200 nautical miles, respectively. The abovementioned domestic legislation stipulated the sovereignty and fishery jurisdiction of Japan, and also had an evident effect on international law. How legislation is evaluated in light of international law depends on the interpretation of relevant international law currently in force. This section therefore first examines the trends of postwar international law of the sea, while considering the issues of territorial sea, continental shelves, and fishery zones.

---

[10]International Court of Justice. 1951. *Reports of Judgments, Advisory Opinions and Orders*, p. 132.

It will then look at what constitutes unilateral measures under international law and their significance, and finally, review the two now-lapsed maritime laws of 1977.

Trends in the Law of the Sea Leading Up to the Emergence of a 200 Nautical Mile Fishery Zone

1. Overview

It was the Truman Proclamation that spurred other countries to assert their maritime claims after World War II, and subsequently to successively issue their respective statements on continental shelves that highlighted the dependence of their coastal citizens on marine resources or stressed the urgency of protecting their fishery resources from destructive exploitation by foreign pelagic fisheries. Moreover, once it became evident that calls for placing the seabed resources of continental shelves under the rule of coastal States would likely be gradually integrated into international law as new rules and without any opposition from major marine nations, the claims of coastal States moved toward new and strong demands expanding their jurisdiction in fisheries.

The International Law Commission (ILC), which organized the UN Conference on the Law of the Sea I, first deliberated the issue of continental shelves and fishery on the high seas. However, faced with the reality of the postwar claims of coastal States on continental shelves and fishery being merely one aspect of a move towards expanding their territorial sea, the issue was addressed in its entirety. Consequently, the ILC draft of the law of the sea included rules on a general system for territorial seas and high seas. Regrettably, despite 8 years of studies on the matter, the ILC left several issues unresolved, the most important of which, it goes without saying, was the issue of the territorial sea breadth. The draft of the law of the sea recognized that each country had varying customary practices in regard to its territorial sea breadth, while also clarifying that expanding the territorial sea to beyond 12 nautical miles was not permitted in international law.

The UN Conference on the Law of the Sea I and II, held in 1958 and 1960, respectively, failed to produce a consensus on the issue of territorial sea breadth, which can be regarded as the core of the maritime system. Despite this, the conferences achieved landmark results in the history of international law with the formation of four key conventions covering all areas of the law of the sea. As for the issue of the territorial sea breadth, given the fact that the interests of fisheries and strategic interests were closely entwined, it is well known that several compromises were proposed including a combined territorial sea and fishery zone within 12 nautical miles of the coast. The United States and Canada put forth an amended proposal at the 1960 Conference; it was approved by 54 States and opposed by 28, with 5 States abstaining from voting. Although this proposal fell just short of the majority vote required, the fact that it was approved in such large numbers indicated that the institutionalization of the 12 nautical mile fishery zone contained in the proposal had considerable support. The codification of the continental shelf regime in the 1958 convention therefore turned the interest of other nations toward fishery zones.

2. Legal nature of the 12 nautical mile fishery zone

The following is an excerpt from the ICJ's judgment in the Fisheries Jurisdiction Case, which the United Kingdom filed against Iceland in July 1972 in regard to a dispute over the expansion of an exclusive fishery jurisdiction to 50 nautical miles.

Legislation developed from State practices based on the discussions and near-agreements at UN Conference on the Law of the Sea II, namely "Two concepts have crystallized as customary law in recent years ... The first is the concept of the fishery zone, the area in which a State may claim exclusive fishery jurisdiction independently of its territorial sea; the extension of that fishery zone up to a 12-mile limit from the baselines appears now to be generally accepted. The second is the concept of preferential rights of fishing."[11] This fishery zone was specified by the Court as a *"tertium genus* between the territorial sea and the high seas."

Incidentally, the ICJ gave no grounds for its judgment in the July 1974 case, most likely because it regarded such grounds as irrelevant considering the concepts were firmly established as customary law. However, here several customary practices of States shall be described in order to understand the facts supporting this judgment.

The countries that unilaterally established a 12 nautical mile fishery zone from 1960 onwards are listed below. It should be noted that at the time Japan's two laws of the sea were enacted in 1977, about half of these countries established a 12 or 200 nautical mile territorial sea. The following countries successively established a 12 nautical mile fishery zone: Albania (1960); Norway, Senegal (1961); Mauritania, Morocco, Tunisia (1962); Uruguay, South Africa, Yemen (1964); Denmark, New Zealand (1965); Pakistan, Portugal, the United States, Brazil, Mexico (1966); Spain, France, Australia, Dominican Republic, Côte d'Ivoire, Monaco (1967); Nauru, Sweden (1968); Poland (1970); and Malta (1971).

On May 18, 1966, 5 months prior to the establishment of the United States' own 12 nautical mile fishery zone, the US State Department expressed its view that, in light of the progression of international practices from 1960 onwards, establishing a 12 nautical mile fishery zone was not in violation of international law. This view was not solely based on such unilateral domestic legislation; rather, it had taken into consideration international practices including international treaties such as the Great Britain-Norway Fishery Agreement of November 17, 1960, the Soviet Union-Norway Fishery Agreement of 1961, the European Fisheries Convention of March 9, 1964, and the agreement concluded with

---

[11] International Court of Justice. 1974. *Reports of Judgments, Advisory Opinions and Orders*, p. 23.

Norway and exchange of notes between the UK, Poland, and the Soviet Union to facilitate the approval of a British 12 nautical mile fishery zone that became effective on September 30, 1964.

Against this backdrop Japan negotiated with other countries and concluded the following agreements: the Japan-US Fisheries Agreement on May 9, 1967; the Japan-New Zealand Fisheries Agreement on July 12, 1967; the Japan-Mexico Fisheries Treaty on March 7, 1968; and the Japan-Australia Fisheries Agreement on November 17, 1968. However, each of these agreements carefully avoided approving the 12 nautical mile fishery zone of the partner country (a shelving style of agreement). The only exception to this was the Japan-ROK Fisheries Agreement concluded on June 22, 1965. Japan took a different position to the US and did not recognize a 12 nautical mile fishery zone as an established system in international law.

Incidentally, the territorial sea and fishery zone are interconnected in a rather interesting way. The establishment of a 12 nautical mile fishery zone peaked in 1966 and 1967, while the setting of a 12 nautical mile territorial sea became prevalent after that, namely in 1966 with three countries, 1967 with eight countries, 1968 with three countries, 1969 with eight countries, and 1970 with three countries; and as previously mentioned, some countries switched over from a fishery zone to a territorial sea. Hence, the regulations on territorial sea in international law in the 1970s included a permissible rule that allowed each country to unilaterally establish a fishery zone from 3 to 12 nautical miles.

In light of this, even the unilateral establishment of a 12 nautical mile fishery zone, which was initially considered to be illegal, was on an individual level an infringement of the rights and interests of other nations while also seemingly in violation of the high seas regime. However, it came to constitute a new customary law as a result of being practiced widely and being given tacit approval by other states.

The 12 nautical mile fishery zone system has countervailing power against all nations, and it is a zone of a coastal State in which it can exercise its jurisdiction for the purpose of its fisheries. While there are examples of interpreting this system to permit foreign fisheries inside this zone for an indefinite or fixed period (phase out style), nevertheless these foreign fisheries were still under the jurisdiction of the coastal State.[12]

3. Emergence of a 200 nautical mile fishery zone

The claims of coastal States on marine resources were not, however, confined to within a 12 nautical mile fishery zone. In 1972, Kenya proposed the concept of an economic zone, and various Caribbean countries put forth the Patrimonial Sea Concept; these were some of the assertions that emerged at the time for jurisdiction over resources in a 200 nautical mile zone. The concept of an economic zone was first advocated as a single draft and revised draft at UN Conference on the

---

[12] Oda, Shigeru. 1971. *Umi no shigen to kokusaihō* (Ocean Resources and International Law) I. Tokyo: Yūhikaku.

Law of the Sea III, which commenced its substantive session in 1974. The following is a list of countries that unilaterally established a 200 nautical mile zone before May 1977, when Japan's two maritime laws were promulgated.

A total of 28 countries: Bangladesh in 1974 (economic zone; EZ); Costa Rica, Iceland in 1975 (fishery zone; FZ); Senegal (FZ), Benin (formerly the Republic of Dahomey, territorial sea), Mexico, Guatemala, Mozambique, Pakistan, Liberia, Angola (all EZ) in 1976; and by May 1997, seven countries in the European Community (EC) (the UK, France, West Germany, the Netherlands, Belgium, Denmark, Ireland: FZ); Norway (FZ); Canada (FZ); India, Sri Lanka, Cuba (all EZ); the US, the Soviet Union, Burma, Japan (all FZ); and Vietnam (EZ). Adding to this the ten countries with a 200 nautical mile territorial sea before the economic zone concept emerged (Chile, Peru, El Salvador, Ecuador, Panama, Argentina, Uruguay, Brazil, Sierra Leone, Somalia), as well as Nicaragua (which had a 200 nautical mile fishery zone), meant that 39 countries actually had, in some way, unilaterally established a 200 nautical mile zone at the time Japan's two maritime laws were enacted in 1977.

In a word, this trend can be summarized as the unilateral measures exemplified by the establishment of a 200 nautical mile zone by the EC, the US, the Soviet Union, and Japan. While these measures dominated the discussions at UN Conference on the Law of the Sea III, they were fundamentally different to the economic zone concept. The following is an examination of why this was the case.

The first crucial point to note here is that conserving and securing marine resources was becoming a matter of urgency. At the first substantive session of UN Conference on the Law of the Sea III in 1974, just 1 month after the judgment on the Iceland Fisheries Jurisdiction Case, a 200 nautical mile economic zone received clear and overwhelming majority support at the close of the Caracas session. A single informal negotiation draft was subsequently distributed at the Geneva session in 1975, and after 8 weeks of discussions at the New York spring session in 1976, relevant sections of the single draft were kept as is.

According to the second section of the revised single draft at the New York spring session in 1976, the rights exercised by a coastal State in an economic zone were: (1) sovereign rights over the exploration, exploitation, conservation, and management of all living and non-living resources in the seabed, soil, and waters of the zone, (2) exclusive jurisdiction over the installation and usage of artificial islands, equipment, and structures, (3) exclusive jurisdiction over the economic exploitation and exploration of the zone, along with other activities and scientific research, and (4) jurisdiction over the preservation of the marine environment. Hence, the legal standing of an economic zone was stipulated as a third zone that is different from the high seas and territorial sea.[13] To summarize this simply and somewhat boldly, this was an assertion of the jurisdiction of coastal States over marine and mining resources, and their right to carry out

---

[13] Articles 44 and 75.

scientific research and preserve the marine environment (the other side of the coin being, the right to regulate navigation).

When broken down in this way, in terms of positive law, the jurisdiction over mining resources noted in the second section means that each nation can actually access these resources based on the current international law of the continental shelf regime. Canada established an antipollution zone in 1970, with the US moving towards similar legislation without any apparent sense of urgency to make it a domestic law. That said, the general postwar trend was to settle the issues concerning continental shelves, and so the remaining issue to be addressed was the coastal States' assertion of their jurisdiction over fishery resources. Such was the urgency of this fishery issue that it could not wait for the conclusions reached at the UN Conference on the Law of the Sea sessions, which is why from 1973 to 1974 major States took legislative action. In the US, a bill was submitted to the two chambers of Congress proposing an expansion of the country's fishery jurisdiction to beyond 12 nautical miles; it was an interim measure until a consensus was reached on an international agreement. Supreme Soviet law and Japanese legislation followed suit with provisional measures taken as a unilateral act under international law.

Incidentally, each nation's legislation limited the rights that could be exercised within a 200 nautical mile zone as exclusive fishery jurisdiction over all living creatures in the zone[14] and jurisdiction over fisheries and the like.[15] It did not include jurisdiction over the exploitation of mining resources in continental shelves, scientific research, or the prevention of marine pollution. Even if such areas were included, they would be handled as secondary to other rights. Hence, this could be interpreted as enabling the expansion of the 12 nautical mile fishery zone established in customary law to 200 nautical miles.

However, the problem remained of whether a State could unilaterally act to expand its 12 nautical mile fishery zone to 200 nautical miles, or establish a new 200 nautical mile fishery zone; in other words, was the establishment of a 200 nautical mile fishery zone regarded as customary law? If a 200 nautical mile fishery zone was deemed a system in customary law, then each nation had the right to unilaterally establish a 200 nautical mile fishery zone.

1977 Act on Temporary Measures Concerning Fishery Waters

On April 13, 1976, US President Gerald Ford signed the Fishery Conservation and Management Act of 1976, Public Law 94-265. The US then began to exercise its fishery regulatory authority in its 200 nautical mile zone on March 1, 1977. The US Coast Guard carried out an on-board inspection on April 9 of a Soviet trawler

---

[14] 1976 US Law Article 102 (1).

[15] Act on Temporary Measures Concerning Fishery Waters, Article 1.

suspected of fishing more than the regulated quantity and detained the ship. It has been pointed out that this law has several problematic areas, and the unilateral expansion of a fishery zone by a coastal State (as per in this law) is noted as being a violation of international law. Moreover, this point was also discussed in the US Congress, citing the July 1974 ICJ judgment on the Iceland Fisheries Jurisdiction Case.

At the time of Japan's enactment of the 1977 Act on Temporary Measures Concerning Fishery Waters, as previously mentioned, there were already 28 countries (39 when including the countries with a 200 nautical mile territorial sea) that had unilaterally set a 200 nautical mile zone, including the US, the Soviet Union, Japan, and the EC (the nations that stood to gain the most from doing so). Moreover, the conclusion of agreements such as those between the US and the Soviet Union, the US and Japan, and Japan and the Soviet Union, meant that upon the enactment of Japan's two laws of the sea of 1977 which recognized a 200 nautical mile zone, the 200 nautical mile fishery zone had become a system in customary law.

However, at the time the US had established its 200 Nautical Mile Fishery Conservation and Management Act, there were only a few nations with 200 nautical mile zones, and so it was difficult to consider that such a system had become customary law. Hence, by making a 200 nautical mile zone a domestic law, the US can be regarded as violating customary law, namely, the freedom of the seas principle noted in Article 2 of the Convention on the High Seas in international law. The US held countervailing power against other nations it had concluded bilateral treaties with and that approved its 200 nautical mile zone, or that gave their tacit consent by not protesting it. In international law, as long as a State does not violate *jus cogens* (the freedom of seas principle is not *jus cogens*), all types of treaties, even those that violate general international law, can be concluded and are hence valid.[16] Therefore, the aforesaid comments on the US 200 nautical mile zone legislation can be applied similarly to the Soviet Union 200 nautical mile zone.

That being the case, how does this apply to Japan's two laws, the Territorial Waters Act and the Fishery Zone Temporary Measures Act (the Fishery Zone Act)? As for the former, although issues can arise with the interpretation and setting of baselines, such as in Sagami Bay and the West Channel of the Tsushima Strait, these are not notable problems in international law. Therefore, the discussion from hereon

---

[16] See the Vienna Convention on the Law of Treaties, Article 53.

will focus on the latter.[17, 18] The main fishery nations in the waters surrounding Japan are the Soviet Union (at the time; now Russia), the ROK, and China. These are all concerned nations of the past and present.

In short, this legislation, when read together with the draft Cabinet Order, can be regarded as having been only applicable to the Soviet Union and its citizens, which can also be gleaned from the fact that it emerged as a part of negotiations between Japan and the Soviet Union.

Incidentally, the legal system of a fishery zone is, as has already been discussed, *opposable à tous* towards all other nations as an area under the jurisdiction of a coastal State. The US Fishery Conservation and Management Act was in violation of international law at the time of its establishment and had no general countervailing power; despite this, the US insisted on such a power *erga omnes* (towards all other nations). So, if a 200 nautical mile zone had been confirmed as becoming customary law in 1977, this fishery zone would also have general countervailing power towards all other nations.

---

[17] Structure of the Fishery Zone Act: Article 3(3) of the Act stipulates Japan's fishery zone to be the waters from the baseline to a breadth of 200 nautical miles; however, Cabinet Order-designated waters are not a fishery zone. This means that Japan's fishery zone is wholly determined by a Cabinet Order, under a system in which it may suddenly change in size one day as the government decrees. The waters designated by a draft Cabinet Order and that do not constitute Japan's fishery zone are the area westward off the coast of Fukui Prefecture on the Sea of Japan side and westward off the coast of Kagoshima Prefecture on the Pacific Ocean side (*Yomiuri Shimbun*, April 20, 1977 edition), or the western section of the Sea of Japan, the Eastern Sea, the Yellow Sea, and part of the south-western section of the Pacific Ocean contiguous to the Eastern Sea side (*Mainichi Shimbun*, April 27, 1977 edition). Also, the areas included in the aforementioned fishery zone within the designated waters noted in Clause 2 of the Territorial Waters Act supplementary provisions are only the Sōya Strait and Tsugaru Strait; these designated waters form the 12 nautical mile exclusive fishery zone (EFZ) that foreign fisheries are prohibited from entering (Article 5(1)). Foreign fisheries are able to operate in the other designated waters within the 12 nautical mile area. However, Article 1 of the 1965 Japan-ROK Fishery Agreement stipulates these waters to also be an EFZ.

It should be noted that the regulations on foreign fishery in the fishery zone (Articles 5 to 11) do not apply to Koreans or Chinese (Article 14 and the draft Cabinet Order). Moreover, neither do they apply to the waters of the four Northern Islands (*Asahi Shimbun*, May 25, 1977 edition).

[18] Legality of the Fishery Zone Act: It is difficult to simply brand this unilateral measure by Japan as a violation of international law, as is the case with the United States and the Soviet Union. This is mainly because the two superpowers established a 200 nautical mile zone, while Japan did not recognize this zone and alleged the illegality of the 1976 US law right up until the first and second rounds of negotiations with the United States in August and November 1976, respectively.

However, Japan appeared to have accepted the US claims at the third round of negotiations in December 1976 in Washington, D.C. Subsequently, it signed an interim agreement on February 10, 1977 (an exchange of notes, Ministry of Foreign Affairs Notification No. 50, Official Gazette of March 3, 1977, No. 15042), which was followed by the provisional signing of a long-term agreement on March 18. Then, at the House of Representatives Foreign Affairs Committee on April 27, 1977, Director-General Nakajima of the Treaties Bureau of the Ministry of Foreign Affairs commented, "A new norm in international law is gradually emerging; it is now possible to set not a 12 nautical mile but a 200 nautical mile fishery zone, as has become the common international practice."

Furthermore, as Japan's Fishery Zone Act was only applicable to the then Soviet Union and its citizens by Cabinet Order (mandated by national law), it seems to have been designed to only have countervailing power towards the Soviet Union. If, however, the unilateral establishment of a 200 nautical mile zone was in violation of international law at the time of its enactment in Japan as well, then Japan would have also established an illegal 200 nautical mile zone just as the Soviet Union had done, by a Cabinet Order that was only applicable to the Soviet Union.

Hence, in this view, Japan carried out a unilateral measure generally recognized as a reprisal in international law. Of course, the Cabinet Order mandate also took into consideration the interests of Japan's fisheries in the waters surrounding the ROK and China, as well as the territorial issue of the attribution of Takeshima and the Senkaku Islands. However, when the Cabinet Order of Article 14 in the Fishery Zone Act is included, Japan's unilateral measure appears to be an act of self-help in the nature of reprisals in international law. In that sense, Japan's unilateral establishment of a 200 nautical mile zone ensures legality towards the Soviet Union, as well as countervailing power. This is no more than a trump card for use in diplomatic negotiations, however; it is not an assertion of a fishery zone in the general sense. It therefore loses all significance once diplomatic negotiations are concluded.

Meanwhile, the Cabinet Order of Article 3(3) in the Fishery Zone Act states that if waters are not designated, then Japan's fishery zone will be the waters (including the exclusive fishery zone in the designated zone) that are 200 nautical miles (or, according to the situation, up to the median line or agreed upon line) from the territorial sea baseline away from the coast. This fishery zone asserts an *erga omnes* countervailing power, which is congruent with the legal principles of the fishery zone system in customary law.

This analysis of Japan's Fishery Zone Act has revealed its two-tiered structure of a reprisal-like nature entwined with an assertion of a general fishery zone system, through its linkage with Cabinet Orders. Furthermore, the reprisal-like nature of the Act came to the forefront during fishery negotiations between Japan and the Soviet Union. However, it was already predicted that the general fishery zone assertion would surface in light of the foreseen issues of ROK fishing vessels operating in Japanese waters and Soviet Union fishing vessels operating in a Cabinet Order-designated zone in the not too distant future. From that perspective, Japan's Fishery Zone Act had a different legal nature due to its linkage with Cabinet Orders. Moreover, as of June 6, 1977, when I had finished the special feature article on the law of the sea that *Hōritsu no Hiroba*, a general law journal, asked me to contribute and the June Cabinet Order had not yet been issued, the impression I was left with was that the Act was a quick-fix without any principles, although it was difficult to determine.

Regarding the legality of a 200 nautical mile fishery zone, the US Fishery Conservation and Management Act was the trigger for a succession of unilateral measures to establish such a zone, which Japan also recognized for the US in the Japan-US Fishery Agreement on March 18 and for the Soviet Union in the Japan-Soviet Union Fishery Provisional Agreement on May 24. Such actions were taken between superpowers, with each nation taking what it called interim measures within its domestic law. Underlying this was the general consensus reached on economic zones in the legal sense at UN Conference on the Law of the Sea III. Furthermore, the 200 nautical mile fishery zone also had the subjective element of being established in international customary law, namely *opinio juris sive necessitatis* (an opinion of law or necessity), as well as the objective element of a rapid succession of individual practices that at first were in violation of the freedom of the high seas. Despite this, a new customary law had been established. This fishery zone was positioned as a third category (*tertium genus*) between the high seas and territorial sea.

Need for Review from the Perspective of Securing and Distributing Protein Resources of the World

If the 200 nautical mile fishery zone were to become a system in customary law as a zone under the jurisdiction of a coastal State, then ensuring Japan's fishery in the 200 nautical mile zone of countries such as Australia, New Zealand, the ROK, and China would thus be a political issue centering on diplomatic negotiations.

A general issue warranting additional discussion is the fishery resources that belong to a coastal State once a 200 nautical mile zone is established. It is preferable to review this from the perspective of securing and distributing protein resources of the world, rather than only taking the view that these are simply resources of a coastal State.

EEZ Enclosing Marine Resources

United Nations Conferences on the Law of the Sea

As previously mentioned, it was the Truman Proclamation issued by the US immediately after World War II that triggered further claims from a number of countries, including countries in Latin America and the Caribbean, asserting their rights to the marine resources offshore from their coast and declaring a 200 nautical mile territorial sea. Another example of this is the Syngman Rhee Line that was the main issue at the fishery negotiations held between Japan and the ROK from 1952 to 1965.[19] As a result, the traditional maritime order—namely a narrow territorial sea and vast high seas, based on the freedom of the high seas—was in disarray. Hence, the UN held the UN Conference on the Law of the Sea I in 1958, at which the

---

[19] Oda, Shigeru. 1972. *Kaiyōhō no genryū o saguru* (Exploring the Origins of UNCLOS). Tokyo: Japan Fisheries Association; and Kawakami, Kenzō. 1972. *Sengo no kokusai gyogyō seido* (The Postwar International Fisheries System). Tokyo: Japan Fisheries Association.

following four conventions of the law of the sea were adopted: Convention on the Territorial Sea and Contiguous Zone, Convention on the High Seas, Convention on Fishing and Conservation of Living Resources of the High Seas, and Convention on the Continental Shelf. The first two Conventions were a codification of customary law, while the latter two were new international legislation put in place to address new circumstances that had arisen.

Agreement on the breadth of the territorial sea could not be reached, however, owing to a clash of fishery interests as well as differences between the United States and the Soviet Union stemming from their military strategies; and so, the UN Conference on the Law of the Sea II in 1960 also ended without a successful outcome. During this period, the 12 nautical mile fishery zone system was being established, as described earlier in this chapter.

As space exploration progressed in the 1960s, the interest of developed nations naturally turned toward marine exploration. Remarkable advancements in science and technology also meant the seabed was in danger of being partitioned among developed nations, as pointed out by the small Mediterranean country of Malta. At the 1967 United Nations General Assembly (UNGA), Malta proposed the peaceful use of the seabed and ocean floor, as well as their resources, as a "common heritage of mankind," while also taking into consideration the interests of developing nations. Then, the Committee on the Peaceful Uses of the Seabed and Ocean Floor was set up the following year, and issues concerning the exploration and exploitation of these areas in the sea were discussed at the UN. In 1969, Malta proposed a conference to review the Convention on the Continental Shelf, although the US, the Soviet Union, Western European nations, and Japan were not so keen on the proposal. Developing countries in Asia, Africa, and Latin America, many of which gained independence in the 1960s, called for a comprehensive revision of the law of the sea to take into account the interests of developing nations, considering that the 1958 Conventions are codification of the traditional law of the sea, which favors developed nations. As a result, a resolution was passed at the 25th UNGA in 1970 to hold UN Conference on the Law of the Sea III in 1973.

Incidentally, as described earlier, the reference to a 200 nautical mile zone was seen first in the assertions for a 200 nautical mile territorial sea made by countries in Latin America and the Caribbean. However, it wasn't until 1972 that the concept of an economic zone was proposed, as a claim for jurisdiction over resources in a 200 nautical mile zone. That year, at the Yaoundé Convention held by African nations, these countries adopted the recommendation to establish an EEZ outside of the territorial sea where a State can exercise its exclusive jurisdiction over the exploration and exploitation of all living and non-living resources. Furthermore, the Santo Domingo Declaration was adopted at the 1972 Specialized Conference of Caribbean Countries on Problems of the Sea; a sub-section of that Declaration entitled the "patrimonial sea" established waters in which a coastal State has sovereign rights over all natural resources in a 200 nautical mile zone from the outer edge of its territorial sea.

This formed the basis for the proposal put forward in 1972 to the Committee on the Peaceful Uses of the Seabed and Ocean Floor. At the first substantive session of

UN Conference on the Law of the Sea III in 1974, most nations advocated with one voice the establishment of a 200 nautical mile EEZ; only Japan stood out for its opposition to the proposal. This led to many nations enacting domestic legislation, with such names as the 200 nautical mile Exclusive Economic Zone Act or 200 nautical mile Exclusive Fishery Zone Act, and establishing a 200 nautical mile fishery zone enclosing fishery resources. Although debate on such a zone went through a difficult process at UN Conference on the Law of the Sea III, UNCLOS was established in 1982.

EEZ as a System Derived from Fishery Zones

The Convention comprehensively covers the bulk of the law of the sea in 17 sections with 320 articles and is supplemented with the following nine annexes: Highly Migratory Species; Commission on the Limits of the Continental Shelf; Basic Conditions of Prospecting, Exploration and Exploitation; Statute of the Enterprise; Conciliation; Statute of the International Tribunal for the Law of the Sea; Arbitration; Special Arbitration; and Participation by International Organizations. UNCLOS was adopted on April 30, 1982, as was a resolution[20] to set up a Preparatory Commission for the International Seabed Authority and the International Tribunal on the Law of the Sea, and a resolution on preliminary investment in multiple metallic masses. However, the US, the UK, (the former) West Germany, and a number of other countries, expressing dissatisfaction over Part XI of the Convention on the deep seabed, did not sign it. The world underwent dramatic political and economic upheaval in the years after the adoption of the Convention. In particular following the conclusion of the Cold War, there was a growing dependence on market economy principles primarily by former socialist countries and developing nations. Hence, nations held unofficial talks from 1990 to 1994, presided over by the UN Secretary General, with the aim of modifying Part XI of the Convention. These talks led to the Agreement Relating to the Implementation of Part XI of the Convention on the Law of the Sea to revise Part XI, which was adopted on July 28, 1994 and came into effect on July 28, 1996.

UNCLOS includes provisions on EEZs and the continental shelf in Part V (Articles 55 to 75) and Part VI (Articles 76 to 85), respectively. The provisions on the continental shelf stipulate the distance to be 200 nautical miles from the baseline to a maximum of 350 nautical miles, and they outline the establishment of a Commission on the Limits of the Continental Shelf for determining the outer limit of those shelves that exceed 200 nautical miles, as well as state the allocation of proceeds from the exploitation of that section of the continental shelf. While basically following the Convention on the Continental Shelf, UNCLOS contains

---

[20]The resolution on a preparatory commission for the deep seabed authority.

highly detailed provisions on EEZ, as it is a newly created concept with an outer limit of 200 nautical miles (Article 55).

Article 56 stipulates the following rights of a coastal State in an EEZ:

1. *In the exclusive economic zone, the coastal State has:*

 (a) *sovereign rights for the purpose of exploring and exploiting, conserving and managing the natural resources, whether living or non-living, of the waters superjacent to the seabed and of the seabed and its subsoil, and with regard to other activities for the economic exploitation and exploration of the zone...;*

 (b) *jurisdiction as provided for in the relevant provisions of this Convention with regard to:*

 (i) *the establishment and use of artificial islands, installations and structures;*
 (ii) *marine scientific research;*
 (iii) *the protection and preservation of the marine environment.*

In summary, a coastal State firstly has sovereign rights over living and non-living resources, secondly has jurisdiction over the establishment and use of artificial islands, installations and structures, and thirdly has the right to marine scientific research[21] and the protection and preservation of the marine environment.[22] As for the sovereign rights over non-living resources, from the perspective of positive law, each nation already has access to these resources via vested interests, in accordance with the continental shelf system in current international law. Hence, the scope of application of the newly established Part XI of the Convention on the deep seabed system—namely, the issue arising from delimiting the border of the deep seabed that is a "common heritage of mankind" and the continental shelf of each nation—is newly regulated in Part VI on the continental shelf (although fundamentally, it does not differ from the Convention on the Continental Shelf).[23] Provisions on coordinating the rights of other countries in an EEZ are specified in Articles 58 and 59, while Article 60 contains relatively detailed provisions on artificial islands, etc. Furthermore, the provisions on EEZs are quite specific in regard to living resources.

The provisions on fisheries in the EEZ of the Convention from the draft stage include those relating to maximum sustainable yield, optimal usage, total catch, surplus, catch quota, and fishing fees that had been invoked in fishery negotiations of some states. Hence, historically, the EEZ is a system derived from fishery zones, as described above.

---

[21] UNCLOS, Part XIV, Articles 238 to 265.

[22] UNCLOS, Part XII, Articles 192 to 237.

[23] For further discussion of this parallel principle, see Nakamura, Kō. 1986. "Haitateki keizai suiiki to tairikudana no kankei (The Relationship between EEZs and Continental Shelves)" in Yamamoto, Sōji (ed). *Kaiyōhō no rekishi to tenbō* (The History and Developments of UNCLOS, Oda Shigeru 60th birthday edition). Tokyo: Yūhikaku.

Japan-ROK Agreement on the Continental Shelf and EEZ

Oda Shigeru pointed out early on that the parallel principle of the UNCLOS provisions on an EEZ (Part V) and continental shelf (Part VI) was a problem;[24] it remains an issue that is relatively difficult to resolve of two regimes occurring within and outside an EEZ. Outside an EEZ, the coastal State can establish the outer edge of the continental margin to a maximum of 350 nautical miles wherever the margin extends beyond 200 nautical miles.[25] It is in this area that the continental shelf regime exists.

Even if within an EEZ, because the Convention itself defines the continental shelf as "the seabed and subsoil of the submarine areas that extend . . . to the outer edge of the continental margin, or to a distance of 200 nautical miles. . .," there exist such seabed and subsoil without the topography and geological features of a continental shelf.[26] Hence, "An EEZ and continental shelf each have different origins, and therefore cannot be assumed to have the same breadth." This is due to the Convention stipulating the delimitation of an EEZ and continental shelf to achieve an "equitable resolution" of this issue. "However, the 'equity' of a continental shelf border and EEZ border are not necessarily always the same."[27] Accordingly, if seeking to set the same border for both an EEZ and continental shelf, logically this will give rise to the problem of which "equity" should take precedence.

Incidentally, in 1974 Japan and the ROK concluded two agreements on the continental shelf adjoining both countries. These are the Agreement between Japan and the Republic of Korea Concerning the Establishment of Boundary in the Northern Part of the Continental Shelf Adjacent to the Two Countries (Northern Part Agreement), which is considered to be based on an equidistant median line, and the Agreement between Japan and the Republic of Korea Concerning Joint Development of the Southern Part of the Continental Shelf Adjacent to the Two Countries (Southern Part Agreement).

The latter Southern Part Agreement is based on an overlap of Japan's assertion of an equidistant median line and the ROK's assertion of a natural prolongation of the shelf, which created a zone for joint development within the Japan-side of the median line of the continental shelf adjoining both countries; the agreement was reached "[d]esiring to promote the friendly relations existing between the two countries; [c]onsidering their mutual interest in carrying out jointly exploration and exploitation of petroleum resources in the southern part of the continental shelf adjacent to the two countries, [and] [r]esolving to reach a final practical

---

[24] In his dissenting opinion in the ICJ judgment on the 1982 Tunisia-Libya Continental Shelf Incident.

[25] UNCLOS, Article 76.

[26] Ibid.

[27] Oda, Shigeru. 1985. *Chūkai kokuren kaiyōhō jōyakujō* (Commentary on UNCLOS). Tokyo: Yūhikaku.

solution to the question of the development of such resources."[28] The Southern Part Agreement was signed on January 30, 1974 and came into effect on June 22, 1978, 4 years before UNCLOS was adopted. Although it will remain valid for 50 years, Article 28 of the Agreement stipulates, "Nothing in this Agreement shall be regarded as determining the question of sovereign rights over all or any portion of the Joint Development Zone, or as prejudicing the positions of the respective Parties with respect to the delimitation of the continental shelf." Hence, it does not address the delimitation issue.

Furthermore, until the conclusion of the new Japan-ROK Fishery Agreement that came into effect in 1999, the original Fishery Agreement concluded in 1965 designated a 12 nautical mile fishery zone and jointly regulated waters. However, due to the enactment of the 1977 Territorial Sea Act that set Japan's territorial sea at 12 nautical miles, and the absence of protests from the ROK to this, the fishery zone of this Agreement only applied to the designated zone that set Japan's territorial sea to be no more than 3 nautical miles. The ROK also took similar measures to Japan in accordance with the 1977 Territorial Sea Act. It should be noted that both Japan and the ROK are parties to the 1982 UNCLOS.

So, based on these facts, how should the relation between an EEZ and continental shelf be viewed? The Northern Part Agreement sets out 35 coordinates, with the straight lines connecting those coordinates in sequence being the boundary line of the continental shelves appertaining to both countries. Furthermore, Article 7(1) of the new Japan-ROK Fishery Agreement that came into effect in 1999 stipulates the EEZ border in the northern part of the Japan-ROK continental shelf as being the line that connects the same 35 coordinates in Article 1(1) of the Northern Part Agreement. Why is it, however, that the border of the new EEZ and the border of the continental shelf are the same? Although it is not entirely clear from the details of the negotiations, it can only be surmised that at the very least, upon the conclusion of the 1974 Convention, the same continental shelf existed in the northern waters; and as there were no special circumstances then, it was considered "equitable" to base delimitation on an equidistant median line. Moreover, at the 1998 Convention, as there were also no special circumstances during the delimitation of the EEZ based on distance, it can only be surmised that both Japan and the ROK agreed that an equidistant median line was "equitable."

Now, with regard to the situation in the southern waters, as already mentioned, the Southern Part Agreement was concluded amid opposing views of the two sides, and was based on an overlap of both countries' claims that created a joint development zone; it did not address the delimitation issue. Subsequently, the diplomatic negotiations on delimitation of an EEZ in the new Japan-ROK Fishery Agreement were in accordance with UNCLOS, to which both countries are parties. The

---

[28] No. 19778 Japan and Republic of Korea: Agreement concerning joint development of the southern part of the continental shelf adjacent to the two countries (with map, appendix, agreed minutes and exchanges of notes). Signed at Seoul on 30 January 1974. https://treaties.un.org/doc/Publication/unts/Volume%201225/volume-1225-I-19778-English.pdf. Accessed on December 3, 2022.

Convention stipulates that delimitation of an EEZ shall be done by consensus and in accordance with international law, in order to achieve an equitable resolution.

In international law, an equitable delimitation is achieved when a delineation is reached based on "a combined equidistance-special circumstances rule."[29] Therefore, if both countries reach consensus on an equidistant median line or on an amended equidistant line taking into account special circumstances, then the continental shelf within the EEZ is defined by joint development, not by the drawing of a border based on the Southern Part Agreement in 1974. Hence, an EEZ and continental shelf exist as two separate regimes. In reality, however, Japan and the ROK were unable to reach a consensus on the border, and Article 9(2) of the new Japan-ROK Fishery Agreement established a "provisional measures zone." The northwest line of this "provisional measures zone" (that Japan asserted was an equidistant median line) ran slightly along the north of the ROK-side line stipulated in the Southern Part Agreement. Meanwhile, the southeast line (that the ROK asserted was an equidistant median line) ran through the joint development zone of which over three-quarters was drawn as being on the Japan side. Based on paragraph 2 of Annex II, each country's zone marked by these lines was deemed to be an EEZ. Accordingly, for Japan, the seabed of the EEZ stipulated in the new Japan-ROK Fishery Agreement (in other words, part of the continental shelf) remained as a continental shelf zone for joint development based on the Southern Part Agreement and throughout the period of its validity.

This is reflected in the fact that throughout the world there are agreements on continental shelf delimitation and joint development. However, in reality it is not likely that any issues will arise, primarily because petroleum development is being carried out in these zones based on agreements reached between nations, or prospecting there reveals no petroleum to be exploited.

As is well known, prospecting was previously carried out in the joint development zone stipulated in the Southern Part Agreement concluded between Japan and the ROK, but no successful outcome was reported. It is generally said that non-renewable petroleum resources will dry up within the next 50 years, and once that happens the continental shelf regime will no longer be significant in reality. In that sense, signs of the end of the continental shelf regime are already being seen. From that perspective, the current concomitant systems of the EEZ and continental shelf are not so much a newly posed problem arising from unclear provisions on the relationship between them as stipulated in UNCLOS, but rather an issue of the relationship between the systems established in the agreements of each nation, such as the current agreement on continental shelf delimitation and joint development, and the newly established EEZ regime in accordance with UNCLOS.

In fact, prior to the new Japan-ROK Fishery Agreement that entered into force in January 1999, there was also the Japan-ROK Fishery Agreement concluded in 1965. This agreement emerged from negotiations on fisheries, which was one of the key

---

[29] Serita, Kentarō. 1999. *Shima no ryōyū to keizai suiiki no kyōkai kakutei* (Sovereignty over Islands and the Delimitation of Economic Zones). Tokyo: Yūshindo Kōbunsha.

issues of the talks on normalizing bilateral relations between Japan and the ROK that commenced in February 1952, along with basic relations, claims, and the legal status of ROK nationals living in Japan. The central theme of these fishery negotiations was how to handle the Syngman Rhee Line.[30] At the time, Japanese fishermen who would fish in the waters on the ROK side experienced problems due to these provisions. The Japan-ROK Fishery Agreement was effective for 5 years, and included stipulations such as "[d]esiring that the maximum sustained productivity of the fishery resources in waters of their common interest be maintained; [b]eing convinced that the conservation of the said resources and their rational exploitation and development will serve the interest of both countries; [and c]onfirming that the principle of the freedom of the high seas shall be respected unless otherwise specifically provided in the present Agreement . . ." It was agreed to terminate the Agreement 1 year after a notification of intent to do so was issued; in January 1998, Japan issued a notification of termination to that effect (Fig. 5.1).

First of all, the Agreement stated the territorial sea of both countries is 3 nautical miles and established a fishery zone spanning up to 12 nautical miles from the respective coastal baselines offshore on the high seas. Secondly, the Agreement went even further to establish a "joint regulation zone" in the ROK coastal waters where fishery is regulated. Furthermore, both countries are to consult with each other if either one uses the straight baseline method to establish its fishery zone, and an exchange of notes was effected concerning the straight baseline of the ROK fishery zone. Thirdly, the Agreement also implies that a coastal State naturally has the right of regulation and jurisdiction in its fishery zone, but that as the waters outside the zone constitute the high seas, these waters fall under the flag State doctrine.[31] Either way, the Agreement took into consideration the disparate fishery capacity of Japanese and ROK fishing vessels. The ROK's fishery industry continued to develop, and as the fishery environment was changing with trouble between local fishermen and ROK fishing vessels operating along the Hokkaidō coast, along with the deteriorating situation of resources in the waters around the ROK's Jeju Island, both Japan and the ROK agreed to self-regulate activities in the waters from October 1980 to January 1998. It should be noted that the ROK also expanded the breadth of its territorial sea in 1977 to 12 nautical miles in accordance with the Territorial Sea Act (using the straight baseline method); subsequently, until Japan's full application of the EEZ regime in January 1997, the remaining fishery zone for both countries covered only specified parts of the West Channel of the Tsushima Strait and of the area around Jeju Island.[32]

Diplomatic negotiations between the Japan and the ROK based on the EEZ regime fully took into account the provisions stipulated in the original Japan-ROK Fishery Agreement and the two nations' fishery relations, including self-regulation

---

[30] Oda, Shigeru. 1956. *Kaiyō no kokusaihō kōzō* (The International Legal Structure of the Oceans). Tokyo: Yūshindō Kōbunsha; and Kawakami, op. cit.

[31] See the section on the flag State doctrine earlier in this chapter.

[32] See Fig. 5.1 depicting the relations outlined in the original Japan-ROK Fishery Agreement.

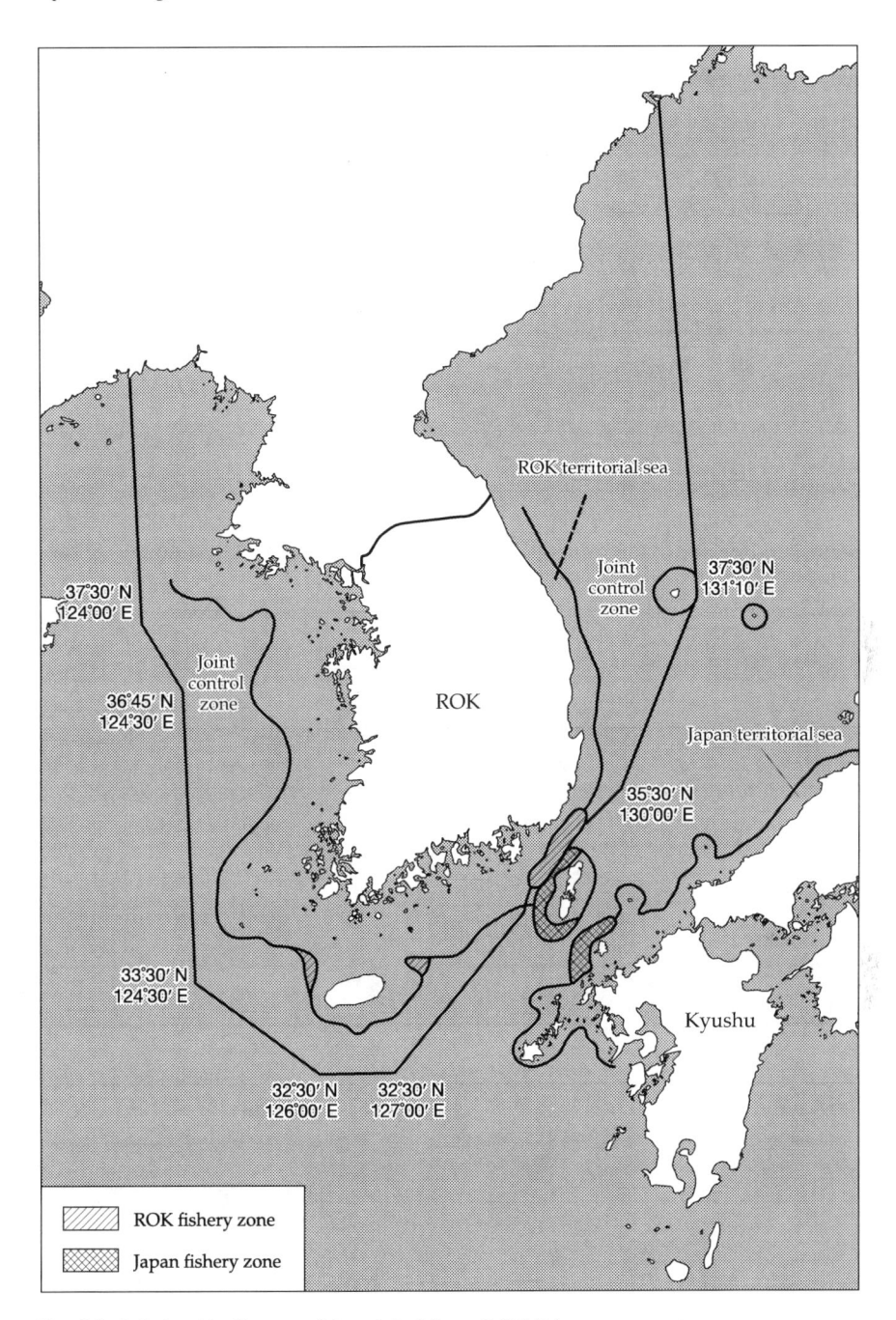

Fig. 5.1 Relationship diagram of the original Japan-ROK fishery agreement

on both sides, as described above. When read together with the previously analyzed continental shelf relations of Japan and the ROK, one could say that fishery considerations take precedence over those of the continental shelf. Within the international rulings on fisheries, one case worth highlighting is the Maritime Delimitation in the Area between Greenland and Jan Mayen (Denmark v. Norway; Jan Mayen) case, in which the ICJ ruled that among access to resources, population, socio-economic factors, and security, access to resources was the only relevant matter that should be taken into consideration in delimitation. Furthermore, although there was scarce information on seabed mining resources, saltwater (smelt) fishery was covered in detail, and the ICJ ruled it was necessary to ensure such fishery so as not to impart a catastrophic effect on the welfare of the citizens of the nations concerned. Also, in the Delimitation of the Maritime Boundary in the Gulf of Marine Area (Canada/United States; US-Canada Gulf of Maine) case, regarding the second section of the sea for delimitation, the ICJ ruled that fishery, navigation, defense, and the exploration and exploitation of petroleum could not be considered as relevant matters in delimitation. It should be noted that the Court also examined whether there is no fundamental inequality that will have a catastrophic effect on the welfare and daily lives of the citizens of the nations concerned.[33]

What is particularly important when considering the state of resources in the future is that, more than non-renewable resources, the focus should be on how to utilize the renewable resources of fisheries, which relates not only to Japan and the ROK, but the world in general. From that viewpoint as well, rather than exploiting mining resources and several years' worth of petroleum, priority should be placed on living resources that can potentially provide a perpetually sustainable yield so long as there is no imminent danger of overfishing or environmental degradation. Furthermore, due consideration should be paid to vulnerable fishing communities, in which the daily lives and welfare of the residents are affected by the reserves of their fish species and performance of their fishery industry.

Hence, an EEZ can still be cultivated as a regime for conserving and utilizing fishery resources including sedentary fish species (which are currently regarded as continental shelf resources). This is still possible even when viewed concomitantly with the continental shelf regime for the time being, and even after the eventual end of the continental shelf as a regime for the exploitation of non-living resources. In that sense, in the present day, whereby in UNCLOS living resources are also recognized as a common heritage left to mankind, it is incumbent on the wisdom of mankind to once again give consideration to the next generation by shifting from a stance of enclosing resources to the joint use of resources.

---

[33] For more details on these incidents see Serita, op. cit.

Military Use and Scientific Research in EEZs

UNCLOS stipulates the rights of a coastal State in an EEZ in the following three categories:

1. *Sovereign rights for the purpose of exploring and exploiting, conserving and managing the natural resources, whether living or non-living, of the waters superjacent to the seabed and of the seabed and its subsoil, and with regard to other activities for the economic exploitation and exploration of the zone, such as the production of energy from the water, currents and winds.*
2. *Jurisdiction as provided for in the relevant provisions of this Convention with regard to the establishment and use of artificial islands, installations and structures; marine scientific research; and the protection and preservation of the marine environment.*
3. *The Convention also states that a coastal State must give due regard to the rights and duties of other States in exercising its rights and performing its duties. This section does not cover the rights and duties of a coastal State in regard to the use and conservation of living resources, and particularly focuses on the authority of a coastal State concerning provisions on scientific research and navigation.*

In regard to the rights of other States in an EEZ, the Convention first stipulates the freedom "of navigation and overflight and the laying of submarine cables and pipelines, and other internationally lawful uses of the sea related to these freedoms ... and compatible with the other provisions of this Convention."[34] It then outlines the right to conduct marine scientific research.[35] These freedoms are the rights of all nations in the high seas. However, the Convention states an EEZ is neither territorial sea nor the high seas, but a "specific legal regime."[36] Therefore, the high seas regime for these freedoms in an EEZ is not a suitable approach to take. Moreover, marine scientific research in the EEZ is subject to Part XIII of the Convention.

Military Use

While it goes without saying that the freedom of navigation that causes marine pollution in a country's EEZ is out of the question, the issue here is military use, such as for fleet exercise and live-fire training. Military use in the high seas has traditionally been recognized alongside the four archetypal freedoms cited as the freedom of the high seas in the 1958 Convention on the High Seas, as "[other freedoms] which are recognized by the general principles of international law." However, as was evident in the 1954 incident involving the *Daigo Fukuryū Maru*,[37] the setting of an

---

[34] Article 58.

[35] Article 238.

[36] As positioned in Article 55.

[37] The *Daigo Fukuryū Maru*, a tuna fishing boat from the Port of Yaizu in Shizuoka Prefecture, was exposed to nuclear fallout on March 1, 1954 from the US *Castle Bravo* thermonuclear weapon test at Bikini Atoll in the South Pacific Ocean. At the time, the boat was outside the extensive danger

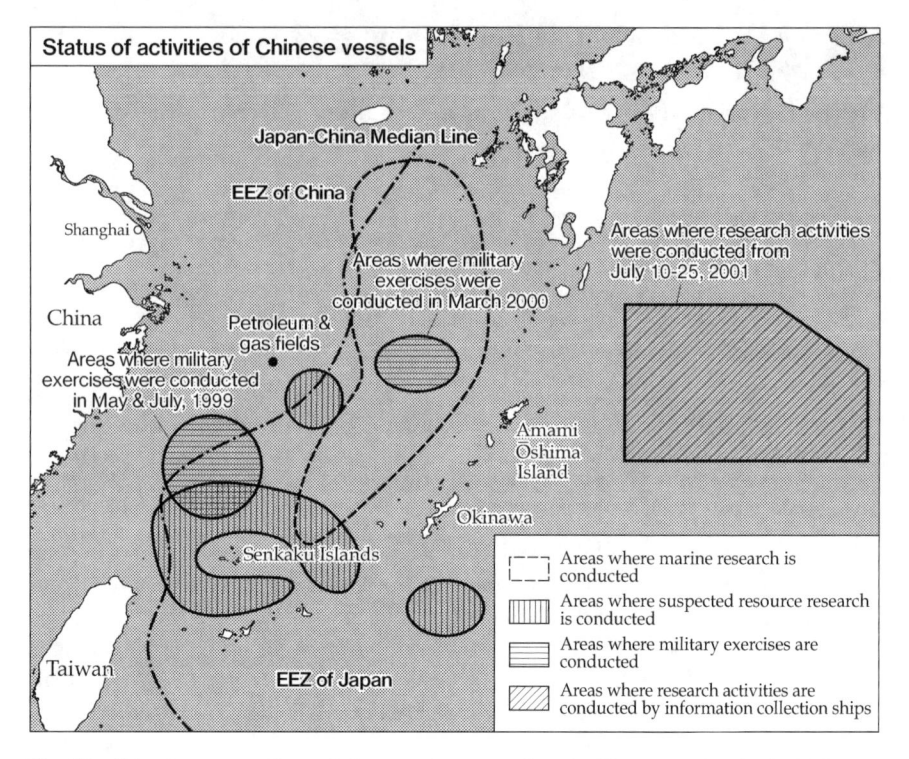

Fig. 5.2 China has repeatedly carried out marine research and military exercises in the high seas

extensive and long-term danger zone for nuclear tests is considered an abuse of rights and therefore problematic. Hence, the 1958 Convention on the High Seas restrictively legalized military use, stating that such freedoms "shall be exercised by all States with reasonable regard to the interests of other States in their exercise of the freedom of the high seas" (Fig. 5.2).

Similar provisions were outlined in UNCLOS, in addition to generally stipulating the *bona fides* (good faith) principle. UNCLOS also states, "In exercising their rights and performing their duties under this Convention, States Parties shall refrain from any threat or use of force against the territorial integrity or political independence of any State, or in any other manner inconsistent with the principles of international law embodied in the Charter of the United Nations,"[38] and particularly notes in a separate Article that "the high seas shall be reserved for peaceful purposes."[39]

---

zone that the United States set up in the high seas for carrying out the hydrogen bomb test. One of the Japanese crew died as a result of exposure to the nuclear fallout. This incident led to heightened debate in Japan on banning atomic and hydrogen bombs. Meanwhile, in order to quell the backlash from the *Bravo* test, the US expressed its remorse over the incident on April 9 that year, and paid compensation to the victims the following year.

[38] Article 301.

[39] Article 88.

Therefore, it is questionable as to whether the freedom of military use is included as is within the conventional freedom of the high seas. (That said, without the context of the Convention's provisions, and commenting only on the interpretation of the phrase "peaceful usage," similar to the Outer Space Treaty and the like, it can be interpreted as such. In other words, it can be said that the interpretation that all military use is not for peaceful purposes is the minority view. Thus, it must stand that the prevailing interpretation is that military use that does not violate the UN Charter is consistent with peaceful purposes. Nevertheless, there needs to be further consideration of the significance of incorporating Article 88, in addition to the general provision of Article 301.)

As already discussed, although an EEZ is a superjacent zone, it is not regarded as having the same features as the high seas, and so military use of an EEZ by a foreign country cannot be regarded as fundamentally the same as the right of all countries for military use, as per the freedom of the high seas. Essentially, since it is not clear if military exercises conducted in another country's EEZ can be described as for "internationally lawful uses," countries must not conduct exceedingly dubious military exercises in an EEZ. Any military exercises carried out in an EEZ without prior consent will, at the very least, be viewed as unfriendly acts.

Scientific Research

The other principal freedom of the high seas stipulated in the 1958 Convention on the High Seas is the freedom of scientific research. Part XIII was included in UNCLOS from the perspective of international cooperation in marine research and publishing and disseminating the findings resulting from it. All countries have the right to conduct marine scientific research, provided it is "exclusively for peaceful purposes." However, scientific research itself does not constitute legal grounds for asserting the claim to the marine environment and its resources.

The high seas stipulated in the 1958 Convention on the High Seas is all of the sea not including the 3 nautical mile territorial sea of each nation and the internal waters. However, as discussed earlier, a coastal State is able to expand its territorial sea breadth up to 12 nautical miles, and furthermore, establish an EEZ up to 200 nautical miles from the baseline. Consequently, the conventional zone for scientific research is now primarily the EEZ of a coastal State, and hence the provisions of UNCLOS exclusively apply to scientific research in an EEZ and continental shelf. In principle, all countries and international organizations with the authority to conduct scientific research have the right to carry out marine scientific research;[40] such international organizations include the Food and Agriculture Organization; Intergovernmental Oceanographic Commission of the United Nations Educational, Scientific and

---

[40] Article 238.

Cultural Organization; United Nations Environment Programme; International Maritime Organization; and the World Meteorological Organization.

First, coastal States have the right to regulate, authorize, and conduct scientific research in their EEZ and on the continental shelf, and that research can only be carried out with the consent of the coastal State. It has always been the case that coastal States grant consent "in normal circumstances," which may exist in spite of the absence of diplomatic relations between the coastal State and the researching State. It should be noted that coastal States may at their discretion withhold their consent to the conduct of a marine scientific research project that has direct impact on the exploration and exploitation of natural resources in its EEZ and continental shelf.[41]

Next, research States and international organizations have a duty to provide information to a coastal State at least 6 months prior to the scheduled start date of the marine scientific research project. This information must fully describe the project and include: the nature and objectives of the project; the method and means to be used, including name, tonnage, type, and class of vessels, and a description of scientific equipment; the precise geographical areas in which the project is to be conducted; the expected date of first appearance and final departure of the research vessels, or deployment of the equipment and its removal, as appropriate; the name of the sponsoring institution, its director, and the person in charge of the project; and the extent to which it is considered that the coastal State should be able to participate or to be represented in the project. The research States and international organizations may proceed with a marine scientific research project 6 months after the date upon which the required information was provided to the coastal State.[42] Furthermore, the research States and international organizations must ensure the right of the coastal State, if it so desires, to participate or be represented in the marine scientific research project, especially on board research vessels and other craft or scientific research installations, when practicable.[43]

This is how marine scientific research is carried out in an EEZ and continental shelf, namely by striking a balance between the rights of coastal States and the rights of research States. In essence, however, a coastal State has sovereign rights in its EEZ and continental shelf, and so a research State must act in accordance with the principle of respecting its sovereign rights and jurisdiction.

Above all, it is paramount that marine scientific research is carried out not for the national interest of one country, but for the interest of all humankind.

As for marine scientific research carried out in Japan's EEZ and continental shelf, domestic legislation on this matter requires the research States to publish the research project details and results; this is both a right and a duty. Furthermore, a coastal State has the right to request the suspension or completion of a research project, and it can board a research vessel in its waters to check if the research is

---

[41] Article 246.

[42] Article 252.

[43] Article 249.

being conducted in accordance with the information provided by the research country.

1996 Exclusive Economic Zone and Continental Shelf Act

Enactment, Revision, and Abolition of Domestic Legislation Pursuant to Japan's Ratification of UNCLOS

In preparation to ratify UNCLOS, Japan first amended its 1977 Territorial Sea Act, established a contiguous zone, and then established the Act on Amending the Act on Territorial Waters and Contiguous Water Area[44] which entered into force on July 20, 1996. The designated areas were set at the standard territorial sea breadth of 3 nautical miles, and the straight baseline method was newly adopted.[45] The current ordinance on the straight baseline method was put into force across the board on January 1, 1997.

Japan then successively enacted the following legislation: Act on the Exclusive Economic Zone and Continental Shelf;[46] Act on the Exercise of the Sovereign Right for Fishery, etc. in the Exclusive Economic Zone;[47] and Act on the Preservation and Control of Living Marine Resources.[48] The Act on the Exercise of the Sovereign Right for Fishery, etc. in the Exclusive Economic Zone led to the abolishment[49] of the aforementioned Act on Temporary Measures Concerning Fishery Waters.[50] All of these laws were put into force from July 20, 1996, when UNCLOS entered into force in Japan (Fig. 5.3).

In short, all of these laws led to Japan adopting the straight baseline method for its territorial sea, and fully establishing an EEZ. As for the living resources in the waters and continental shelf on the perimeter of the EEZ designated in the Act on the Exclusive Economic Zone and Continental Shelf, according to the Act on the Exercise of the Sovereign Right for Fishery, etc. in the Exclusive Economic Zone, "the provisions of Article 3 through to the preceding Article shall apply *mutatis mutandis* to the Fishery, the harvest of aquatic animals and plants, and the Survey pertaining to sedentary species,"[51] and "Japan shall have the primary interest and responsibility under 1 of Article 66 of the United Nations Convention on the Law of

---

[44] June 14, 1996, Act No. 73.

[45] Enforcement ordinance of the Act on Territorial Waters and Contiguous Water Area (1977 Ordinance No. 210, last revised on December 28, 2001 Ordinance No. 434).

[46] June 14, 1996, Act No. 74.

[47] June 14, 1996, Act No. 76.

[48] June 14, 1996, Act No. 77.

[49] Article 3 of the Annex of the same Act.

[50] 1977, Act No. 31.

[51] Article 14.

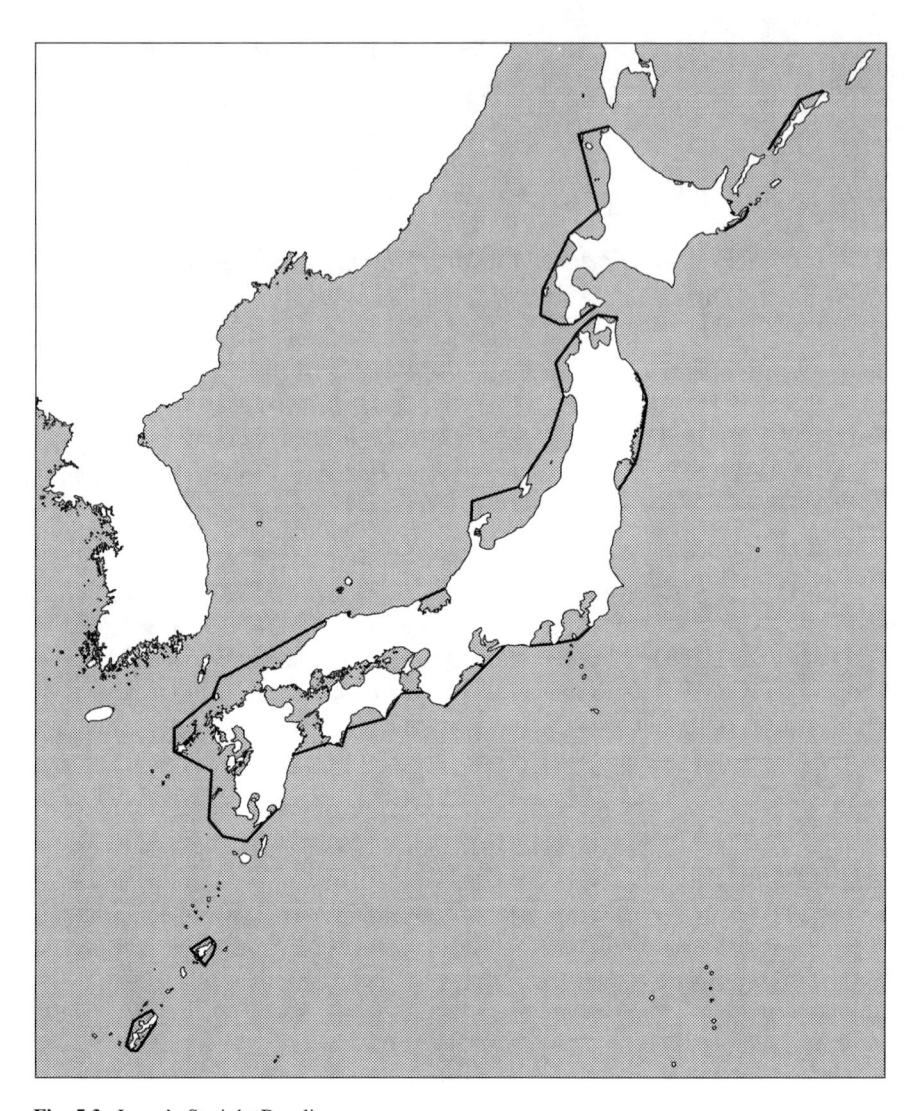

Fig. 5.3 Japan's Straight Baseline

the Sea even in the sea area outside the Exclusive Economic Zone with regard to anadromous stock that lay eggs in Japan's inland water."[52]

---

[52] Article 15.

Adoption of the Straight Baseline Method for the Territorial Sea

The straight baseline method came into force in Japan from January 1, 1997. As discussed previously, the outer limit of the territorial sea line at any point is the line that is equidistant from the closest point above the baseline. Normally, the baseline is the low-water line along the coast, as marked on the large-scale charts officially recognized by a coastal State. However, if the coastline is deeply indented or cut into, or if there is a series of islands along the coast in its immediate vicinity, straight baselines may be used to join appropriate points along the coastline. The principle behind this is the ICJ ruling on the 1951 Fisheries Case concerning a conflict of interests between the Norwegian coastal fishery and the UK pelagic trawler fishery.

The particular problem in this case was Norway's two coves with an entrance of over 40 nautical miles. It was ruled that the baseline of these waters was within a rational limit from the general direction of the coast, and furthermore the fishery in these waters was indispensable to the livelihood of the citizens and a long-established customary practice. The wording of this ruling was adopted as is in the 1958 Convention on the Territorial Sea and the Contiguous Zone; it was also emulated in the 1982 UNCLOS. Japan did not adopt the straight baseline method until the law was revised in 1996. The Convention established a category for archipelagic nations, including both coastal archipelagos and oceanic archipelagos such as Indonesia, and recognized the adoption of a maximum 125 nautical mile straight baseline (archipelagic baseline) for such countries.

Incidents Involving Foreign Fishing Vessels Operating in New Territorial Seas

On September 11, 1998, the Hiroshima High Court ruled on nine incidents involving ROK fishing vessels that were detained by the Japan Coast Guard for operating in the new territorial sea off the Hamada coast in Shimane Prefecture, which extended to 12 nautical miles from the straight baseline. In five of these cases a summary order for the payment of a fine was issued, in two cases a suspended indictment was issued, and the remaining two cases are currently still on trial for the violation of foreign fishery regulations.[53]

Regarding the August 15, 1997 ruling of the Hamada branch of the Matsue District Court on the incident involving an ROK fishing vessel that was detained in the new territorial sea off the Hamada coast in Shimane Prefecture, although the waters in which the vessel was operating became part of the territorial sea from January 1997 onwards, the area was still outside Japan's fishery zone stipulated in

---

[53] *Sankei Shimbun*, September 11, 1998, evening edition.

the 1965 Japan-ROK Fishery Agreement. Hence, as the Agreement stated that the flag State has the right of regulation in the waters outside the fishery zone, the Court concluded "the treaty of the Japan-ROK Fishery Agreement takes precedence over the domestic legislation of the amended Territorial Sea Act; therefore, the jurisdiction does not cover the waters in which the vessels were detained"; the case was then dismissed.[54]

Conversely, in the June 24, 1998 ruling of the Nagasaki District Court on the incident involving an ROK fishing vessel that was detained while operating in the new territorial sea off the Gotō coast in Nagasaki Prefecture, irrespective of the Japan-ROK Fishery Agreement, Japan was deemed to have the right of regulation and jurisdiction in the new territorial sea that had been extended by adopting the straight baseline method in accordance with Article 2(1) of the enforcement ordinance of the new Territorial Sea Act that came into effect in January 1997.[55] Although the defendant appealed the ruling, the appeal was dismissed by the Fukuoka High Court on April 28, 1999.

The prosecutor appealed the ruling of the Hamada branch of the Matsue District Court. The ruling of the Matsue branch of the Hiroshima High Court on September 11, 1998 stated, "the jurisdiction of Japan in the new territorial sea is a matter of course under international law, and is not subject to the limitations of the Japan-ROK Fishery Agreement"; consequently, the first ruling was annulled, and the trial returned to the Matsue District Court, upon which the defendant immediately filed a final appeal.

Although the ruling of the Hamada branch of the Matsue District Court recognized the right of a coastal State to exercise its sovereign right in the territorial sea, it also interpreted Article 4(1) of the Japan-ROK Fishery Agreement as a provision that limits Japan's right of regulation and jurisdiction, despite the fact that it was only later on that the waters outside the fishery zone were designated part of the territorial sea. In other words, in cases limited only to fishery, the ruling interpreted this provision as renouncing Japan's right to exercise its sovereign right in the territorial sea in the waters outside the fishery zone.

However, as was also stated by the Hiroshima High Court, this interpretation is incorrect. As it stands now, until an EEZ is systemized, in international law the ocean is divided into the territorial sea under the sovereignty of a coastal State, and the high seas that are open for use by all people as a free zone which no country can claim as its territory. It was also stipulated that a coastal State is able to establish a fishery zone, where it can exercise exclusive jurisdiction in fishery, in a certain area of the high seas that is contiguous to its territorial sea. Accordingly, as was recognized by the Hiroshima High Court, it is not possible for this fishery zone to overlap with the territorial sea. Within this certain area of the high seas that is contiguous to its territorial sea, in addition to a fishery zone, a coastal State is able to establish a

[54] See the morning editions of various Japanese newspapers on August 16, 1998 for more details.

[55] *Asahi Shimbun*, June 25, 1998, morning edition; for details on the verdict see *Hanrei jihō* (Chronicle of Legal Rulings) 1648: p. 158, and *Hanrei taimuzu* (Legal Ruling Times) 998: p. 279.

contiguous zone where it can exercise authority to "prevent infringement of its customs, fiscal, immigration or sanitary laws and regulations within its territory or territorial sea."

At any rate, although a fishery zone creates some restriction of movement in the high seas, it does not do so in a territorial sea, nor does it form an exception to the territorial sea. The Japan-ROK Fishery Agreement regulates the high seas, and the right of regulation and jurisdiction in the waters outside the fishery zone, namely the high seas, are in accordance with the flag State doctrine as per the freedom of the high seas principle. As such, the Agreement only confirmed that which is a matter of course in international law.

In regard to Japan's current use of the straight baseline method, the ruling of the Hamada branch of the Matsue District Court raised some questions on legality in its relation to the duty of consultation stipulated in the provision of Article 1 of the Japan-ROK Fishery Agreement. However, the ROK is also a party to UNCLOS, and hence follows the Convention in legally expanding its territorial sea. Therefore, there are no particular problems in terms of the procedures taken. There are currently over 70 countries around the world (compared to only 21 in 1977 when the original Territorial Sea Act was enacted), including Japan's neighbors the ROK and China, that have adopted the straight baseline method. Although, as was stated in the ruling on the previously discussed Norway Fisheries Case, "The delimitation of waters is normally of an international nature, and therefore cannot be in accordance solely with the intentions of a coastal State as expressed in its domestic law." In that sense, it does not mean one cannot argue whether Japan's adoption of the straight baseline method is appropriate in light of international law.

However, in this incident, it was also stated in the opposing argument to the appellant's (original defendant) written reason for an appeal on January 27, 1998 (1997, c., no. 32), "As a lawyer, in this appeal I will not argue if the Act on Territorial Waters and Contiguous Water Area is legal in accordance with the provisions of UNCLOS." Therefore, since the use of the straight baseline method was not argued, it was deemed a matter of course in international law for a coastal State to exercise its sovereign right in its territorial sea within a set zone from the baseline. As such, the ruling of the Hamada branch of the Matsue District Court was deemed an incorrect interpretation due to insufficient knowledge of rudimentary treaty law and the law of the sea.

In the final appeal, the defendant completely reversed his position and argued the legality of Japan's adoption of the straight baseline method, stating, "At present (1998), Japan's straight baseline consists of a total 194 points spanning the country's entire coast. When analyzing this by similar examples, 60% are baselines set mostly due to the existence of islands, 32% are baselines set according to the complexity of the coastline, and 8% are baselines set by the closing line of a bay entrance. In terms of length, the most common is baselines of under 10 nautical miles with 100 points, while baselines of 40 nautical miles and over have 21 points, baselines of 24 nautical miles and under have 117 points, and baselines over 24 nautical miles have 46 points." Furthermore, the defendant asserted that the straight baseline of the zone in question in this incident was not set in accordance with the standards stipulated in UNCLOS, and hence could not be regarded as legal in international law. However, the Supreme Court dismissed the final appeal with the ruling of "the appeal is simply a claim of the violation of the law, including a breach of the Constitution, and therefore does not constitute a grounds for appeal in accordance with Article 405 of the Criminal Procedure Code."[56]

Treatment of the Seabed Zone in the Act on the Exclusive Economic Zone and Continental Shelf

Article 1(1) of the Act on the Exclusive Economic Zone and Continental Shelf states, "In accordance with the United Nations Convention on the Law of the Sea (UNCLOS), there is hereby established the exclusive economic zone, as a zone in which Japan exercises its sovereign rights and other rights as a coastal State as prescribed in Part V of UNCLOS." This is clearly a provision stipulating the new establishment of an EEZ. Meanwhile, Article 2 confirms the content of a continental shelf, stating "The continental shelf over which Japan exercises its sovereign rights and other rights as a coastal State in accordance with UNCLOS (the continental shelf) comprises the seabed and its subsoil subjacent to the following areas of the sea."

According to Article 1(2) of the Act, an EEZ "comprises the areas of the sea extending from the baseline of Japan (as defined in the amended Act on the Territorial Sea and the Contiguous Zone) to the line every point of which is 200 nautical miles from the nearest point on the baseline of Japan (excluding therefrom the territorial sea) and its subjacent seabed and its subsoil." It also states the median line to be the line between Japan and the foreign coast that is opposite the coast of Japan. Furthermore, if there is such a median line (or a substitute line for the median line, which is agreed upon between Japan and a foreign country), an EEZ is the area of the sea extending up to the agreed upon line and its subjacent seabed and subsoil. Article 2 first stipulates the continental shelf to be the seabed and its subsoil extending 200 nautical miles from the baseline of Japan, or the median line (or a substitute line for the median line) as mentioned in Article 1. Article 2 also stipulates the continental shelf to be "the areas of the sea adjacent seaward to the areas of the sea referred to in the preceding subparagraph (limited to the part of the sea delimited by the line every point of which is 200 nautical miles from the nearest point on the baseline of Japan), as prescribed by Cabinet Order in accordance with Article 76 of UNCLOS" (Fig. 5.4)[57]

---

[56] Supreme Court of Japan. *Saikōsai keiji hanrei shū* (Collection of Supreme Court Rulings) 53, No. 8, p. 1045.

[57] With regard to the continental shelf that extends beyond 200 nautical miles, Japan conducted scientific research and submitted a report to the Commission on the Limits of the Continental Shelf on November 12, 2008. In the August/September session of the Commission, a subcommittee was

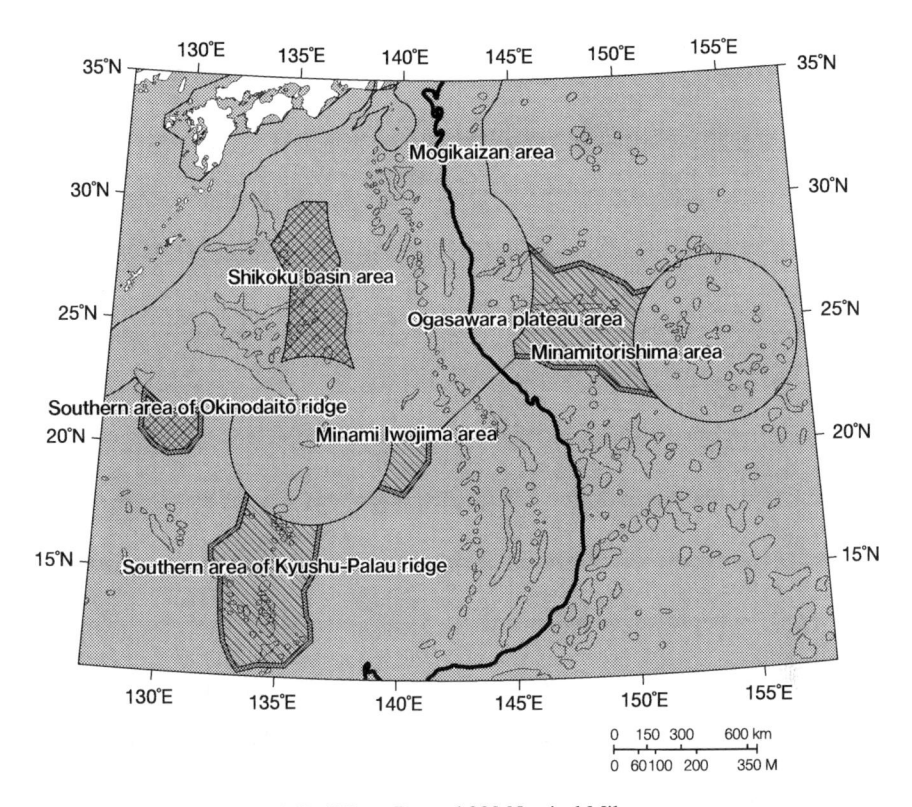

Fig. 5.4 Japan's Continental Shelf Zone Beyond 200 Nautical Miles

According to the above, the continental shelf as stipulated in Japanese law is firstly a designated area of the sea, and the seabed and subsoil subjacent to it. This is different from the continental shelf of a coastal State as stipulated in Article 76(1) of UNCLOS, which "comprises the seabed and subsoil of the submarine areas that extend beyond its territorial sea throughout the natural prolongation of its land territory to the outer edge of the continental margin, or to a distance of 200 nautical miles from the baselines from which the breadth of the territorial sea is measured where the outer edge of the continental margin does not extend up to that distance." Basically, in Japanese law, the continental shelf is positioned as the seabed and subsoil of the designated superjacent area of the sea; in that sense, it is based on the assumption of this superjacent area being an EEZ.

Incidentally, Japan has not ratified the Convention on the Continental Shelf, although the continental shelf regime has been established as customary law and appears to apply the concept of natural prolongation as grounds in the establishment

---

set up and deliberations were initiated. The final decision will be made after consultations with the Commission.

of a continental shelf.[58] However, as previously mentioned, this concept does not exist in Japanese law, and a continental shelf is simply defined as the seabed and subsoil subjacent to an EEZ. Thus, if nothing else, it can be said that a continental shelf within a 200 nautical mile area has no relevance as a continental shelf in customary law.

Principle of Delimitation in the Act on the Exclusive Economic Zone and Continental Shelf

According to Article 1(2) of the Act, an EEZ "comprises the areas of the sea extending from the baseline of Japan (as defined in the amended Act on the Territorial Sea and the Contiguous Zone) to the line every point of which is 200 nautical miles from the nearest point on the baseline of Japan (excluding therefrom the territorial sea) and its subjacent seabed and its subsoil." It also states the median line to be the line between Japan and the foreign coast that is opposite the coast of Japan. Furthermore, if there is such a median line (or a substitute line for the median line, which is agreed upon between Japan and a foreign country), an EEZ is the area of the sea extending up to the agreed upon line and its subjacent seabed and subsoil. Furthermore, Article 2 states the continental shelf to be the seabed and its subsoil extending 200 nautical miles from the baseline of Japan, or the median line (or a substitute line for the median line) as mentioned in Article 1. Article 2(2) also stipulates the continental shelf to be "the areas of the sea adjacent seaward to the areas of the sea referred to in the preceding subparagraph (limited to the part of the sea delimited by the line every point of which is 200 nautical miles from the nearest point on the baseline of Japan), as prescribed by Cabinet Order in accordance with Article 76 of UNCLOS."

Although the Act does not include any specific clauses on delimitation, Articles 1 and 2 clearly specify the median line to be "the line every point of which is equidistant from the nearest point on the baseline of Japan, and the nearest point on the baseline from which the breadth of the territorial sea pertaining to the foreign coast which is opposite the coast of Japan is measured." Originally, the median line has also been defined in parentheses as "a substitute line for the median line, which is agreed upon between Japan and a foreign country"; hence, although it is a median line in principle, it can be regarded as a line that is determined through diplomatic negotiations and by taking into consideration a range of circumstances.

This has been a traditional assertion of Japan, and one that is clearly adopted in domestic legislation as a delimitation method for defining borders with adjacent countries. In that sense, the concept of natural prolongation has no longer been regarded as relevant since the emergence of a 200 nautical mile EEZ. As is known, Articles 74 (EEZ) and 83 (continental shelf) of UNCLOS include provisions on

---

[58] See the ICJ judgment on the North Sea Continental Shelf cases.

delimitation that state in paragraph 1, "the delimitation of the exclusive economic zone (continental shelf) between States with opposite or adjacent coasts shall be effected by agreement on the basis of international law, as referred to in Article 38 of the Statute of the International Court of Justice, in order to achieve an equitable solution."

Changing Relevance of the "Median Line" Claim

In regard to the issue of delimitation of the continental shelf, Japan belongs to the "equidistant median line" group, as opposed to the "natural prolongation principle" group with the ROK and other countries.

Article 6 of the 1958 Convention on the Continental Shelf stipulates that delimitation of the continental shelf as being determined by the agreement of the concerned States. Specifically, "[w]here the same continental shelf is adjacent to the territories of two or more States whose coasts are opposite each other, the boundary of the continental shelf appertaining to such States shall be determined by agreement between them. In the absence of agreement, and unless another boundary line is justified by special circumstances, the boundary is the median line ..."[59] In reality, however, until the 1969 ICJ rulings on the North Sea Continental Shelf cases, and even afterwards, there have been numerous international agreements concluded on the basis of an equidistant median line.[60]

Incidentally, although agreements based on an equidistant median line were concluded between countries for the North Sea continental shelf, in the course of negotiations involving West Germany and its neighbors Denmark and the Netherlands, West Germany asserted the just and equitable share of an undelimited area, while the other two countries insisted on using the equidistance method. The three-nation dispute reached the ICJ in 1967, with the Court ruling that the continental shelf is the appurtenance of a coastal State, and in accordance with its rights, the continental shelf comprises the area of natural prolongation in the direction of the sea of the coastal State's land domain. The Court ruled that this fact is rooted in the sovereignty of the coastal State's land territory, and it has always been as such. Moreover, if the seabed area is not a part of the natural prolongation of the coastal State's territory, it does not belong to the coastal State irrespective of how close it may be to the State's territory. Accordingly, the equidistance method was clarified as not being inherent to the continental shelf regime.[61]

---

[59] https://legal.un.org/ilc/texts/instruments/english/conventions/8_1_1958_continental_shelf.pdf. Accessed on December 10, 2022.

[60] For further details on a combined equidistance-special circumstances rule, see Serita, op. cit.

[61] International Court of Justice. 1969. *Reports of Judgments, Advisory Opinions and Orders*, p. 3.

Fig. 5.5 Median Line of the
Okinawa Trough

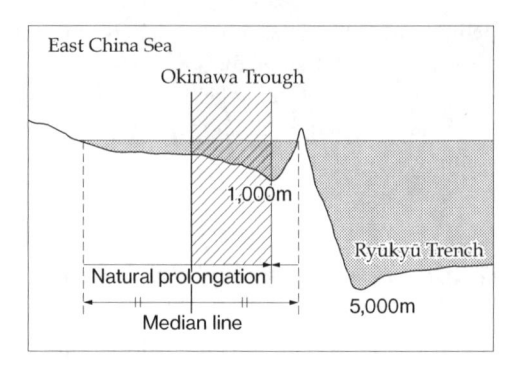

As for the East China Sea, its continental shelf extends out from the continent until the Pacific Ocean side beyond the Ryūkyū Islands spanning the southern tip of Kyūshū to Taiwan. At the northeast end of the East China Sea on the northwest side of the Amami Islands lies the approximately 1000 m deep Okinawa Trough, while on its northwest side facing the Pacific Ocean is the Ryūkyū Trench reaching a depth of 5000 m (Fig. 5.5).

"This continental shelf extends from the direction of China and the Korean Peninsula towards Japan in the east and right in front of the Ryūkyū Islands. It is a large, initial back-arc rifting basin stretching out toward the Pacific Ocean, and beyond it lies the Ryūkyū Islands. This is Japan's understanding of this single continental shelf" ... hence, "Japan regards the median line method as appropriate for delimitation."[62] The ROK's response was to assert its continental shelf to be the area extending to the Okinawa Trough, in accordance with the principle of natural prolongation of land territory; namely, the continental shelf ended at the large, initial back-arc rifting basin, as described by Japan. A joint development zone was subsequently set up in the overlapping area based on the assertions of Japan and the ROK, with both countries then concluding the Southern Part Agreement.[63]

This is how the median line used in the delimitation of a continental shelf became a marker denoting the boundary beyond which a coastal State could not assert its rights. Correspondingly, Article 57 of UNCLOS recognized the right of a coastal State to extend its EEZ up to 200 nautical miles, and the overlapping area in which

---

[62] House of Representatives Committee on Foreign Affairs, April 1, 1977.

[63] Mizukami, op. cit.

both countries could assert their rights for up to 200 nautical miles is the appropriate area for delimitation. The median line method is one method of dividing the area of overlapping claims.

Japan's domestic legislation of the Act on the Exclusive Economic Zone and Continental Shelf states that an EEZ is the area of the sea extending up to 200 nautical miles from the baseline of Japan; it also stipulates that it extends up to the median line or agreed upon line between Japan and an adjacent foreign country. However, this median line is merely a line provisionally drawn in the absence of an agreement, as was expressed in the ICJ ruling on the Jan Mayen case[64] that the conjoint conduct of both Parties of restraining the exercise of jurisdiction beyond the median line cannot be interpreted to mean that a delimitation line has already been defined. Accordingly, the ICJ independently determined the delimitation line for both countries in this case.

In the case that the countries concerned are unable to reach an agreement, the median line used in the delimitation of a continental shelf effectively becomes a line for limiting a country's claim. In contrast, the median line used in the delimitation of an EEZ is the line that curtails the exercise of a country's jurisdiction. This difference in the nuance of assertions on the median line must be recognized in discussions of this matter (Fig. 5.6).

---

[64] A delimitation dispute over an approximately 250 nautical mile area of water between Denmark's territory of Greenland and Norway's territory of the solitary Jan Mayen Island (no resident population). In June 1980, Denmark extended its 200 nautical mile fishery zone, which it partially established in 1976, as far as the east coast of Greenland. Although it did not exercise its fishery jurisdiction beyond the median line in accordance with its relation to Jan Mayen Island, in 1981 Denmark fully asserted its rights in the entire 200 nautical mile fishery zone. Meanwhile, in May 1980, Norway established a 200 nautical mile fishery zone surrounding Jan Mayen Island; however, in accordance with its relation to Greenland, Norway did not extend its zone beyond the median line. Subsequently, from June 1980 to August 1981, the median line was the effective delimitation line for both countries in exercising their fishery jurisdiction.

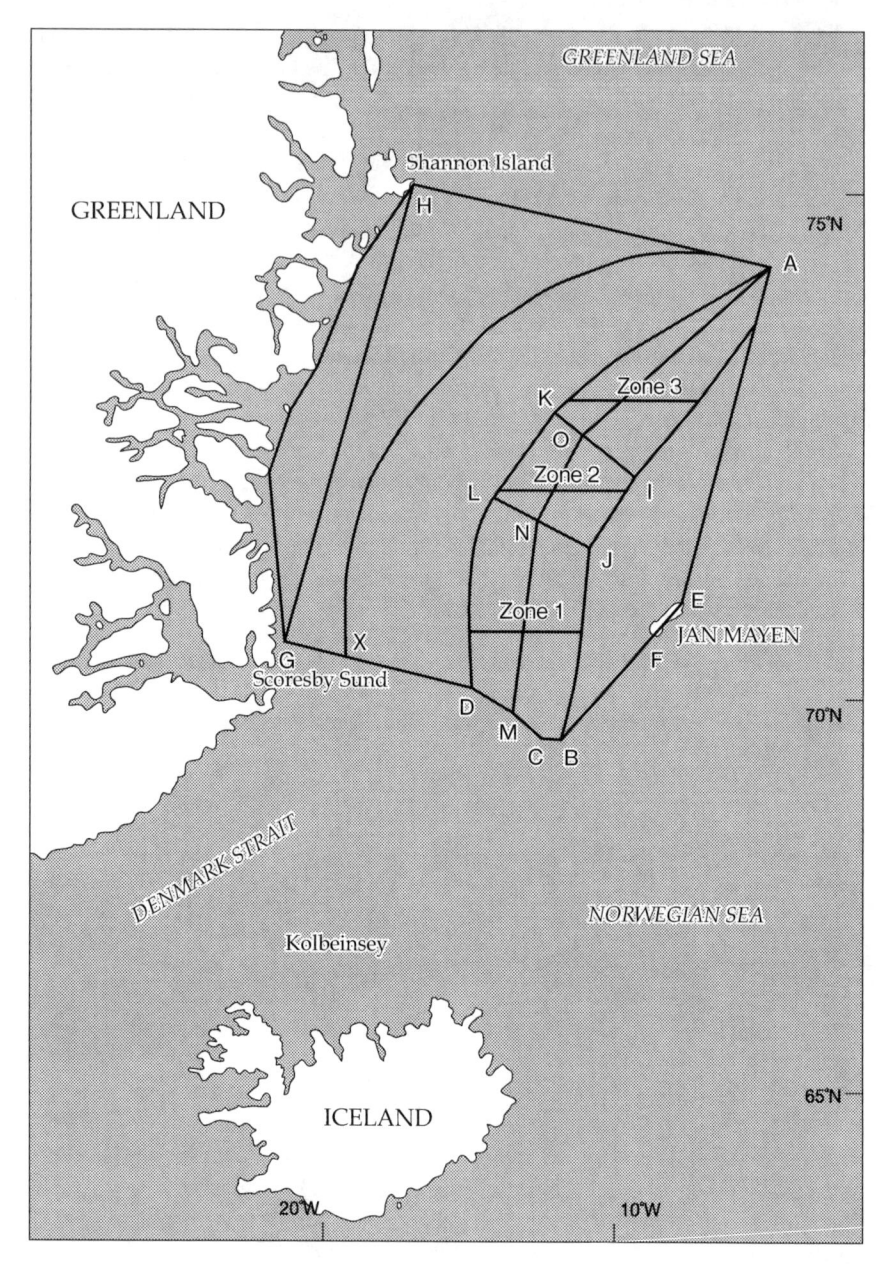

Fig. 5.6 Border between Greenland and Jan Mayen. Created by Serita from maps 1 and 2 of the lines drawn in the Judgment. A-X represents the 200 nautical mile line from Jan Mayen, A-I-J-B represents the 200 nautical mile line from Greenland, and A-K-L-D represents the median line

Chapter 6
Exclusive Economic Zones Between Japan and the Republic of Korea, and Japan and China

Main Causes of Difficulties with Demarcation of Boundaries

In principle, the obstacles to determining the boundaries of the exclusive economic zones (EEZs) between Japan and China and between Japan and the Republic of Korea (ROK) are that firstly, China is contesting Japan's exclusive sovereignty over the Senkaku Islands, and secondly, that the ROK occupies Takeshima, over which Japan asserts its sovereignty.

Furthermore, as a State practice, continental shelf boundary delimitation serves as a reference when delimiting the boundaries of EEZs, but "islands" on continental shelves are known to significantly affect boundary delimitations. Nevertheless, if looked at from the perspective of what impact and effect "islands" have had, there are discrepancies in the assertions respective States make with regard to the effect "islands" have when delimiting boundaries.[1] Above all else, islands that are in the middle of disputes cannot be considered as a datum point for delimiting boundaries. In other words, such islands are assigned no effect whatsoever in boundary delimitations.

Furthermore, looked at from the perspective of international law, Takeshima and the Senkaku Islands may well fall under this category.

Additionally, according to Article 121, Paragraph 3 of the United Nations Convention on the Law of the Sea (UNCLOS), "Rocks which cannot sustain human habitation or economic life of their own shall have no exclusive economic zone or continental shelf." Under international law, an "island" is "a naturally formed area of land, surrounded by water, which is above water at high tide,"[2] so even if an area that is only around the size of two tatami mats (equivalent in size to a double bed) is above the water at high tide (as is the case with Okinotorishima

---

[1] For details, see Serita, Kentarō. 1999. *Shima no ryōyū to keizai suiiki no kyōkai kakutei* (Sovereignty over Islands and the Delimitation of Economic Zones). Tokyo: Yūshindo Kōbunsha.

[2] UNCLOS, Article 121, Paragraph 1.

© Kreab K.K. 2023
K. Serita, *The Territory of Japan*, https://doi.org/10.1007/978-981-99-3013-5_6

Island), it constitutes an island that possesses territorial seas, an EEZ, and a continental shelf. "Rocks" do not constitute "islands," however. Even so, there is no definition of "rocks" in UNCLOS, and definitions of "rocks" are extremely varied.[3] If Takeshima and the Senkaku Islands are considered to constitute rocks, then they will have no impact on boundary delimitations. In addition, where islands are concerned, there also appear to be conflicting interpretations regarding the effects that they exert, including which of the islands that exist between two countries should be taken as datum points, and whether they should be considered to have a 100% effect or a 50% effect.[4]

Gap Between the Claims of Japan and the ROK

Incidentally, in the negotiations between the ROK and Japan, for argument's sake, if the ROK side were to propose a compromise and state that "Dokdo (i.e., Takeshima) corresponds to what are called 'rocks' in UNCLOS, so it is not necessary to take Dokdo into consideration," would the Japanese side be able to accept this compromise proposal?

The answer is probably "no." That is because from Japan's standpoint, it would have to consider what the repercussions of accepting this proposal would be. In other words, what ramifications would it have for the Senkaku Islands? Moreover, what ramifications would it have for the remote Okinotorishima Island, far off in the Pacific Ocean? Because given that Takeshima is about the size of Hibiya Park in Tokyo, if the island were designated as "rocks" then it would clearly be untenable to argue that Okinotorishima Island, an area only about the size of two tatami mats at high tide, were not. Furthermore, if Okinotorishima Island were "rocks," it could result in the loss of the extensive EEZ that Japan currently possesses.[5]

Then again, as has already been demonstrated, fishing zones and EEZs are different, and so Okinotorishima Island would no doubt retain the "200 nautical mile fishing zone" established under international customary law.[6] In light of the fact that no country has been protesting the domestic legislative measures that Japan adopted after UNCLOS entered into force, it could be argued that Okinotorishima

---

[3] Serita, op. cit.

[4] See Serita, op. cit.

[5] "Koto Okinotorishima ga kieru—gyogyō suiiki 400,000 heihō kiro ushinau osore (The Risk of Okinotorishima Island Disappearing and the Loss of 400,000 Square Kilometers of Fishing Grounds)," *Kobe Shimbun*, September 2, 1987; "Ryōdo, tetsu no gādo sakusen (Strategy for the Ironclad Guarding of Japan's Territories)," *Yomiuri Shimbun*, May 21, 1988, evening edition; "Burokku 8950-ko de hōi—Okinotorishima, keizai suiiki 400,000 heihō kiro no meiun nigiru (Taking Control of the Fate of Okinotorishima Island and 400,000 Square Kilometers of Economic Zone, with an 8950 Block Enclosure)," *Yomiuri Shimbun*, May 21, 1988, evening edition.

[6] See the Preamble to UNCLOS: "Affirming that matters not regulated by this Convention continue to be governed by the rules and principles of general international law," etc.

Island would continue to maintain an EEZ. Conversely, this hypothetical ROK proposal could in itself potentially saddle the ROK side with problems also, such as how Heuksando off the northwest coast of Jeju Island would be dealt with when negotiating the boundary delimitations of the economic zone between the ROK and China. That being the case, these are questions well worth asking even though sufficient information does not exist.

What would the outcome be if the Japanese side were to propose that "Takeshima is currently in dispute, so let's both stop using it a datum point"? As already shown, insofar as the ROK side adopts the position that the matter of Takeshima, which it occupies, is not in dispute, the ROK would probably be unable to accept this proposal.

However, when considered in this way, it appears to suggest that it would be possible for Japan and the ROK to both agree to remove Takeshima (i.e., "Dokdo") as a datum point so long as the basis for doing so were not questioned. Thus, the future is not necessarily completely bleak.

What would be the outcome if Takeshima (i.e., "Dokdo") were acknowledged as a datum point? In one case, full 100% effect would be given to the island in the delimitation process; in another case, only partial (half) effect would be given to it, following the example set in the arbitration decision over the channel between the United Kingdom and France. In either case, because delimitation as ROK territory and delimitation as Japanese territory would occur simultaneously, it would surely give rise to overlapping areas of ocean where rights are claimed. Conceivably it would be possible to propose to designate these areas of overlapping claims as joint use maritime areas. However, this concept assumes that the ROK side recognizes that the sovereignty over Takeshima (i.e., "Dokdo") is in dispute, which the ROK side would have difficulty accepting, it must be said. A joint use maritime area concept that would be acceptable to the ROK would undoubtedly take the form of a maritime area where claims overlap, and a form that recognizes a broader joint use maritime area to take into account the track record of ROK's fisheries industry, and a form in which the influence or effect of Takeshima's existence is not discernable. Such a case would have to take the form of a jointly administered fisheries area, and delimiting the boundaries of EEZs would be difficult.

In fact, as is discussed later, the new Japan-ROK Fisheries Agreement that took effect on January 22, 1999 was applied to both Japan's and the ROK's EEZs overall and employed a regime of "reciprocal access" in which each country permits fishing by the other country's citizens in its own EEZ. However, a Provisional Measures Zone (PMZ)—a maritime area where the reciprocal access measure is not adopted— was established in part of the Sea of Japan as a result of the two sides being at a loss over how to handle Takeshima and Yamatotai. Furthermore, they could not reach agreement on how to determine a datum point in the East China Sea, and so a PMZ was also established here. The agreement stipulates that boundary delimitation negotiations will continue, but there are many difficulties.

Gap Between the Claims of Japan and China

The circumstances between Japan and China are the same as well. The Japanese side's assertion is that the median line is between the Senkaku Islands and the Chinese mainland. China's argument is vague at present, but like the ROK, China too has been adopting the concept of natural prolongation in relation to continental shelves. In reality, however, China is not behaving in a way that will deliberately cause disputes in developing its continental shelf: it seems to be granting exploration and prospecting rights for developing the continental shelf in areas of ocean that are closer to the continent than the median line between the Senkaku Islands and the China mainland. Incidentally, China enacted the Law on the Territorial Sea and the Contiguous Zone in February 1992, which designates Taiwan and islands such as Uotsuri Island as Chinese territory. Japan immediately lodged an official protest stating it could not accept this measure.

Bathymetric charts of Japan's coastal waters show very clearly that the Nansei Shotō Islands and the Ryūkyū Trench run from mainland China and Kagoshima to Taiwan on either side of the East China Sea, and they face one another. As is widely known, Point 6[7] (established in Article 2 of the Agreement Between Japan and the Republic of Korea Concerning Joint Development of the Southern Part of the Continental Shelf Adjacent to the Two Countries) is said to be the equidistant midpoint of Japan, China, and the ROK. Furthermore, in the new Japan-China Fisheries Agreement of September 1997, it was agreed that the coverage would be north of 27° north latitude, the same as in the Japan-China Fisheries Agreement of August 15, 1975, while the line at 30°40′ north latitude was designated as the northern limit. In other words, care was taken that the agreements would not have an impact on the equidistant midpoint of Japan, China, and the ROK (Fig. 6.1).

However, the southern limit of the 27° north latitude parallel was agreed upon in the Japan-China Fisheries Agreement of 1975. Reportedly, this took into account relations with Taiwan, since delineation between Japan and China north of this line would not affect Taiwan. That being the case, this approach was probably followed in this new agreement as well. However, even though this line is derived by drawing a median line between Japan and China while ignoring the Senkaku Islands as a datum point (as opposed to drawing a median line between the Senkaku Islands and mainland China as the Japanese side argues for), more of the Japanese side's portion is designated as a joint-use maritime area, temporarily, than it would be if it was based on a median line drawn between the Senkaku Islands and China by awarding the Senkaku Islands full 100% effect and including the Japanese side's portion (and naturally including the Chinese side also). In any event, a temporary agreement appears to have been reached within parameters where the Senkaku Islands would not have a major impact, or rather, by setting the Senkaku Islands aside even while acknowledging it. In that respect, it has to be said that delineating the boundaries of the EEZs between Japan and China is extremely difficult.

---

[7] 30°46.2′ north latitude, 125°55.5′ east longitude; shown as Point E in Fig. 6.1.

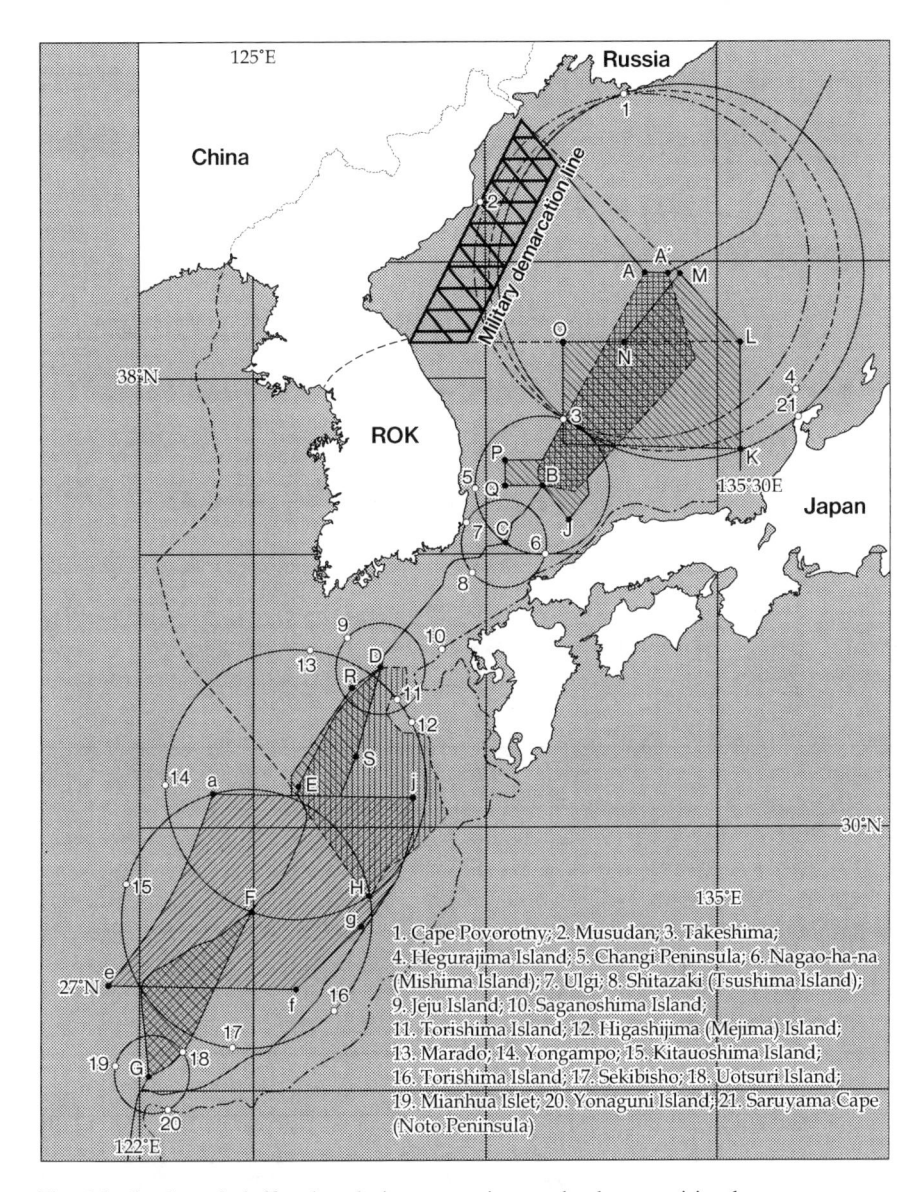

Fig. 6.1 Continental shelf and exclusive economic zone borders, provisional measures zones, hypothetical median lines, etc., in the Sea of Japan/East China Sea. (*Source*: Japan Coast Guard Chart Application No. 140024)

New Fisheries Agreements Between Japan and China, and Japan and the ROK, and the Establishment of PMZs

Regulations Leading up to the New Fisheries Agreements

In addition to Japanese, Koreans, and Chinese, these waters are fished by Taiwanese and Russians. Japan and Russia already had a shared history in this regard from 1976, which marked the opening of the 200 nautical mile era. Japan's Act on Temporary Measures Concerning Fishery Waters of 1977 was applied to the Pacific overall, and in the Sea of Japan, to the seas east of 135° east longitude only. Furthermore, it only covered the citizens of Russia (then the Soviet Union).[8] The ROK and China had been regulated through the respective fisheries agreements.[9]

A fundamental flaw of bilateral treaties is that, by nature, they only regulate the two countries, and cannot restrain third countries. As just mentioned, Japan's fishery zone was not enforced in the Sea of Japan west of 135° east longitude. Consequently, it was not possible to control either Taiwanese or Chinese fishing boats fishing there. Furthermore, the old Japan-ROK Fisheries Agreement was concluded in the era of 12 nautical mile fishery zones, which meant that in principle, ROK fishing boats that were in the high seas 12 nautical miles or further from each other's territorial sea baselines could only be controlled based on the flag State doctrine, in accordance with the principles of international law. Self-regulatory measures were employed between Japan and the ROK from 1980; in the seas in the vicinity of Hokkaido, ROK trawlers were banned from operating within Japan's otter trawl prohibition line, and a self-restraint period was established for each ROK trawler. In the seas in the vicinity of Western Japan, a fixed area of sea where trawl-fishing operations were prohibited was added; guidance and supervision was strengthened, but there were said to be constant violations.[10] In other words, the situation could be described as being almost completely uncontrolled from the standpoint of preserving fisheries resources.

The same circumstances also exist in the Yellow Sea and East China Sea, with a mix of Japanese, Koreans, Chinese, and Taiwanese operating in these fishing grounds, too. How to deal with Taiwan posed a problem in both the Japan-China negotiations and the China-ROK negotiations. Accordingly, the Japan-China fisheries agreement was considered to only cover the area of ocean north of 27° north latitude, an area not affected by Taiwan. The same is true of the latest Japan-China fisheries agreement.

---

[8] See Chapter 5, in particular the section on the 1977 Act on Temporary Measures Concerning Fishery Waters onwards.

[9] However, the Japan-ROK Fisheries Agreement of 1965 ended in January 1999 and the new agreement came into force. A new fisheries agreement between Japan and China was established in November 1997.

[10] This triggered calls to the Government of Japan from Japanese fishermen for the Japan-ROK Fisheries Agreement to be revoked.

Provisional Measures Under the New Fisheries Agreements

In the negotiations on the new Japan-China Fisheries Agreement, one problem was related to the Senkaku Islands and another problem was delineating the area of ocean where the 200-mile EEZ claims overlap. As has already been shown, the principle of boundary delimitations adopted in Japan's Continental Shelf and EEZ Act is "up to the median line" or "up to an agreed line" with the foreign country being faced. In Japan's boundary delimitations with China, however, reaching an agreement over what should be taken as a datum point is difficult to begin with, and the two sides even have opposing opinions on the "median line" itself. Agreeing on "an agreed line" is also difficult. That being the case, setting the boundaries of the PMZ in the areas of overlapping claims naturally proved challenging in the Japan-China negotiations. The two sides' opinions are said to have clashed in the negotiations, with the Chinese side demanding broader boundaries to allow its current hauls to be maintained, and the Japanese side keen to broaden the boundaries to which its own jurisdiction extended.[11]

In the end, it was decided that the new agreement would apply to both Japan's and China's EEZs overall (the previous agreement had only applied to the East China Sea and part of the Yellow Sea).[12] However, boundary delimitation of the EEZs did not occur, and the PMZ was designated as being the area of ocean between a line at 30°40′ north latitude and a line of 27° north latitude, comprising an area of ocean that excludes areas up to roughly 52 nautical miles from the baselines of both countries' territorial seas.[13] The excluded waters are the countries' respective EEZs, and the agreement states[14] that to operate there requires the permission, etc., of the partner country, as stipulated in UNCLOS. In the PMZ, the flag State doctrine is employed so the supervisory authority lies with the flag State; however, management of fisheries and marine resources is to be carried out jointly.[15] A Japan-China Joint Fisheries Committee, newly established under Article 11 of the new agreement, oversees specific regulatory measures. The area south of 27° north latitude and water area west of 125°30′ east longitude to the south of the East China Sea (excluding the People's Republic of China's EEZ in the East China Sea) had not been covered by the Japan-China Fisheries Agreement in the past; in the new agreement, it was decided that "essentially the existing fisheries order will be maintained," and so the area was considered to be outside the coverage of the coastal State principle.

---

[11] See articles published on September 4, 1997 in the *Asahi Shimbun* and *Yomiuri Shimbun*, respectively.

[12] New China-Japan Fisheries Agreement, Article 1.

[13] More accurately, the waters enclosed by a line formed by using a series of straight lines to connect the 11 points cited in Paragraph 1, Article 7 of the Agreement.

[14] New China-Japan Fisheries Agreement, Article 1 and 2.

[15] Ibid., Article 7, Paragraphs 2 and 3.

But what about the area of ocean between Japan and the ROK? For a clear understanding of the points at issue, it is worthwhile examining the points that were in question on September 5, 1998, when the Japan-ROK negotiations reached their final stages, based on newspaper reports that had appeared up to then. It can probably be surmised from the reports that in principle, as with the new Japan-China Agreement, the applicable water area under the new Japan-ROK agreement was considered to be all of the EEZs of both Japan and the ROK, with a PMZ to be established in areas of ocean where the EEZs overlapped.

To begin with, one point that the two countries were conceivably in agreement on was that the line delineating the Sea of Japan's central portion is the median line of North Korea, the ROK, Russia, and Japan. (This is based on the arguments that appeared in newspaper reports[16] before the Japanese side announced in January 1998 that the agreement had been completed, in other words, during the period when the negotiations had broken down.) Where the lines of the ROK's east coast and Japan's north coast are concerned, it appears that the ROK was asserting a line 34 nautical miles from the coast, while Japan was asserting a line 35 nautical miles from the coast. The ROK asserted the eastern tip of the Sea of Japan to be at 136° east longitude and Japan asserted it to be the 135th meridian east.[17] Moreover, according to one report,[18] the compromise plan consisted of the Japanese side accepting the ROK side's argument regarding the boundaries west of 135° east longitude, in return for the ROK accepting Japan's proposal to set the eastern tip of the PMZ as 135° east longitude. The other content of the agreement relates to issues such as ensuring the previous fishing catch levels remain the same, as argued by the ROK, and approaches to resource management within the PMZ.

What can be surmised from this is that the areas up to just over 35 nautical miles from the respective coasts were considered to be the respective country's EEZ, and vessels operating there would require the approval, etc., of the partner country. Furthermore, other areas of ocean west of 135° east longitude were designated to be a PMZ where the flag State doctrine would apply and the supervisory authority would lie with the flag State, but with management of fisheries and marine resources to be conducted jointly. Where specific regulatory measures are concerned, as before, an ROK-Japan joint fisheries committee was to be set up for that purpose. Incidentally, there are no reports whatsoever mentioning the East China Sea from the Tsushima Strait, but based on the line that was established in the Agreement Between Japan and the Republic of Korea Concerning Joint Development of the Southern Part of the Continental Shelf Adjacent to the Two Countries, a median line would be drawn here, or alternatively because it involves boundary delimitation with

---

[16]*Asahi Shimbun*, January 24, 1998, morning edition; *Kōbe Shimbun*, January 23, 1998, morning edition.

[17]Serita, Kentarō. 1998. "Nikkan gyogyo kyotei haki no ho to gaiko (Law and Diplomacy relating to the Abolition of the Japan-ROK Fisheries Agreement)." *Jurist*, March 15.

[18]*Kōbe Shimbun*, August 31, 1998, morning edition.

China, it was considered to be an area of water excluded from the coverage of the agreement. This is completely unclear from newspaper reports.

Therefore, after ratifying UNCLOS, Japan and the ROK began diplomatic negotiations in May 1996 on the new Japan-ROK Fisheries Agreement, which was an outstanding issue for the two countries. Following a temporary suspension in those negotiations, an agreement was reached early on the morning of September 25, 1998, and the negotiations concluded for the first time in 2 years and 9 months. The agreement was subsequently signed on November 28 and entered into force on January 22, 1999. This new Japan-ROK Fisheries Agreement comprises a Preamble, 17 Articles that form the body of the agreement, and concluding clause, as well as Annexes I and II, which form an indivisible part of the main agreement. Other related documents include the agreed minutes, which record items relating to the areas of sea established in the East China Sea, an exchange of notes concerning measures for instances when vessels are operated in violation of the provisions of the agreement, and a Japanese note concerning catch quotas for ROK citizens and fishing boats.

The areas of sea that this agreement applies to are considered to be the EEZs of Japan and the ROK in their entirety.[19] As with the New Japan-China Fisheries Agreement, a regime of "reciprocal access" was adopted whereby each contracting party permits the citizens and fishing boats of the other contracting party to fish within its own EEZ.[20] In areas of sea where the reciprocal access measure is not adopted, a PMZ was established in part of the Sea of Japan and part of the East China Sea.[21] (According to Annex II, in this zone each country will respectively take measures based on the flag State doctrine.)

135°30′ east longitude was designated as the eastern limit of the Sea of Japan's PMZ, but a portion north of 38°37 north latitude was protruded in order to include Yamatotai, a good fishing area, in the PMZ.[22] This resulted in approximately 45% of Yamatotai being included in the PMZ, which is said to have angered Japanese fishermen.

Additionally, the area of sea in the vicinity of Takeshima, which is an area of mutually overlapping claims, was included in the PMZ in the Sea of Japan, and portions of the EEZs that could be described as inherent to each party were also included. Was this potentially influenced by the fact that Japan's Act on Temporary Measures Concerning Fishery Waters of 1977 had not established a 200 nautical mile area of sea west of 135° east longitude? Additionally, is the PMZ's legal status the high seas? Incidentally, the latitude/longitude point of intersection at the 38°37′ north latitude and 131°40′ east longitude[23] that is the western limit of the PMZ is conceivably the median point between the ROK and the Democratic People's

---

[19] New Japan-ROK Fisheries Agreement, Article 1.

[20] Ibid., Article 2 to Article 6.

[21] Ibid., Article 8 and 9.

[22] Ibid., Article 9, Paragraph 1.

[23] Shown as Point O in Fig. 6.1.

Republic of Korea (North Korea).[24] Based on further conjecture, it is also possible to imagine that conceivably, the apex of the protruded triangular portion is the median point between Russia's Cape Povorotny, Takeshima, and Saruyama Cape on the Japan side, not Hegurajima Island on the Noto Peninsula coast, with the protruding portion forming an isosceles triangle.[25]

Partly because the same line as the boundary established in the agreement between Japan and the ROK Concerning the Establishment of the Boundary in the Northern Part of the Continental Shelf was employed[26] as the boundary of the two countries' EEZs, the end point in this agreement on the northern part of the continental shelf (which is also the starting point of the Agreement Concerning Joint Development of the Southern Part of the Continental Shelf) was adopted as the starting point of the East China Sea's PMZ.[27] This can be thought of as the median line linking the ROK's Jeju Island and Torishima Island in Japan's Danjo Archipelago. However, where other points are concerned, although there appears to be agreement between the two countries with regard to drawing median lines, the northwest line is drawn slightly north of the line established in the Agreement Concerning Joint Development of the Southern Part of the Continental Shelf, for example. This conceivably reflects the Japanese side arguing for the ROK's Marado off the coast of Jeju Island and Japan's Torishima Island as datum points, while the southeast line conceivably reflects the ROK side arguing for its own Marado and Ujishima Island and Kusagakishima Island as datum points and for Japan's Danjo Archipelago to be ignored. No agreement between the two countries over which islands should be used as datum points can be detected, and as a result, conceivably, the area where the countries' claims overlap was designated as a PMZ. Incidentally, the southern limit is only designated to be "north of the southernmost parallel of the ROK's EEZ." Since it is not presented as a latitude, it is not necessarily clear. At the same time, because Point 6[28] (established in Article 2 of the Agreement Concerning Joint Development of the Southern Part of the Continental Shelf) is said to be the median point between Japan, China, and the ROK, if this point were taken to be the southernmost point of the ROK's EEZ, the East China Sea PMZ established in the Japan-ROK Fisheries Agreement would be to the north of the PMZ established in the Japan-China Fisheries Agreement, so the two areas of sea would not overlap.

In these PMZs in the Sea of Japan and the East China Sea, the two countries decided that with regard to their own citizens and fishing boats[29] they would take the necessary measures to ensure appropriate management, including conserving living

---

[24] At the same time, North Korea does not recognize the new Japan-ROK Fisheries Agreement, claiming it to be invalid.

[25] Some areas of sea on the northern side of Points M, N, and O in Fig. 6.1 are excluded from the coverage of the agreement under Appendix II.

[26] New Japan-ROK Fisheries Agreement, Article 7.

[27] Ibid., Article 9, Paragraph 2.

[28] Shown as Point E in Fig. 6.1.

[29] New Japan-ROK Fisheries Agreement, Appendix I.

marine resources and setting the maximum numbers of vessels by fishing category that may operate there, in accordance with the decisions of the ROK-Japan Joint Fisheries Committee.

Incidentally, decisions regarding the conditions, etc., for operating in each sea area in 2010 were made at the Japan-China Joint Committee on Fisheries held in Beijing in December 2009, and the Japan-ROK Fisheries Joint Committee held in Seoul in February 2010.

Chapter 7
A Proposal for Stability and Coexistence in East Asia

Acknowledging the Issues: Looking Squarely at the Causes of Instability

Territorial disputes are inclined to make people emotional, lose their power of reason, and lose their composure. Moreover, there are even those who exploit this provocative effect that territorial disputes have on people, fiercely stirring up the disputes with the nationalistic goal of inflaming the situations.

The factors causing instability between Japan and the Republic of Korea (ROK), and Japan and China include a number of issues relating to Japan's former colonial rule such as the problem of the perceptions of history and the textbook issue, as well as the issue of Japanese prime ministers visiting Yasukuni Shrine, where war criminals are enshrined. However, the disputes relating to Takeshima and the Senkaku Islands, insofar as they are territorial problems, are major flashpoints that will not readily disappear. Furthermore, untangling the knotted threads of this issue will require an extraordinary effort given that it also involves the utilization of both living and non-living resources in the exclusive economic zones (EEZs) in the vicinity of these islands. A thorough examination of the respective facts and what surrounds them should yield some clues as to resolving these problems, however.

As is well known and as has already been noted, the Senkaku Islands suddenly came to the attention of the countries of the world after a scientific seafloor survey by the Economic Commission for Asia and the Far East raised the possibility of a deposit of crude oil resources in the continental shelf of the East China Sea. In considering how to go about reaching a desirable solution, it will be necessary to return to this starting point. Furthermore, what triggered Takeshima to emerge as a problem was the ROK's attempt to use the Syngman Rhee Line to preserve its fishery resources by standing up to, and shutting out of its coastal sea areas, Japanese fishing boats whose superior technical strengths were enabling them to operate off the coast of the Korean Peninsula and catch large quantities of fish. These developments coincide with a general trend in post-World War II international law of the sea

© Kreab K.K. 2023
K. Serita, *The Territory of Japan*, https://doi.org/10.1007/978-981-99-3013-5_7

of coastal States seeking to secure the use of maritime resources, particularly fishery resources and oil resources.

Where fishery resources are concerned, we have managed to conclude a new Japan-China Fisheries Agreement and a new Japan-ROK Fisheries Agreement for the 200 nautical mile era, and to establish Provisional Measures Zones (PMZs), for the time being, and efforts are being made to have a clearer outlook for managing and preserving those resources. Accordingly, the major problem that remains in the East Asia ocean area is the development of the continental shelf in the vicinity of the Senkaku Islands and the struggle between Japan and China over the continental shelf. In other words, behind the problem of sovereignty over the Senkaku Islands lies the problem of continental shelf boundary delimitation in connection with the exploitation of petroleum, as well as marine resources surveys in economic zones. This is the biggest challenge.

Neither, however, can these two new fisheries agreements escape the constraints that arise from bilateral treaties, namely, that treaties only impose obligations on the State parties to the treaties. In other words, the Japan-China agreement naturally applies to Japanese and Chinese fishing boats: it establishes that in the PMZs the State parties have supervisory authority over their own vessels and can caution the partner State's vessels, but it does not apply to ROK or Taiwanese fishing boats. In this respect it is insufficient from the standpoint of preserving resources and conserving the environment. In the same way, the Japan-ROK agreement applies to ROK and Japanese fishing boats, but Chinese and Taiwanese fishing boats also operate in the sea areas that the agreement covers. The problems of resource management, resource preservation, and environmental conservation will not be resolved by Japan and the ROK alone. As the fishermen know from daily experience, in the field of fishery resources utilization unstable factors also remain.

In the interests of resolving these problems on a realistic basis and in a future-oriented way, I present the following two proposals, which are based on the outcomes of the issues that have been considered up to Chapter 6. The first proposal is to establish a Senkaku Islands nature reserve and a Takeshima nature reserve. The other proposal is that Japan, China, the ROK, and Taiwan should set up joint fishing areas, as an international regime for conserving the resources and environment in the Sea of Japan, Yellow Sea, and East China Sea. The aim of these proposals is to make Japan a stable presence that is trusted in East Asia and the world.

Establishing the Senkaku Islands and Takeshima Nature Reserves

Other Countries' Precedents for Dealing with Island Territories

While keeping the Senkaku Islands and Takeshima in mind, we shall now examine treaties that have addressed and resolved problems of sovereignty over islands in conjunction with continental shelf boundary delimitation.[1]

The first is the agreement between Abu Dhabi and Qatar reached on March 20, 1969. A territorial problem existed between the two countries with regard to three islands: Lasahat (Al Ashat), Shura'awa (Shara'iwah), and Daiyina (Dayyinah). Qatar and Abu Dhabi are adjacent to each other. Daiyina is slightly larger than the other two islands, and it flanks a median line. As a result of negotiations, it was decided that the first two islands, which lie toward Qatar, would be designated as Qatar's territory, and that they would be completely disregarded as datum points when undertaking continental shelf boundary delimitation. Daiyina, however, would be permitted to have 3 nautical mile territorial waters (Qatar and Abu Dhabi both have 3 nautical mile territorial waters). Accordingly, the agreed line is a median line that ignores the presence of the three islands, but with a circular projection to the Qatar side, around the circumference of Daiyina.

The second case is the Treaty between Australia and the Independent State of Papua New Guinea concerning matters of sovereignty and maritime boundaries in the area known as the Torres Strait, and related matters, which was signed in Sydney on December 18, 1978. The islands in the Torres Strait remained Australian territory even after Papua New Guinea became independent, but three islands, namely Boigu, Daunan, and Saibai, were problematic. In all cases the islands are separated from the Australian mainland by distances of 140 km or more, but they are less than 4 km away from the coast of Papua New Guinea, and around 700 people live on them. Following negotiations, it was decided that these three islands' territorial waters would be 3 nautical miles, even if Australia's territorial waters were extended to 12 nautical miles in the future.

What is extremely interesting to note is that the decision resolved four problems altogether—not simply the problem of sovereignty but also the delimitation of the continental shelf, the allocation of fishing zones, and the preservation of the indigenous people's lifestyle—while using a different method for resolving each. The continental shelf's boundary line runs close to Papua New Guinea, but the above-mentioned islands are completely disregarded as datum points. The boundaries of the fishing zones are taken to be the boundaries of the continental shelf, but special judicial authority is established for both countries. To the extent that at one point there was reportedly a proposal to try to make these three islands into a nature reserve, both countries have a duty to preserve and conserve the environment, and

---

[1] See Chapter 1 of Serita, Kentarō. 1999. *Shima no ryōyū to keizai suiiki no kyōkai kakutei* (Sovereignty over Islands and the Delimitation of Economic Zones). Tokyo: Yūshindo Kōbunsha.

mining and commercial fishing are regulated so that traditional fishing by the indigenous people is not interfered with.

In considering the problem of the Senkaku Islands, these two treaties may seem too different to be able to serve as references, given the different circumstances of the countries concerned, the different circumstances that the islands are in, and the different positional relations of the islands at issue. Nevertheless, in terms of providing clues for resolving problems, these treaties are certainly not lacking in value.

Next it is worthwhile to examine the significance of islands in relation to continental shelf boundary delimitation.

As illustrated in *Shima no ryōyū to keizai suiiki no kyōkai kakutei*, practices differ by country, and through various proposals at the Third United Nations Conference on the Law of the Sea as well as some State practices and international precedents, some standards are provided respectively for the size of islands, their position, population, political and economic status, and so on. Of those standards, based on international judicial precedents that emphasize the geography itself, it can be surmised that the "size" of an island and its "position" are of considerable importance. As is well known, Article 121, Paragraph 3 of the United Nations Convention on the Law of the Sea (UNCLOS) stipulates that "Rocks which cannot sustain human habitation or economic life of their own shall have no exclusive economic zone or continental shelf." No definition of any kind is offered for the "rocks" cited here. However, without the addition of artificial means, the Senkaku Islands and Takeshima could not conceivably sustain human habitation.

When the influence and effects that islands exert on continental shelf boundary delimitation are classified on the basis of continental shelf boundary delimitation treaties and other such agreements that countries have concluded thus far, it reveals the following:

1. Islands within a country's own territorial waters and/or running alongside its coast qualify as datum points.
2. When the island in question is located around the median line, which is provisionally drawn without considering the existence of the island, that island is either completely disregarded as a datum point or is granted territorial waters only.
3. In the case of a solitary island in distant seas, such as Rockall Island in British territory, claiming a continental shelf on the basis of that island alone is problematic.
4. Islands that are far removed from the country concerned and close to another country will have territorial seas only, and depending on the circumstances, the territorial seas themselves will also be limited, as is stipulated in the treaty between Australia and Papua New Guinea of December 18, 1978. Or alternatively, the islands will have no territorial seas whatsoever, as with Argentina's small island of Martín García, which is on the Uruguayan side of a boundary line established in a treaty between Argentina and Uruguay on November 19, 1973.

Incidentally, Martín García Island in Argentine territory agreed in the Argentina-Uruguay treaty, is to be used exclusively as a nature reserve intended for the conservation and preservation of indigenous flora and fauna, according to Article 45 of the treaty.

Characterization of the Senkaku Islands and Takeshima

It is possible to characterize the Senkaku Islands and Takeshima as islands under dispute, as uninhabited islands, as islands far from a mainland, and as small islands on and around a median line. In this regard, it must be noted that Tsushima Island and Ikinoshima Island are considered as datum points for measuring the intermediate line stipulated in the Agreement between Japan and the Republic of Korea concerning Establishment of Boundary in the Northern Part of the Continental Shelf Adjacent to the Two Countries (Boundary Agreement), while Takeshima is not taken into account whatsoever. In other words, disputed islands are disregarded as datum points for delimitation of the continental shelf, meaning they have no effect on delimitation.

Additionally, the Senkaku Islands are no more than uninhabited islands with a total land area of a little over 6.3 km^2, comprising the largest island, Uotsuri Island, which has a land area of 4.32 km^2, followed by Kōbisho (1.08 km^2), Minamikojima Island (0.46 km^2), Kitakojima Island (0.31 km^2), and Sekibisho (0.15 km^2). Takeshima meanwhile has a total land area of 0.23 km^2. Tsushima's Kamijima Island, which was taken into account as a datum point in the Japan-ROK Boundary Agreement, has around 40 times the land area of the Senkaku Islands, making it roughly the same size as Iriomote Island or Ishigaki Island.

Understandably, there are islands that, based on their size, population, and geographical location, cannot be completely disregarded when it comes to drawing median lines, while neither is it possible to grant them full effect. In the case of the Anglo-French Continental Shelf Arbitration Award, a precedent existed in State practice of a partial (half) effect approach being adopted, namely that Kharg Island, an island in the Persian (Arabian) Gulf, belongs to Iran. Kharg Island is located approximately 17 miles off the coast of Iran and has a land area of approximately 20 km^2. However, excepting cases where there is a resident population, conceivably it is difficult to grant effect to an uninhabited island.

Under international law, it is possible to argue that both the Senkaku Islands and Takeshima are in all cases islands. Namely, they are "a naturally formed area of land, surrounded by water, which is above water at high tide," and consequently they possess "an exclusive economic zone and continental shelf."[2]

Uotsuri Island is approximately 90 nautical miles from Iriomote Island and approximately 120 nautical miles from Taiwan's Keelung Port, while Takeshima is a distance of 120 nautical miles from the Korean Peninsula and 115 nautical miles from the Japanese mainland. At the same time, there are also examples of an island that is far away from a main island being granted effect. The agreement reached

---

[2]UNCLOS, Article 121, Paragraph 1 and 2.

between Indonesia and Malaysia on October 27, 1969 is one such case. Under this agreement, even though Indonesia's Natuna and Anambas islands in the Borneo Sea are approximately 250 nautical miles away from the Borneo mainland, they are granted full effect in delimiting the boundary of the continental shelf between the Malay Peninsula and Sarawak.

Establishing Joint-Use Nature Reserves

The conclusion that we can reach from the above examination is that even if the sovereignty disputes were resolved, there would have to be cumulative and seemingly endless and futile debate in negotiating boundary delimitations, beginning with the positioning of the datum points. Immeasurable amounts of energy and time would have to be devoted to that.

Unnecessary discord could well emerge during that time. So, it would clearly be more prudent to utilize that energy and time for mutual friendship. Accordingly, the following are proposals for the Senkaku Islands and Takeshima.

The first proposal is the adoption of a collective approach to dealing with the Senkaku Islands through the establishment of a nature reserve and the joint development of the continental shelf.

Rather than Japan and China contesting the Senkaku Islands by both claiming the continental shelf, they should deal with the issues all at once by making the Senkaku Islands a nature reserve, thus redressing the overhunting of albatrosses, which once inhabited the islands in such large numbers that they were dubbed "*baka-dori*" (meaning "idiot birds" in Japanese, so called because they were so easy to catch), while simultaneously developing the continental shelf jointly through economic cooperation. It would undoubtedly be the best policy, since it would put to rest the issue of the Senkaku Islands once again, and, as they apparently had in the past, both Japan and China would mutually benefit from the joint development of the continental shelf in the vicinity of the Senkaku Islands. The only way to reach a final resolution would be to deal with the related issues collectively, not only the territorial right issue alone.

The second proposal is to establish Takeshima as a nature reserve.

No problem relating to continental shelf resources exists in the vicinity of Takeshima, so conceivably the only issue is fishing in the surrounding area. Additionally, as the area of water that encompasses Takeshima is currently a PMZ, this proposal would not involve transferring Takeshima to Japan, and neither would it involve making concessions to Japan over the issue. Consequently, establishing Takeshima as a nature reserve could be assumed to present virtually no emotional difficulties to the ROK people. Rather than blowing up the islands in order to resolve territory problems as a high-level ROK official is reported to have suggested, the best policy would surely be to make the islands into nature reserves, enabling all parties to work together in a forward-looking manner.

As a common proposal for both cases, instead of establishing territorial seas around these Senkaku Islands and Takeshima nature reserves, it would be better to make 3 nautical mile or 12 nautical mile zones into fishing-prohibited areas. Currently fishing is not taking place in the area of water around Takeshima, and fishing is apparently not being carried out around the Senkaku Islands either, so this idea poses no particular obstacles. Above all else, this proposal can be recommended from the perspective of conserving marine resources, and furthermore, it would also generate positive outcomes for fishing and the state of resources in the surrounding ocean areas.

Another proposal is described below regarding the management of the Senkaku Islands nature reserve and Takeshima nature reserve. Since the Senkaku Islands are currently under Japan's control, it would make sense for Japan to manage them, and since Takeshima is currently occupied by the ROK, it would make sense for the ROK to manage it. In that way, the current circumstances would not change greatly, and neither would it be likely to irritate citizens. Researchers should be free to land on these nature reserves in order to conduct international or domestic joint research. Accordingly, the respective authorities should in principle approve such visits and the outcomes of the academic research should be promptly published.

Establishing an International Regime for Preserving the Resources and the Environment in the Sea of Japan, Yellow Sea, and East China Sea: Establishing a Joint Fishing Zone by Japan, China, the ROK, and Taiwan

In addition to Japanese fishermen, there are also ROK, Chinese, and Taiwanese fishermen operating in the Sea of Japan, the Yellow Sea, and the East China Sea; no doubt North Koreans will also be a presence in these seas before long. The Japan-ROK Fisheries Agreement and the Japan-China Fisheries Agreement apply to this area of sea, but as has already been noted, neither agreement can escape the limitations of being a bilateral agreement. Consequently, it would be desirable to develop a regime based on a multilateral treaty. That said, enormous amounts of energy were expended just to negotiate the present agreements, and conceivably even more energy would be needed to adopt a multilateral treaty. Accordingly, a realistic first step would be to begin by utilizing the existing agreements.

So what should be done specifically? The handling of Taiwan becomes an issue in connection with the One China principle. It is an issue that warrants careful discussion, taking into account the 20 million or more people living in Taiwan and the betterment of the relationship across the Taiwan Strait. A good start for the time being might be holding a joint resources protection sub-meeting or joint environmental conservation sub-meeting of the China-Japan Joint Fisheries Committee and the ROK-Japan Joint Fisheries Committee. Or, if this proves too political, the parties could hold a joint scientific research sub-meeting on the state of resources or the situation with regard to environmental destruction. To that end, the ultimate goal must be confirmed.

The ultimate goal (which is sure to be debated, and in fact should be broadly debated) should be the conclusion of a multilateral treaty among the countries/regions of Japan, China, the ROK, and Taiwan that contains the following:

1. Designate the Sea of Japan, Yellow Sea, and East China Sea, west of 135°30′ east longitude as the area of sea that the treaty applies to;
2. Maintain the EEZs of each country/region at 35 to 52 nautical miles offshore, and designate the area beyond the EEZs a joint fishing zone;
3. Establish an international committee, which might be called the East Asian Fisheries Committee, in order to preserve and manage fishery resources and conserve the marine environment; and
4. Grant this joint committee the authority to enforce regulatory measures, such as the fish catches allocated to each country/region, and grant the committee itself the authority to supervise offending vessels rather than entrusting the supervision of vessels violating the treaty to each treaty party according to the flag State doctrine, in order to make the treaty something that is viable.

This proposal is not meant to exclude the Democratic People's Republic of Korea (North Korea), and the door should always remain open. In any event, a start first needs to be made, based on a clear vision of establishing order in East Asia.

Chapter 8
Territorial Air Space and Air Defense Identification Zones

Territorial Air Space and Outer Space

Air space first became an issue in international law in the twentieth century when aircraft were invented and began flying over territorial land. At first, there were two conflicting views on the matter. There were those who believed that the skies were free and open, and those who believed that the sovereignty of an aerial space belonged to the country below it. However, the use of aircraft for military purposes in World War I proved to be the decisive turning point; eventually, following the war, the Convention Relating to the Regulation of Aerial Navigation (Paris Convention) was signed in Paris in 1919. The Convention stipulated that "every Power has complete and exclusive sovereignty over the air space above its territory." The Paris Convention was superseded in 1944 by the Convention on International Civil Aviation (Chicago Convention), which was adopted in Chicago; this convention has been maintained until the present day. The fact that every State has complete and exclusive sovereignty over the air space above its territory is an established principle of international law.

The vertical bound of such territory, however, remains undefined. Given the state of aviation, those at the time did not feel the need to define the term "air space," nor were they particularly hindered by this fact. However, the launch of Sputnik in 1957 marked the start of the space age, and the term "air space" could no longer remain undefined.

Interestingly, there have been many different arguments on this subject. For example, there were some who argued for unlimited territorial air space, in other words that there was no vertical bound on a terrestrial nation's territorial rights. Then again, the fact that the Earth orbits the sun and rotates on its axis obviously renders this argument an irrational one. In addition, because the Paris Convention and the Chicago Convention stipulated that the air space over which every State had sovereignty was "air space," there were those who argued that air space was limited to space in which there was air. There were yet others who argued that territorial air

© Kreab K.K. 2023
K. Serita, *The Territory of Japan*, https://doi.org/10.1007/978-981-99-3013-5_8

space should be limited to the extent that can be reached through buoyant flight using air flow since these conventions recognized sovereignty over air space at a time when people had envisioned conventional aircraft based on aerodynamic buoyance.

By now, however, different States have already launched thousands of artificial satellites. The UN General Assembly adopted the Treaty on Principles Governing the Activities of States in the Exploration and Use of Outer Space, including the Moon and Other Celestial Bodies in 1966, which prohibited national appropriation by claim of sovereignty. In light of this, at the very least, it became the dominant view that territorial air space was limited to the perigee of the orbit of a satellite or other spacecraft around the Earth. In terms of a specific number, this limit was 100 km above sea level. In any case, the boundary between territorial air space and outer space is undefined. Of course, the space above an exclusive economic zone (EEZ) or the high seas does not belong to any State, and it is known as "international air space."[1]

Freedom of Flight for Civil Aircraft

Foreign aircraft cannot freely fly through territorial air space. While the right of innocent passage is recognized in territorial seas, no such right is recognized in territorial air space. Nevertheless, for the sake of international transit, it was deemed necessary to scrap the inconvenient practice of seeking permission from a territorial State every time a flight is made and instead establish a system that permitted flight, however limited it may be. Such a regime, first established under the Paris Convention of 1919, currently is based on the Chicago Convention of 1944. In addition to stipulating the general principles of international civil aviation, the Chicago Convention established the International Civil Aviation Organization (ICAO; headquartered in Montreal, Canada) and its mission.

The Chicago Convention applies only to the civil aircraft of the parties to the Convention, including all types of airplanes, helicopters, and airships, but excluding pilotless aircraft. Military or other government aircraft, however, must not fly over or land in another State's territory, unless so permitted by a special agreement or other means.

Apart from when providing regular air services, civil aircraft hold the right to enter the territory of other parties to the Convention, fly through a territory without landing, or land in the territory for purposes other than transportation such as refueling or maintenance, without needing to seek prior approval. That being said, civil aircraft must of course abide by any landing requests made by the State, follow the flight paths designated by the State, and so on.

---

[1] The development of outer space has advanced significantly in recent years. For more details, see Aoki, Setsuko. 2006. *Nihon no uchū senryaku* (Japan's Space Strategy). Tokyo: Keio University Press.

The Chicago Convention thus made a distinction between irregular flight and regular international air services. The freedom of flight was only recognized for irregular flight, whereas regular flight, which primarily takes the form of international air services, was not liberalized. Regular flight was instead regulated by the International Air Services Transit Agreement and the International Air Transport Agreement; international air services could only be conducted upon the conclusion of bilateral aviation agreements. At present, States around the world have concluded an intricate network of aviation agreements. As things currently stand, negotiations on such agreements impact the interests of the States involved and are therefore usually very problematic.[2]

Air Defense Identification Zones

In general, a coastal State establishes an air defense identification zone (ADIZ) over a fixed area above its EEZ or the high seas for ensuring its own security. In establishing an ADIZ, the State requests all aircraft flying through it to present their flight plans and report their position, in an attempt to swiftly and accurately identify and confirm the position of such aircraft.

This practice was first begun by the United States in 1950. In order to be able to identify, locate, and control all aircraft within a certain distance from the coast, the US required, under domestic law, that all applicable aircraft report their position and other information, and established penal provisions for those who violated the law. Subsequently, many other countries, including Canada, France, Iceland, the United Kingdom, and the Soviet Union, took similar measures.

In Japan's case, this was done for the sake of easily identifying aircraft flying in the vicinity of Japan, which was deemed to assist the implementation of effective measures against aerial incursions of Japan's territory, as stipulated in the Self-Defense Forces (SDF) Act. For the ADIZ implemented by Japan's Defense Agency, the pilots of SDF aircraft that fly through the zone are obligated to report the time and location at which they expect to enter the zone, among other information, to a radar site. The scope of the Act is stipulated in accordance with a government directive on flight in the ADIZ.[3] Civil aircraft, meanwhile, are identified through the reporting of their flight plans and other relevant information by the Ministry of Land, Infrastructure, Transport, and Tourism (Fig. 8.1).

In addition, to avoid accidental collisions between Japanese SDF aircraft and the military aircraft of the Republic of Korea (ROK), a dedicated hotline has been established between the two countries. This was first proposed by the ROK side in 1990, and the two sides voluntarily established measures in July 1995 for preventing

---

[2] Sakamoto, Akio and Miyoshi, Susumu. 1999. *Shin kokusai kōkūhō* (New International Aviation Law). Tokyo: Yūshindō Kōbunsha.

[3] Defense Agency Directive No. 36, 1969.

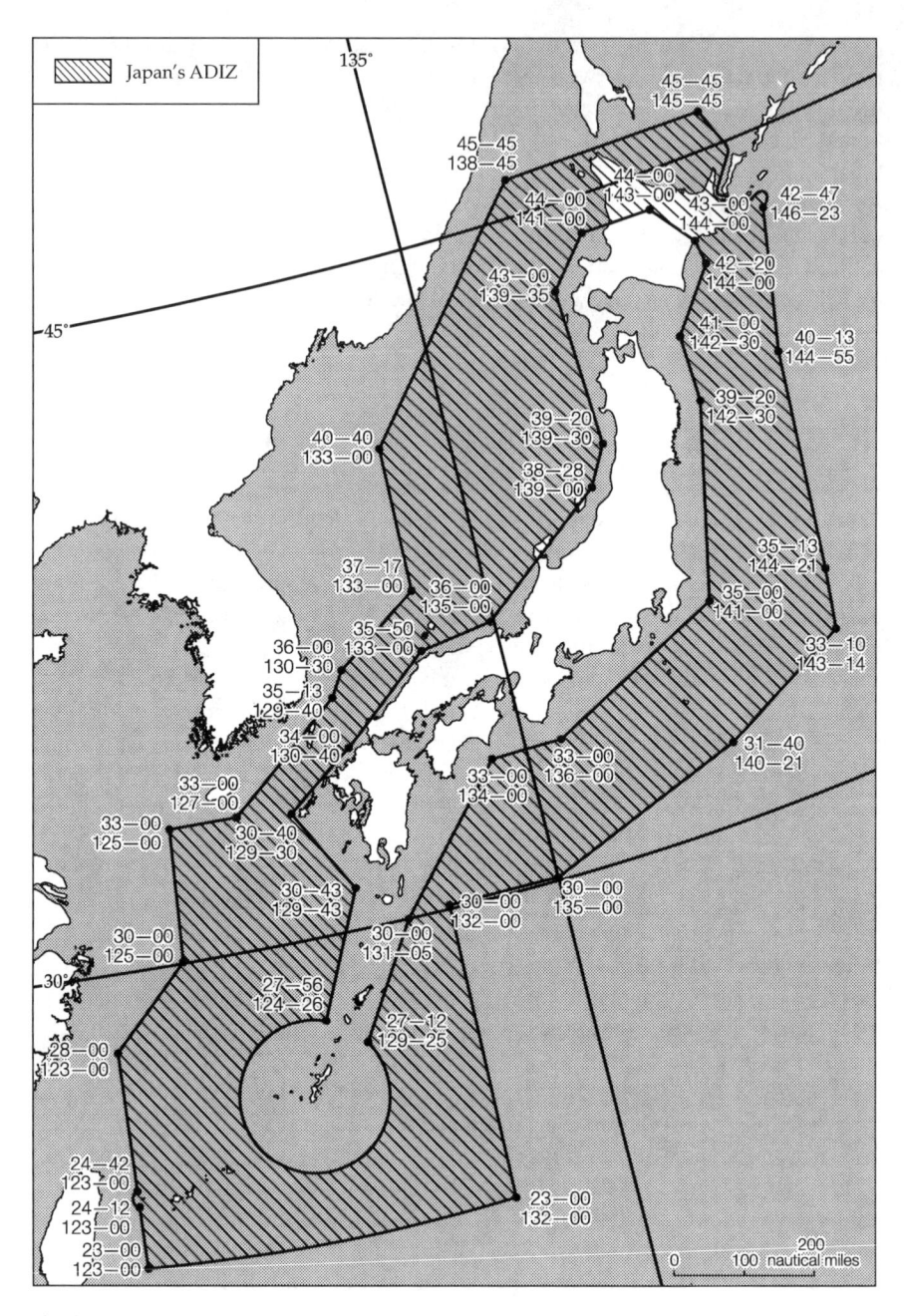

Fig. 8.1 Japan's ADIZ

accidental collisions, whereby each side would inform the other of the flight plans of any of its military aircraft that intended to enter the other's ADIZ. The notification would be made through the Aeronautical Fixed Telecommunication Network (a network for civil aviation) or on-board radio.[4] Therefore, no scramble will be made in principle against applicable aircraft entering the area, provided their flight plans have been notified. Furthermore, aircraft must constantly monitor the international air distress frequency when flying within the ADIZ or in the vicinity of the territorial air space of another country. Consultations between the Japanese and ROK sides continued thereafter, and they decided to set up a dedicated hotline[5] for the notification of flight plans between the two sides in order to prevent accidental collisions more effectively. The hotline went into operation in September 1997.

The issue, in terms of international law, occurs when Japan's ADIZ is applied to foreign aircraft operating beyond Japan's territorial air space in air space above its EEZ or the high seas (not when it is applied internally to SDF aircraft or when issuing scramble orders in response to external information). This is because all aircraft have the freedom to fly in air space above EEZs or the high seas. The grounds for the unilateral establishment of such an ADIZ are not necessarily clear, although some have attempted to justify it by likening it to the case of contiguous zones and calling for the restriction of the freedom of the high seas (in this case the freedom of flight above them) to protect a coastal State's legal interests, or by citing the principle of self-defense.

Another type of air space is flight information regions (FIRs), in which each State has the responsibility to provide aircraft with air traffic control services, flight assistance services, and flight navigation services, to ensure safe and efficient flight. The ICAO-designated FIRs were established for air spaces that include territorial air space and air space over the high seas, with smooth air traffic, rather than sovereignty over air space, in mind. FIRs are not named after any State and are instead named after the control center or flight information center providing the flight services in it. The FIRs under Japanese jurisdiction are the Tokyo FIR and the Naha FIR, and flight services are provided by their respective air traffic control centers. Thus ADIZs and FIRs differ in purpose and usually also scope.

---

[4]The area in question is the space above the EEZ and high seas south of 37° north latitude, which is adjacent to the ADIZs of both countries.

[5]The hotline was set up between Japan Air Self-Defense Force's Kasuga Air Base in Kasuga, Fukuoka Prefecture on the Japanese side and Osan Air Base on the ROK side.

Epilogue

In writing this book, I have sought primarily and in principle to brush up and revise previous works I have authored regarding Japan's territory, while also adding new text to create a clearer overview and give the work a sense of consistency.

In Chapter 1, "Development of Japan's Territory," I have revised an essay written for *Nihon no kokusaihō jirei kenkyū (3): Ryōdo* (Study of Japanese Practices (Vol. 3): Territory) published by Keio University Press in 1990, and which was compiled by Kokusaihō Jirei Kenkyūkai, a study group that analyzes Japanese practices related to international law. I have added several explanatory notes regarding various historical facts and explained specialized terminology in order to illustrate the current state of Japan more clearly.

Chapter 2, "The Northern Territories (Kunashiri Island, Etorofu Island, Habomai Islands, and Shikotan Island)," is a comprehensive description of the state of affairs up to autumn 2001. The reason I have made no mention whatsoever of the "parallel consultation" is because the Russian side has shown no signs of acknowledging it. It is not the case that mention of the parallel consultation has been deleted after the fact owing to the occurrence of a variety of incidents.

Chapter 3, "The Senkaku Islands," and Chapter 4, "Takeshima," are based on the sections on these issues in Serita Kentarō, *Shima no ryōyū to keizai suiiki no kyōkai kakutei* (Sovereignty over Islands and the Delimitation of Economic Zones) published by Yūshindo Kōbunsha in 1999, to which I have added new material and made revisions.

In Chapter 5, "Territorial Sea and Exclusive Economic Zone," I have added new material related to the various principles of the law of the sea to help the reader understand the overall picture more easily and to place the focus of the chapter more clearly on the various issues that Japan faces.

Chapter 6, "Exclusive Economic Zones between Japan and the Republic of Korea, and Japan and China," is also based on the relevant sections of this work.

Chapter 7, "A Proposal for Stability and Coexistence in East Asia," is an attempt to better clarify a long-standing argument of mine. I strongly hope that this proposal will be widely discussed and eventually realized.

© Kreab K.K. 2023

K. Serita, *The Territory of Japan*, https://doi.org/10.1007/978-981-99-3013-5

Chapter 8, "Territorial Air Space and Air Defense Identification Zones," was newly composed for this book. It is worth pointing out that since the completion of this chapter, there has been much coverage of Japan's air defense identification zone—not in relation to its originally intended purpose of facilitating scrambles to prevent aerial incursions into Japanese territory, but in light of its use in pursuing suspicious vessels in the Sea of Japan. As such, I feel the chapter is slightly incomplete.

In fact, that is not the only section that I feel to be incomplete. For example, it is to my regret that while Chapter 5 touches upon internal waters, it should have also made mention of particularly problematic aspects of internal waters, namely the legal status of foreign vessels in a harbor and the rights of coastal States. Issues have, in fact, also occurred in relation to fires onboard foreign vessels at anchor and I hope to add a section on the subject, should the opportunity present itself.

On a side note, my interest in territorial matters first arose while I was studying in France from 1969 to 1971, when I came across a record of lectures on France's territory in a Parisian book shop. Surprised to find that such a work by a scholar of international law existed, I decided to one day write my own book on Japan's territory. Having studied the legal precedents of various territorial disputes, I first had the opportunity to work on territorial matters when I helped to put together a report by the Ministry of Foreign Affairs on the subject, led by the late Prof. Taijudō Kanae, from 1980 to 1981.

I was one of the founders of Kokusaihō Jirei Kenkyūkai and the third topic that we looked at was territorial matters. I was in charge of writing an overview of the topic and studied the related historical developments. Discussions with fellow members of the study group also deepened my understanding of the subject. After writing *Shima no ryōyū to keizai suiiki no kyōkai kakutei*, I presented a copy to my colleague, Professor Iokibe Makoto. At a tennis gathering held to celebrate the publication of this work, Professor Iokibe, perhaps having read the sections on the territorial issues related to the Senkaku Islands and Takeshima, recommended that I publish a work under the title of *Japan's Territory* and took the trouble to introduce me to Asō Akihiko in the editing department of Chūōkōron-Shinsha. Professor Iokibe also asked to write a review of my book once it was published. Unfortunately, the publication was delayed by almost a year and Professor Iokibe is currently carrying out research at Harvard University.

Although I did so for the purpose of studying maritime societies, I found visiting Japan's surrounding islands and exploring various fishing harbors and villages, while maintaining an interest in territorial and security issues, highly valuable for writing about Japan's territories. Not only that, but I was also given access to the facilities of the Japan Coast Guard and the Japan Maritime Self-Defense Force, and I was able to hold hearings with them. I travelled to Tsushima Island, the Sakishima Islands in Okinawa, and even to faraway Yonaguni Island and Hateruma Island. I headed to Hachijōjima Island, too. As a student, I could never have dreamed that I would be doing this: that I would look out at Kaigarajima Island from Cape Nosappu on the Nemuro Peninsula and think to myself how close it was, or look out from Cape Sōya and think of faraway Sakhalin.

Finally, I would like to express my heartfelt gratitude to Professor Iokibe, who took pains to introduce me to Mr. Asō of Chūōkōron-Shinsha, and also to Mr. Asō himself, for being the first person to read this book, and for his scrupulous criticism as well.

May 19, 2002

Bibliography

Aoki, Setsuko. 2006. *Nihon no uchū senryaku* (Japan's Space Strategy). Tokyo: Keio University Press.

Asahi Shimbun, August 11, 1970.

———, September 4, 1997.

———, January 24, 1998a, morning edition.

———, April 21, 1998b.

———, June 25, 1998c, morning edition.

———, October 7, 2001.

"Burokku 8,950-ko de hōi—Okinotorishima, keizai suiiki 400,000 heihō kiro no meiun nigiru (Taking Control of the Fate of Okinotorishima and 400,000 Square Kilometers of Economic Zone, with an 8,950 Block Enclosure)." *Yomiuri Shimbun*, May 21, 1988, evening edition.

Department of Transportation, Ministry of Railways of Japan. 1926. *Shina tetsudō kankei jōyaku isan* (Collection of Treaties related to Chinese Railways), September.

Hamashita, Takeshi. 1997. *Chōkō shisutemu to kindai ajia* (The Tributary System and Modern Asia). Tokyo: Iwanami Shoten.

Hanrei jihō (Chronicle of Legal Rulings) 1648.

Hanrei taimuzu (Legal Ruling Times) 998.

Hokkaidō Shimbun, September 4, 2001.

Hori, Kazuo. 1987. "1905-nen Nihon no Takeshima ryōdo hennyū (Japan's Incorporation of Takeshima into its Territory in 1905)." *Chōsenshi kenkyūkai ronbunshū (Bulletin of Society for Study in Korean History)* 24, March.

Ikeshima, Taisaku. 2000. *Nankyoku jōyaku taisei to kokusaihō* (The Antarctic Treaty Regime and International Law). Tokyo: Keio University Press.

Inō, Kanori. 1965. *Taiwan bunkashi (3)* (Cultural History of Taiwan [Vol. 3]). Tokyo: Tōkō Shoin, reprint.

Inoue, Kiyoshi. 1972. *Senkaku rettō* (The Senkaku Islands). Tokyo: Gendai hyōronsha.

International Court of Justice. 1951. *Reports of Judgments, Advisory Opinions and Orders.*

———. 1953. *Reports of Judgments, Advisory Opinions and Orders.*

———. 1969. *Reports of Judgments, Advisory Opinions and Orders.*

———. 1974. *Reports of Judgments, Advisory Opinions and Orders.*

Irie, Keishirō. 1951. *Nihon kōwa jōyaku no kenkyū* (Study of the Treaty of Peace with Japan). Tokyo: Itagaki Shoten.

Japanese Society of International Law. 1952. *Heiwa jōyaku no sōgōteki kenkyū* (Comprehensive Studies of the Treaty of Peace with Japan) 1.

© Kreab K.K. 2023
K. Serita, *The Territory of Japan*, https://doi.org/10.1007/978-981-99-3013-5

————. 1955. *Okinawa no chii* (The Position of Okinawa). Tokyo: Yūhikaku.

Kawakami, Kenzō. 1966. *Takeshima no rekishi chirigakuteki kenkyū* (A Geographical Study of the History of Takeshima). Tokyo: Kokon Shoin.

————. 1972. *Sengo no kokusai gyogyō seido* (The Postwar International Fisheries System). Tokyo: Japan Fisheries Association.

Kikan Okinawa. (Okinawa Quarterly) 56.

Kim, Myung-ki. 1991. *Dokudo to kokusaihō* (Takeshima and International Law). Original Korean edition: Kim, Myung-ki. 1987. *Dokdo wa gukjebeop*. Seoul: Hwahaksa.

Kishaba, Kazutaka. "Senkaku shotō to sakuhōshi roku (The Senkaku Islands and Chinese Envoys)." *Kikan Okinawa (Okinawa Quarterly)* 63.

Kōbe Shimbun, January 23, 1998a, morning edition.

————, August 31, 1998b, morning edition.

————, July 18, 2001.

Kokusaihō Jirei Kenkyūkai. 1983. *Kokka shōnin* (Recognition of States). Japan Institute of International Affairs.

————. 1988. *Kokkō saikai, seifu shōnin* (Restoration of Diplomatic Relations and Recognition of Governments). Tokyo: Keio University Press.

————. 1990. *Nihon no kokusaihō jirei kenkyū (3): Ryōdo* (Japanese Practices [Vol. 3]: Territory). Tokyo: Keio University Press.

————. 2001. *Nihon no jirei kenkyū (5): Jōyaku hō* (Japanese Practices [Vol. 5]: Law of Treaties). Tokyo: Keio University Press.

"Koto Okinotorishima ga kieru—gyogyō suiiki 400,000 heihō kiro ushinau osore (The Risk of Okinotorishima Disappearing and the Loss of 400,000 Square Kilometers of Fishing Grounds)." *Kōbe Shimbun*, September 2, 1987.

Lin, Chin-ching. 1987. *Sengo no nikka kankei to kokusaihō* (Postwar Japan-Republic of China Relations). Tokyo: Yūhikaku Publishing.

Mainichi Shimbun, April 4, 1996.

Matsui, Yoshirō. "International Law of Territorial Acquisition and the Dispute over the Senkaku (Diaoyu) Islands," *The Japanese Annual of International Law 40*.

Minagawa, Takeshi. 1963. "Takeshima funsō to kokusai hanrei (The Takeshima Dispute and International Precedent)" in *Kokusaihōgaku no shomondai: Maehara Mitsuo kyōju kanreki kinen* (Issues of International Law: In Commemoration of Professor Maehara Mitsuo's 60th Birthday). Tokyo: Keio University Press.

Ministry of Foreign Affairs of Japan. *Teikoku hanto kankei zakken* (Miscellaneous Matters Related to Imperial Territory).

————. 2001. *Warera no hoppō ryōdo* (Our Northern Territories).

Miyanaga, Masamori. 1930. *Yaeyama gōi* (Lexicon of the Yaeyama Islands). Tokyo: Tōyō Bunko.

Mizukami, Chiyuki. 1995. *Nihon to kaiyōhō* (Japan and UNCLOS). Tokyo: Yūshindō Kōbunsha.

Oda, Shigeru. 1956. *Kaiyō no kokusaihō kōzō* (The International Legal Structure of the Oceans). Tokyo: Yūshindō Kōbunsha.

————. 1971. *Umi no shigen to kokusaihō* (Ocean Resources and International Law) I. Tokyo: Yūhikaku.

————. 1972. *Kaiyōhō no genryū o saguru* (Exploring the Origins of UNCLOS). Tokyo: Japan Fisheries Association.

————. 1985. *Chūkai kokuren kaiyōhō jōyakujō* (Commentary on UNCLOS). Tokyo: Yūhikaku.

Okuhara, Toshio. "Senkaku rettō no ryōdo hennyū keii (The Circumstances Leading to Territorial Incorporation of the Senkaku Islands)." *Kokushikan daigaku seikei gakkaishi (Journal of the Politics and Economics Society of Kokushikan University)* 4.

————. 1978. "Senkaku shotō ryōyūken no konkyo (Evidence for the Territorial Rights over the Senkaku Islands)." *Chūō kōron (The Central Review)*, July.

Ōyama, Azusa (ed). 1980. *Nihon gaikōshi kenkyū* (Studies in Japanese Diplomatic History). Tokyo: Ryōsho fukyūkai.